YOUTH:
ITS EDUCATION, REGIMEN, AND HYGIENE

By
G. STANLEY HALL

Youth:
Its Education, Regimen, And Hygiene

by G. Stanley Hall

Copyright © 2023

All Rights reserved.
No part of this publication may be reproduced, stored in a retrieval system, or transmitted in any form or by any means, electronic, mechanical, photocopying or Otherwise, without the written permission of the publisher.

The author/editor asserts the moral right to be identified as the author/editor of this work.

ISBN: 978-93-58595-66-6

Published by

DOUBLE 9 BOOKS
2/13-B, Ansari Road, Daryaganj
New Delhi – 110002
info@double9books.com
www.double9books.com
Tel. 011-40042856

This book is under public domain

ABOUT THE AUTHOR

Granville American psychologist and educator Stanley Hall (February 1, 1846 - April 24, 1924) was a trailblazer who graduated from Harvard College with the nation's first psychology degree in the nineteenth century. He was particularly interested in the evolution of the human life span and these ideas. Hall served as the first president of both Clark University and the American Psychological Association. Hall was raised on a farm by his parents, Granville Bascom Hall, a former member of the Massachusetts assembly, and Abigail Beals, a former student of the Albany Female Seminary who later became a teacher. Hall was born in Ashfield, Massachusetts. He began his career by instructing English and philosophy at Antioch College in Yellow Springs, Ohio, before moving on to Williams College in Massachusetts to instruct philosophical history. Hall has two marriages. Cornelia Fisher served as his first wife. Julia Fisher Hall was born on May 30, 1882, and Robert Granville Hall was born on February 7, 1881. They were married in September 1879 and had two kids together. Julia and Cornelia asphyxiated unintentionally and died in 1890. Robert's father reared him starting at age four. On April 24, 1924, Hall passed away in Worcester, Massachusetts.

CONTENTS

PREFACE 7

CHAPTER I - PRE-ADOLESCENCE 8

CHAPTER II - THE MUSCLES AND MOTOR POWERS IN GENERAL 12

CHAPTER III - INDUSTRIAL EDUCATION 27

CHAPTER IV - MANUAL TRAINING AND SLOYD 31

CHAPTER V - GYMNASTICS 42

CHAPTER VI - PLAY, SPORTS, AND GAMES 55

CHAPTER VII - FAULTS, LIES, AND CRIMES 86

CHAPTER VIII - BIOGRAPHIES OF YOUTH 99

CHAPTER IX - THE GROWTH OF SOCIAL IDEALS 153

CHAPTER X - INTELLECTUAL EDUCATION AND SCHOOL WORK 173

CHAPTER XI - THE EDUCATION OF GIRLS 205

CHAPTER XII - MORAL AND RELIGIOUS TRAINING 235

INDEX 265

PREFACE

I have often been asked to select and epitomize the practical and especially the pedagogical conclusions of my large volumes on Adolescence, published in 1904, in such form that they may be available at a minimum cost to parents, teachers, reading circles, normal schools, and college classes, by whom even the larger volumes have been often used. This, with the coöperation of the publishers and with the valuable aid of Superintendent C.N. Kendall of Indianapolis, I have tried to do, following in the main the original text, with only such minor changes and additions as were necessary to bring the topics up to date, and adding a new chapter on moral and religions education. For the scientific justification of my educational conclusions I must, of course, refer to the larger volumes. The last chapter is not in "Adolescence," but is revised from a paper printed elsewhere. I am indebted to Dr. Theodore L. Smith of Clark University for verification of all references, proof-reading, and many minor changes.

G. STANLEY HALL.

CHAPTER I - PRE-ADOLESCENCE

Introduction: Characterization of the age from eight to twelve—The era of recapitulating the stages of primitive human development—Life close to nature—The age also for drill, habituation, memory, work and regermination—Adolescence superposed upon this stage of life, but very distinct from it.

The years from about eight to twelve constitute a unique period of human life. The acute stage of teething is passing, the brain has acquired nearly its adult size and weight, health is almost at its best, activity is greater and more varied than it ever was before or ever will be again, and there is peculiar endurance, vitality, and resistance to fatigue. The child develops a life of its own outside the home circle, and its natural interests are never so independent of adult influence. Perception is very acute, and there is great immunity to exposure, danger, accident, as well as to temptation. Reason, true morality, religion, sympathy, love, and esthetic enjoyment are but very slightly developed.

Everything, in short, suggests that this period may represent in the individual what was once for a very protracted and relatively stationary period an age of maturity in the remote ancestors of our race, when the young of our species, who were perhaps pygmoid, shifted for themselves independently of further parental aid. The qualities developed during pre-adolescence are, in the evolutionary history of the race, far older than hereditary traits of body and mind which develop later and which may be compared to a new and higher story built upon our primal nature. Heredity is so far both more stable and more secure. The elements of personality are few, but are well organised on a simple, effective plan. The momentum of these traits inherited from our indefinitely remote ancestors is great, and they are often clearly distinguishable from those to be added later. Thus the boy is father of the man in a new sense, in that his qualities are indefinitely older and existed, well compacted, untold ages before the more distinctly human attributes were developed. Indeed there are a few faint indications of an earlier age node, at about the age of six, as if amid the instabilities of health we could detect signs that this may have been the age of puberty in remote ages of the past. I have also given reasons that lead me to the conclusion that, despite its dominance, the function of sexual maturity and procreative power is peculiarly mobile up and down the age-line independently of many of the qualities usually so closely associated with it, so that much that sex created in the phylum now precedes it in the individual.

Rousseau would leave prepubescent years to nature and to these primal hereditary impulsions and allow the fundamental traits of savagery their fling till twelve. Biological psychology finds many and cogent reasons to confirm this view *if only a proper environment could be provided*. The child revels in savagery; and if its tribal, predatory, hunting, fishing, fighting, roving, idle, playing proclivities could be indulged in the country and under conditions that now, alas! seem hopelessly ideal, they could conceivably be so organized and directed as to be far more truly humanistic and liberal than all that the best modern school can provide. Rudimentary organs of the soul, now suppressed, perverted, or delayed, to crop out in menacing forms later, would be developed in their season so that we should be immune to them in maturer years, on the principle of the Aristotelian catharsis for which I have tried to suggest a far broader application than the Stagirite could see in his day.

These inborn and more or less savage instincts can and should be allowed some scope. The deep and strong cravings in the individual for those primitive experiences and occupations in which his ancestors became skilful through the pressure of necessity should not be ignored, but can and should be, at least partially, satisfied in a vicarious way, by tales from literature, history, and tradition which present the crude and primitive virtues of the heroes of the world's childhood. In this way, aided by his vivid visual imagination, the child may enter upon his heritage from the past, live out each stage of life to its fullest and realize in himself all its manifold tendencies. Echoes only of the vaster, richer life of the remote past of the race they must remain, but just these are the murmurings of the only muse that can save from the omnipresent dangers of precocity. Thus we not only rescue from the danger of loss, but utilize for further psychic growth the results of the higher heredity, which are the most precious and potential things on earth. So, too, in our urbanized hothouse life, that tends to ripen everything before its time, we must teach nature, although the very phrase is ominous. But we must not, in so doing, wean still more from, but perpetually incite to visit, field, forest, hill, shore, the water, flowers, animals, the true homes of childhood in this wild, undomesticated stage from which modern conditions have kidnapped and transported him. Books and reading are distasteful, for the very soul and body cry out for a more active, objective life, and to know nature and man at first hand. These two staples, stories and nature, by these informal methods of the home and the environment, constitute fundamental education.

But now another remove from nature seems to be made necessary by the manifold knowledges and skills of our highly complex civilization. We should transplant the human sapling, I concede reluctantly, as early as eight, but not before, to the schoolhouse with its imperfect lighting, ventilation, temperature. We must shut out nature and open books. The child must sit on unhygienic benches and work the tiny muscles that wag the tongue and pen, and let all the others, which constitute nearly half its weight, decay. Even if it be prematurely, he must be subjected to special disciplines and be apprenticed to the higher qualities of adulthood; for he is not only a product of nature, but a candidate for a highly developed humanity. To many, if not most, of the influences here there can be at first but little inner response. Insight, understanding, interest, sentiment, are for the most part only nascent; and most that pertains to the true kingdom of mature manhood is embryonic. The wisest requirements seem to the child more or less alien, arbitrary, heteronomous, artificial, falsetto. There is much passivity, often active resistance and evasion, and perhaps spasms of obstinacy, to it all. But the senses are keen and alert, reactions immediate and vigorous; and the memory is quick, sure and lasting; and ideas of space, time, and physical causation, and of many a moral and social licit and non-licit, are rapidly unfolding. Never again will there be such susceptibility to drill and discipline, such plasticity to habituation, or such ready adjustment to new conditions. It is the age of external and mechanical training. Reading, writing, drawing, manual training, musical technic, foreign tongues and their pronunciations, the manipulation of numbers and of geometrical elements, and many kinds of skill have now their golden hour; and if it passes unimproved, all these can never be acquired later without a heavy handicap of disadvantage and loss. These necessities may be hard for the health of body, sense, mind, as well as for morals; and pedagogic art consists in breaking the child into them betimes as intensely and as quickly as possible with minimal strain and with the least amount of explanation or coquetting for natural interest, and in calling medicine confectionery. This is not teaching in its true sense so much as it is drill, inculcation, and regimentation. The method should be mechanical, repetitive, authoritative, dogmatic. The automatic powers are now at their very apex, and they can do and bear more than our degenerate pedagogy knows or dreams of. Here we have something to learn from the schoolmasters of the past back to the middle ages, and even from the ancients. The greatest stress, with short periods and few hours, incessant insistence, incitement, and little reliance upon interest, reason or work done without the presence of the teacher, should be the guiding principles for pressure in these essentially formal and, to the child, contentless elements of knowledge. These should be sharply distinguished from the indigenous, evoking, and more truly educational factors described in the last paragraph, which are meaty, content-full, and relatively formless as to time of day, method, spirit, and perhaps environment and personnel of teacher, and possibly somewhat in season of the year, almost as sharply as work differs from play, or perhaps as the virility of man that loves to command a phalanx, be a martinet and drill-master, differs from femininity which excels in persuasion, sympathetic insight, story-telling, and in the tact that discerns and utilizes spontaneous interests in the young.

Adolescence is a new birth, for the higher and more completely human traits are now born. The qualities of body and soul that now emerge are far newer. The child comes from and harks back to a remoter past; the adolescent is neo-atavistic, and in him the later acquisitions of the race slowly become prepotent. Development is less gradual and more saltatory, suggestive of some ancient period of storm and stress when old moorings were broken and a higher level attained. The annual rate of growth in height, weight, and strength is increased and often doubled, and even more. Important functions, previously non-existent, arise. Growth of parts and organs loses its former proportions, some permanently and some for a season. Some of these are still growing in old age and others are soon arrested and atrophy. The old measures of dimensions become obsolete, and old harmonies are broken. The range of individual differences and average errors in all physical measurements and all psychic tests increases. Some linger long in the childish stage and advance late or slowly, while others push on with a sudden outburst of impulsion to early maturity. Bones and muscles lead all other tissues, as if they vied with each other; and there is frequent flabbiness or tension as one or the other leads. Nature arms youth for conflict with all the resources at her command—speed, power of shoulder, biceps, back, leg, jaw—strengthens and enlarges skull, thorax, hips, makes man aggressive and prepares woman's frame for maternity.

CHAPTER II - THE MUSCLES AND MOTOR POWERS IN GENERAL

Muscles as organs of the will, of character and even of thought—The muscular virtues—Fundamental and accessory muscles and functions—The development of the mind and of the upright position—Small muscles as organs of thought—School lays too much stress upon these—Chorea—vast numbers of automatic movements in children—Great variety of spontaneous activities—Poise, control and spurtiness—Pen and tongue wagging—Sedentary school life *vs* free out-of-door activities—Modern decay of muscles, especially in girls—Plasticity of motor habits at puberty.

The muscles are by weight about forty-three per cent. of the average adult male human body. They expend a large fraction of all the kinetic energy of the adult body, which a recent estimate places as high as one-fifth. The cortical centers for the voluntary muscles extend over most of the lateral psychic zones of the brain, so that their culture is brain building. In a sense they are organs of digestion, for which function they play a very important rôle. Muscles are in a most intimate and peculiar sense the organs of the will. They have built all the roads, cities, and machines in the world, written all the books, spoken all the words, and, in fact, done everything that man has accomplished with matter. If they are undeveloped or grow relaxed and flabby, the dreadful chasm between good intentions and their execution is liable to appear and widen. Character might be in a sense defined as a plexus of motor habits. To call conduct three-fourths of life, with Matthew Arnold; to describe man as one-third intellect and two-thirds will, with Schopenhauer; to urge that man is what he does or that he is the sum of his movements, with F.W. Robertson; that character is simply muscle habits, with Maudsley; that the age of art is now slowly superseding the age of science, and that the artist will drive out with the professor, with the anonymous author of "Rembrandt als Erzicher";[1] that history is consciously willed movements, with Bluntschli; or that we could form no conception of force or energy in the world but for our own muscular effort; to hold that most thought involves change of muscle tension as more or less integral to it—all this shows how we have modified the antique Ciceronian conception *vivere est cogitari*, [To live is to think] to *vivere est velle*, [To live is to will] and gives us a new sense of the importance of muscular development and regimen.[2]

Modern psychology thus sees in muscles organs of expression for all efferent processes. Beyond all their demonstrable functions, every change of attention and of psychic states generally plays upon them unconsciously, modifying their tension in subtle ways so that they may be called organs of thought and feeling as well as of will, in which some now see the true Kantian thing-in-itself the real substance of the world, in the anthropomorphism of force. Habits even determine the deeper strata of belief; thought is repressed action; and deeds, not words, are the language of complete men. The motor areas are closely related and largely identical with the psychic, and muscle culture develops brain-centers as nothing else yet demonstrably does. Muscles are the vehicles of habituation, imitation, obedience, character, and even of manners and customs. For the young, motor education is cardinal, and is now coming to due recognition; and, for all, education is incomplete without a motor side. Skill, endurance, and perseverance may almost be called muscular virtues; and fatigue, velleity, caprice, *ennui*, restlessness, lack of control and poise, muscular faults.

To understand the momentous changes of motor functions that characterize adolescence we must consider other than the measurable aspects of the subject. Perhaps the best scale on which to measure all normal growth of muscle structure and functions is found in the progress from fundamental to accessory. The former designates the muscles and movements of the trunk and large joints, neck, back, hips, shoulders, knees, and elbows, sometimes called central, and which in general man has in common with the higher and larger animals. Their activities are few, mostly simultaneous, alternating and rhythmic, as of the legs in walking, and predominate in hard-working men and women with little culture or intelligence, and often in idiots. The latter or accessory movements are those of the hand, tongue, face, and articulatory organs, and these may be connected into a long and greatly diversified series, as those used in writing, talking, piano-playing. They are represented by smaller and more numerous muscles, whose functions develop later in life and represent a higher standpoint of evolution. These smaller muscles for finer movements come into function later and are chiefly associated with psychic activity, which plays upon them by incessantly changing their tensions, if not causing actual movement. It is these that are so liable to disorder in the many automatisms and choreic tics we see in school children, especially if excited or fatigued. General paralysis usually begins in the higher levels by breaking these down, so that the first symptom of its insidious and never interrupted progress is inability to execute the more exact and delicate movements of tongue or hand, or both. Starting with the latest evolutionary level, it is a devolution that may work downward till very many of the fundamental activities are lost before death.

Nothing better illustrates this distinction than the difference between the fore foot of animals and the human hand. The first begins as a fin or paddle or is armed with a hoof, and is used solely for locomotion. Some carnivora with claws use the fore limb also for holding well as tearing, and others for digging. Arboreal life seems to have almost created the simian hand and to have wrought a revolution in the form and use of the forearm and its accessory organs, the fingers. Apes and other tree-climbing creatures must not only adjust their prehensile organ to a wide variety of distances and sizes of branches, but must use the hands more or less freely for picking, transporting, and eating fruit; and this has probably been a prime factor in lifting man to the erect position, without which human intelligence as we know it could have hardly been possible. "When we attempt to measure the gap between man and the lower animals in terms of the form of movement, the wonder is no less great than when we use the term of mentality."[3] The degree of approximation to human intelligence in anthropoid animals follows very closely the degree of approximation to human movements.

The gradual acquirement of the erect position by the human infant admirably repeats this long phylogenetic evolution.[4] At first the limbs are of almost no use in locomotion, but the fundamental trunk muscles with those that move the large joints are more or less spasmodically active. Then comes creeping, with use of the hip muscles, while all below the knee is useless, as also are the fingers. Slowly the leg and foot are degraded to locomotion, slowly the great toe becomes more limited in its action, the thumb increases in flexibility and strength of opposition, and the fingers grow more mobile and controllable. As the body slowly assumes the vertical attitude, the form of the chest changes till its greatest diameter is transverse instead of from front to back. The shoulder-blades are less parallel than in quadrupeds, and spread out till they approximate the same plane. This gives the arm freedom of movement laterally, so that it can be rotated one hundred and eighty degrees in man as contrasted to one hundred degrees in apes, thus giving man the command of almost any point within a sphere of which the two arms are radii. The power of grasping was partly developed from and partly added to the old locomotor function of the fore limbs; the jerky aimless automatisms, as well as the slow rhythmic flexion and extension of the fingers and hand, movements which are perhaps survivals of arboreal or of even earlier aquatic life, are coördinated; and the bilateral and simultaneous rhythmic movements of the heavier muscles are supplemented by the more finely adjusted and specialized activities which as the end of the growth period is approached are determined less by heredity and more by environment. In a sense, a child or a man is the sum total of his movements or tendencies to move; and nature and instinct chiefly determine the basal, and education the accessory parts of our activities.

The entire accessory system is thus of vital importance for the development of all of the arts of expression. These smaller muscles might almost be called organs of thought. Their tension is modified with the faintest change of soul, such as is seen in accent, inflection, facial expressions, handwriting, and many forms of so-called mind-reading, which, in fact, is always muscle-reading. The day-laborer of low intelligence, with a practical vocabulary of not over five hundred words, who can hardly move each of his fingers without moving others or all of them, who can not move his brows or corrugate his forehead at will, and whose inflection is very monotonous, illustrates a condition of arrest or atrophy of this later, finer, accessory system of muscles. On the other hand, the child, precocious in any or all of these later respects, is very liable to be undeveloped in the larger and more fundamental parts and functions. The full unfoldment of each is, in fact, an inexorable condition precedent for the normal development to full and abiding maturity of the higher and more refined muscularity, just as conversely the awkwardness and clumsiness of adolescence mark a temporary loss of balance in the opposite direction. If this general conception be correct, then nature does not finish the basis of her pyramid in the way Ross, Mercier, and others have assumed, but lays a part of the foundation and, after carrying it to an apex, normally goes back and adds to the foundation to carry up the apex still higher and, if prevented from so doing, expends her energy in building the apex up at a sharper angle till instability results. School and kindergarten often lay a disproportionate strain on the tiny accessory muscles, weighing altogether but a few ounces, that wag the tongue, move the pen, and do fine work requiring accuracy. But still at this stage prolonged work requiring great accuracy is irksome and brings dangers homologous to those caused by too much fine work in the kindergarten before the first adjustment of large to small muscles, which lasts until adolescence, is established. Then disproportion between function and growth often causes symptoms of chorea. The chief danger is arrest of the development and control of the smaller muscles. Many occupations and forms of athletics, on the contrary, place the stress mainly upon groups of fundamental muscles to the neglect of finer motor possibilities. Some who excel in heavy athletics no doubt coarsen their motor reactions, become not only inexact and heavy but unresponsive to finer stimuli, as if the large muscles were hypertrophied and the small ones arrested. On the other hand, many young men, and probably more young women, expend too little of their available active energy upon basal and massive muscle work, and cultivate too much, and above all too early, the delicate responsive work. This is, perhaps, the best physiological characterization of precocity and issues in excessive nervous and muscular irritability. The great influx of muscular vigor that unfolds during adolescent years and which was originally not only necessary to successful propagation, but expressive of virility, seems to be a very plastic quantity, so that motor regimen and exercise at this stage is probably more important and all-conditioning for mentality, sexuality, and health than at any other period of life. Intensity, and for a time a spurty diathesis, is as instinctive and desirable as are the copious minor automatisms which spontaneously give the alphabet out of which complex and finer motor series are later spelled by the conscious will. Mercier and others have pointed out that, as most skilled labor, so school work and modern activities in civilized life generally lay premature and disproportionate strains upon those kinds of movement requiring exactness. Stress upon basal movements is not only compensating but is of higher therapeutic value against the disorders of the accessory system; it constitutes the best core or prophylactic for fidgets and tense states, and directly develops poise, control, and psycho-physical equilibrium. Even when contractions reach choreic intensity the best treatment is to throw activities down the scale that measures the difference between primary and secondary movements and to make the former predominate.

The number of movements, the frequency with which they are repeated, their diversity, the number of combinations, and their total kinetic quantum in young children, whether we consider movements of the body as a whole, fundamental movements of large limbs, or finer accessory motions, is amazing. Nearly every external stimulus is answered by a motor response. Dresslar[5] observed a thirteen months' old baby for four hours, and found, to follow Preyer's classification, impulsive or spontaneous, reflex, instinctive, imitative, inhibitive, expressive, and even deliberative movements, with marked satisfaction in rhythm, attempts to do almost anything which appealed to him, and almost inexhaustible efferent resources. A friend has tried to record every word uttered by a four-year-old girl during a portion of a day, and finds nothing less than verbigerations. A teacher noted the activities of a fourteen-year-old boy during the study time of a single school day[6], with similar results.

Lindley[7] studied 897 common motor automatisms in children, which he divided into 92 classes: 45 in the region of the head, 20 in the feet and legs, 19 in the hands and fingers. Arranged in the order of frequency with which each was found, the list stood as follows: fingers, feet, lips, tongue, head, body, hands, mouth, eyes, jaws, legs, forehead, face, arms, ears. In the last five alone adolescents exceeded children, the latter excelling the former most in those of head, mouth, legs, and tongue, in this order. The writer believes that there are many more automatisms than appeared in his returns.

School life, especially in the lower grades, is a rich field for the study of these activities. They are familiar, as licking things, clicking with the tongue, grinding the teeth, scratching, tapping, twirling a lock of hair or chewing it, biting the nails (Bérillon's onychophagia), shrugging, corrugating, pulling buttons or twisting garments, strings, etc., twirling pencils, thumbs, rotating, nodding and shaking the head, squinting and winking, swaying, pouting and grimacing, scraping the floor, rubbing hands, stroking, patting, flicking the fingers, wagging, snapping the fingers, muffling, squinting, picking the face, interlacing the fingers, cracking the joints, finger plays, biting and nibbling, trotting the leg, sucking things, etc.

The average number of automatisms per 100 persons Smith found to be in children 176, in adolescents 110. Swaying is chiefly with children; playing and drumming with the fingers is more common among adolescents; the movements of fingers and feet decline little with age, and those of eyes and forehead increase, which is significant for the development of attention. Girls excel greatly in swaying, and also, although less, in finger automatism; and boys lead in movements of tongue, feet, and hands. Such movements increase, with too much sitting, intensity of effort, such as to fix attention, and vary with the nature of the activity willed, but involve few muscles directly used in a given task. They increase up the kindergarten grades and fall off rapidly in the primary grades; are greater with tasks requiring fine and exact movements than with those involving large movements. Automatisms are often a sign of the difficulty of tasks. The restlessness that they often express is one of the commonest signs of fatigue. They are mostly in the accessory muscles, while those of the fundamental muscles (body, legs, and arms) disappear rapidly with age; those of eye, brow, and jaw show greatest increase with age, but their frequency in general declines with growing maturity, although there is increased frequency of certain specialized contractions, which indicate the gradual settling of expression in the face.

Often such movements pass over by insensible gradation into the morbid automatism of chorea, and in yet lower levels of decay we see them in the aimless picking and plucking movements of the fingers of the sick. In idiots[8] arrest of higher powers often goes with hypertrophy of these movements, as seen in head-beaters (as if, just as nature impels those partially blind to rub the eyes for "light-hunger," so it prompts the feeble-minded to strike the head for cerebrations), rockers, rackers, shakers, biters, etc. Movements often pass to fixed attitudes and postures of limbs or body, disturbing the normal balance between flexors and extensors, the significance of which as nerve signs or exponents of habitual brain states and tensions Warner has so admirably shown.

Abundance and vigor of automatic movements are desirable, and even a considerable degree of restlessness is a good sign in young children. Many of what are now often called nerve signs and even choreic symptoms, the fidgetiness in school on cloudy days and often after a vacation, the motor superfluities of awkwardness, embarrassment, extreme effort, excitement, fatigue, sleepiness, etc., are simply the forms in which we receive the full momentum of heredity and mark a natural richness of the raw material of intellect, feeling, and especially of will. Hence they must be abundant. All parts should act in all possible ways at first and untrammeled by the activity of all other parts and functions. Some of these activities are more essential for growth in size than are later and more conscious movements. Here as everywhere the rule holds that powers themselves must be unfolded before the ability to check or even to use them can develop. All movements arising from spontaneous activity of nerve cells or centers must be made in order even to avoid the atrophy of disease. Not only so, but this purer kind of innateness must often be helped out to some extent in some children by stimulating reflexes; a rich and wide repertory of sensation must be made familiar; more or less and very guarded, watched and limited experiences of hunger, thirst, cold, heat, tastes, sounds, smells, colors, brightnesses, tactile irritations, and perhaps even occasional tickling and pain to play off the vastly complex function of laughing, crying, etc., may in some cases be judicious. Conscious and unconscious imitation or repetition of every sort of copy may also help to establish the immediate and low-level connection between afferent and efferent processes that brings the organism into direct *rapport* and harmony with the whole world of sense. Perhaps the more rankly and independently they are developed to full functional integrity, each in its season, if we only knew that season, the better. Premature control by higher centers, or coördination into higher compounds of habits and ordered serial activities, is repressive and wasteful, and the mature will of which they are components, or which must at least domesticate them, is stronger and more forcible if this serial stage is not unduly abridged.

But, secondly, many, if not most, of these activities when developed a little, group after group, as they arise, must be controlled, checked, and organized into higher and often more serial compounds. The inhibiting functions are at first hard. In trying to sit still the child sets its teeth, holds the breath, clenches its fists and perhaps makes every muscle tense with a great effort that very soon exhausts. This repressive function is probably not worked from special nervous centers, nor can we speak with confidence of collisions with "sums of arrest" in a sense analogous to that of Herbart, or of stimuli that normally cause catabolic molecular processes in the cell, being mysteriously diverted to produce increased instability or anabolic lability in the sense of Wundt's *Mechanik der Nerven*. The concept now suggested by many facts is that inhibition is irradiation or long circuiting to higher and more complex brain areas, so that the energy, whether spontaneous or reflex, is diverted to be used elsewhere. These combinations are of a higher order, more remote from reflex action, and modified by some Jacksonian third level.[9] Action is now not from independent centers, but these are slowly associated, so that excitation may flow off from one point to any other and any reaction may result from any stimulus.

The more unified the brain the less it suffers from localization, and the lower is the level to which any one function can exhaust the whole. The tendency of each group of cells to discharge or overflow into those of lower tension than themselves increases as correspondence in time and space widens. The more one of a number of activities gains in power to draw on all the brain, or the more readily the active parts are fed at cost of the resting parts, the less is rest to be found in change from one of these activities to another, and the less do concentration and specialization prove to be dangerous. Before, the aim was to wake all parts to function; now it is to connect them. Intensity of this cross-section activity now tends to unity, so that all parts of the brain energize together. In a brain with this switchboard function well organized, each reaction has grown independent of its own stimulus and may result from any stimulation, and each act, e.g., a finger movement of a peculiar nature, may tire the whole brain. This helps us to understand why brain-workers so often excel laborers not only in sudden dynamometric strength test, but in sustained and long-enduring effort. In a good brain or in a good machine, power may thus be developed over a large surface, and all of it applied to a small one, and hence the dangers of specialization are lessened in exact proportion as the elements of our ego are thus compacted together. It is in the variety and delicacy of these combinations and all that they imply, far more than in the elements of which they are composed, that man rises farthest above the higher animals; and of these powers later adolescence is the golden age. The aimless and archaic movements of infancy, whether massive and complex or in the form of isolated automatic tweaks or twinges, are thus, by slow processes of combined analysis and synthesis, involving changes as radical as any in all the world of growth, made over into habits and conduct that fit the world of present environment.

But, thirdly, this long process carried out with all degrees of completeness may be arrested at any unfinished stage. Some automatisms refuse to be controlled by the will, and both they and it are often overworked. Here we must distinguish constantly between (1) those growing rankly in order to be later organized under the will, and (2) those that have become feral after this domestication of them has lost power from disease or fatigue, and (3) those that have never been subjugated because the central power that should have used them to weave the texture of willed action — the proper language of complete manhood — was itself arrested or degenerate. With regard to many of these movements these distinctions can be made with confidence, and in some children more certainly than in others. In childhood, before twelve, the efferent patterns should be developed into many more or less indelible habits, and their colors set fast. Motor specialties requiring exactness and grace like piano-playing, drawing, writing, pronunciation of a foreign tongue, dancing, acting, singing, and a host of virtuosities, must be well begun before the relative arrest of accessory growth at the dawn of the ephebic regeneration and before its great afflux of strength. The facts seem to show that children of this age, such as Hancock[10] described, who could not stand with feet close together and eyes closed without swaying much, could not walk backward, sit still half a minute, dress alone, tie two ends of a string together, interlace slats, wind thread, spin a top, stand on toes or heels, hop on each foot, drive a nail, roll a hoop, skate, hit fingers together rapidly in succession beginning at the little finger and then reversing, etc., are the very ones in whom automatisms are most marked or else they are those constitutionally inert, dull, or uneducable.

In children these motor residua may persist as characteristic features of inflection, accent, or manners; automatisms may become morbid in stammering or stuttering, or they may be seen in gait, handwriting, tics or tweaks, etc. Instead of disappearing with age, as they should, they are seen in the blind as facial grimaces uncorrected by the mirror or facial consciousness, in the deaf as inarticulate noises; and they may tend to grow monstrous with age as if they were disintegrated fragments of our personality, split off and aborted, or motor parasites leaving our psychophysic ego poorer in energy and plasticity of adaptation, till the distraction and anarchy of the individual nature becomes conspicuous and pathetic.

At puberty, however, when muscle habits are so plastic, when there is a new relation between quantity or volume of motor energy and qualitative differentiation, and between volitional control and reflex activities, these kinetic remnants strongly tend to shoot together into wrong aggregates if right ones are not formed. Good manners and correct motor form generally, as well as skill, are the most economic ways of doing things; but this is the age of wasteful ways, awkwardness mannerisms, tensions that are a constant leakage of vital energy, perhaps semi-imperative acts, contortions, quaint movements, more elaborated than in childhood and often highly anesthetic and disagreeable, motor coördinations that will need laborious decomposition later. The avoidable factor in their causation is, with some modification, not unlike that of the simpler feral movements and faulty attitudes, carriage, and postures in children; viz., some form of overpressure or misfit between environment and nature. As during the years from four to eight there is great danger that overemphasis of the activities of the accessory muscles will sow the seeds of chorea, or aggravate predispositions to it, now again comes a greatly increased danger, hardly existing from eight to twelve, that overprecision, especially if fundamental activities are neglected, will bring nervous strain and stunting precocity. This is again the age of the basal, e.g., hill-climbing muscle, of leg and back and shoulder work, and of the yet more fundamental heart, lung, and chest muscles. Now again, the study of a book, under the usual conditions of sitting in a closed space and using pen, tongue, and eye combined, has a tendency to overstimulate the accessory muscles. This is especially harmful for city children who are too prone to the distraction of overmobility at an age especially exposed to maladjustment of motor income and expenditure; and it constitutes not a liberal or power-generating, but a highly and prematurely specialized, narrowing, and weakening education unless offset by safeguards better than any system of gymnastics, which is at best artificial and exaggerated.

As Bryan well says, "The efficiency of a machine depends so far as we know upon the maximum force, rate, amplitude, and variety of direction of its movements and upon the exactness with which below these maxima the force, rate, amplitude, and direction of the movements can be controlled." The motor efficiency of a man depends upon his ability in all these respects. Moreover, the education of the small muscles and fine adjustments of larger ones is as near mental training as physical culture can get; for these are the thought-muscles and movements, and their perfected function is to reflect and express by slight modifications of tension and tone every psychic change. Only the brain itself is more closely and immediately an organ of thought than are these muscles and their activity, reflex, spontaneous, or imitative in origin. Whether any of them are of value, as Lindley thinks, in arousing the brain to activity, or as Müller suggests, in drawing off sensations or venting efferent impulses that would otherwise distract, we need not here discuss. If so, this is, of course, a secondary and late function—nature's way of making the best of things and utilizing remnants.

With these facts and their implications in mind we can next pass to consider the conditions under which the adolescent muscles best develop. Here we confront one of the greatest and most difficult problems of our age. Changes in modern motor life have been so vast and sudden as to present some of the most comprehensive and all-conditioning dangers that threaten civilized races. Not only have the forms of labor been radically changed within a generation or two, but the basal activities that shaped the body of primitive man have been suddenly swept away by the new methods of modern industry. Even popular sports, games, and recreations, so abundant in the early life of all progressive peoples, have been reduced and transformed; and the play age, that once extended on to middle life and often old age, has been restricted. Sedentary life in schools and offices, as we have seen, is reducing the vigor and size of our lower limbs. Our industry is no longer under hygienic conditions; and instead of being out of doors, in the country, or of highly diversified kinds, it is now specialized, monotonous, carried on in closed spaces, bad air, and perhaps poor light, especially in cities. The diseases and arrest bred in the young by life in shops, offices, factories, and schools increase. Work is rigidly bound to fixed hours, uniform standards, stints and piece-products; and instead of a finished article, each individual now achieves a part of a single process and knows little of those that precede or follow. Machinery has relieved the large basal muscles and laid more stress upon fine and exact movements that involve nerve strain. The coarser forms of work that involve hard lifting, carrying, digging, etc., are themselves specialized, and skilled labor requires more and more brain-work. It has been estimated that "the diminution of manual labor required to do a given quantity of work in 1884 as compared with 1870 is no less than 70 per cent."[11] Personal interest in and the old native sense of responsibility for results, ownership and use of the finished products, which have been the inspiration and soul of work in all the past, are in more and more fields gone. Those who realize how small a proportion of the young male population train or even engage in amateur sports with zest and regularity, how very few and picked men strive for records, and how immediate and amazing are the results of judicious training, can best understand how far below his possibilities as a motor being the average modern man goes through life, and how far short in this respect he falls from fulfilling nature's design for him.

For unnumbered generations primitive man in the nomad age wandered, made perhaps annual migrations, and bore heavy burdens, while we ride relatively unencumbered. He tilled the reluctant soil, digging with rude implements where we use machines of many man-power. In the stone, iron, and bronze age, he shaped stone and metals, and wrought with infinite pains and effort, products that we buy without even knowledge of the processes by which they are made. As hunter he followed game, which, when found, he chased, fought, and overcame in a struggle perhaps desperate, while we shoot it at a distance with little risk or effort. In warfare he fought hand to hand and eye to eye, while we kill "with as much black powder as can be put in a woman's thimble." He caught and domesticated scores of species of wild animals and taught them to serve him; fished with patience and skill that compensated his crude tools, weapons, implements, and tackle; danced to exhaustion in the service of his gods or in memory of his forebears imitating every animal, rehearsing all his own activities in mimic form to the point of exhaustion, while we move through a few figures in closed spaces. He dressed hides, wove baskets which we can not reproduce, and fabrics which we only poorly imitate by machinery, made pottery which set our fashions, played games that invigorated body and soul. His courtship was with feats of prowess and skill, and meant physical effort and endurance.

Adolescent girls, especially in the middle classes, in upper grammar and high school grades, during the golden age for nascent muscular development, suffer perhaps most of all in this respect. Grave as are the evils of child labor, I believe far more pubescents in this country now suffer from too little than from too much physical exercise, while most who suffer from work do so because it is too uniform, one-sided, accessory, or performed under unwholesome conditions, and not because it is excessive in amount. Modern industry has thus largely ceased to be a means of physical development and needs to be offset by compensating modes of activity. Many labor-saving devices increase neural strain, so that one of the problems of our time is how to preserve and restore nerve energy. Under present industrial systems this must grow worse and not better in the future. Healthy natural industries will be less and less open to the young. This is the new situation that now confronts those concerned for motor education, if they would only make good what is lost.

Some of the results of these conditions are seen in average measurements of dimensions, proportions, strength, skill, and control. Despite the excellence of the few, the testimony of those most familiar with the bodies of children and adults, and their physical powers, gives evidence of the ravages of modern modes of life that, without a wide-spread motor revival, can bode only degeneration for our nation and our race. The number of common things that can not be done at all; the large proportion of our youth who must be exempted from any kinds of activity or a great amount of any; the thin limbs, collapsed shoulders or chests, the bilateral asymmetry, weak hearts, lungs, eyes, puny and bad muddy or pallid complexions, tired ways, automatism, dyspeptic stomachs, the effects of youthful error or of impoverished heredity, delicate and tender nurture, often, alas, only too necessary, show the lamentable and cumulative effects of long neglect of the motor abilities, the most educable of all man's powers, and perhaps the most important for his well-being. If the unfaithful stewards of these puny and shameful bodies had again, as in Sparta, to strip and stand before stern judges and render them account, and be smitten with a conviction of their weakness, guilty deformity, and arrest of growth; if they were brought to realize how they are fallen beings, as weak as stern theologians once deemed them depraved, and how great their need of physical salvation, we might hope again for a physical renaissance. Such a rebirth the world has seen but twice or perhaps thrice, and each was followed by the two or three of the brightest culture periods of history, and formed an epoch in the advancement of the kingdom of man. A vast body of evidence could be collected from the writings of anthropologists showing how superior unspoiled savages are to civilized man in correct or esthetic proportions of body, in many forms of endurance of fatigue, hardship, and power to bear exposure, in the development and preservation of teeth and hair, in keenness of senses, absence of deformities, as well as immunity to many of our diseases. Their women are stronger and bear hardship and exposure, monthly periods and childbirth, better. Civilization is so hard on the body that some have called it a disease, despite the arts that keep puny bodies alive to a greater average age, and our greater protection from contagious and germ diseases.

The progressive realization of these tendencies has prompted most of the best recent and great changes motor-ward in education and also in personal regimen. Health- and strength-giving agencies have put to school the large motor areas of the brain, so long neglected, and have vastly enlarged their scope. Thousands of youth are now inspired with new enthusiasm for physical development; and new institutions of many kinds and grades have arisen, with a voluminous literature, unnumbered specialists, specialties, new apparatus, tests, movements, methods, and theories; and the press, the public, and the church are awakened to a fresh interest in the body and its powers. All this is magnificent, but sadly inadequate to cope with the new needs and dangers, which are vastly greater.

[Footnote 1: Dieterich. Göttingen, 1886.]

[Footnote 2: See Chap. xii.]

[Footnote 3: F. Burk in From Fundamental to Accessory. Pedagogical Seminary, Oct., 1898, vol. 6, pp. 5-64.]

[Footnote 4: Creeping and Walking, by A.W. Trettien. American Journal of Psychology, October, 1900, vol. 12, pp. 1-57.]

[Footnote 5: A Morning Observation of a Baby. Pedagogical Seminary, December 1901, vol. 8, pp. 469-481.]

[Footnote 6: Kate Carman. Notes on School Activity. Pedagogical Seminary, March, 1902, vol. 9, pp. 106-117.]

[Footnote 7: A Preliminary Study of Some of the Motor Phenomena of Mental Effort. American Journal of Psychology, July, 1896, vol. 7, pp. 491-517.]

[Footnote 8: G.E. Johnson. Psychology and Pegagogy of Feeble-Minded Children. Pedagogical Seminary, October, 1895, vol. 3, pp. 246-301.]

[Footnote 9: Dr. Hughlings Jackson, the eminent English pathologist, was the first to make practical application of the evolutionary theory of the nervous system to the diagnosis and treatment of epilepsies and mental diseases. The practical success of this application was so great that the Hughlings-Jackson "three-level theory" is now the established basis of English diagnosis. He conceived the nervous mechanism as composed of three systems, arranged in the form of a hierarchy, the higher including the lower, and yet each having a certain degree of independence. The first level represents the type of simplest reflex and involuntary movement and is localized in the gray matter of the spinal cord, medulla, and pons. The second, or middle level, comprises those structures which receive sensory impulses from the cells of the lowest level instead of directly from the periphery or the non-nervous tissues. The motor cells of this middle level also discharge into the motor mechanisms of the lowest level. Jackson located these middle level structures in the cortex of the central convolutions, the basal ganglia and the centers of the special senses in the cortex. The highest level bears the same relation to the middle level that it bears to the lowest i.e., no continuous connection between the highest and the lowest is assumed; the structures of the middle level mediate between them as a system of relays. According to this hierarchical arrangement of the nervous system, the lowest level which is the simplest and oldest "contains the mechanism for the simple fundamental movements in reflexes and involuntary reactions. The second level regroups these simple movements by combinations and associations of cortical structure in wider, more complex mechanisms, producing a higher class of movements. The highest level unifies the whole nervous system and, according to Jackson, is the anatomical basis of mind."

For a fuller account of this theory see Burk: From Fundamental to Accessory in the Nervous System and of Movements. Pedagogical Seminary, October, 1898, vol. 6, pp. 17-23.]

[Footnote 10: A Preliminary Study of Some of the Motor Phenomena of Mental Effort. American Journal of Psychology, July, 1896, vol. 7, pp. 491-517.]

[Footnote 11: Encyclopedia of Social Reform, Funk and Wagnalls, 1896, p. 1095]

CHAPTER III - INDUSTRIAL EDUCATION

Trade classes and schools, their importance in the international market — Our dangers and the superiority of German workmen — The effects of a tariff — Description of schools between the kindergarten and the industrial school — Equal salaries for teachers in France — Dangers from machinery — The advantages of life on the old New England farm — Its resemblance to the education we now give negroes and Indians — Its advantage for all-sided muscular development.

We must glance at a few of the best and most typical methods of muscular development, following the order: industrial education, manual training, gymnastics, and play, sports, and games.

Industrial education is now imperative for every nation that would excel in agriculture, manufacture, and trade, not only because of the growing intensity of competition, but because of the decline of the apprentice system and the growing intricacy of processes, requiring only the skill needed for livelihood. Thousands of our youth of late have been diverted from secondary schools to the monotechnic or trade classes now established for horology, glass-work, brick-laying, carpentry, forging, dressmaking, cooking, typesetting, bookbinding, brewing, seamanship, work in leather, rubber, horticulture, gardening, photography, basketry, stock-raising, typewriting, stenography and bookkeeping, elementary commercial training for practical preparation for clerkships, etc. In this work not only is Boston, our most advanced city, as President Pritchett[1] has shown in detail, far behind Berlin, but German workmen and shopmen a slowly taking the best places even in England; and but for a high tariff, which protects our inferiority, the competitive pressure would be still greater. In Germany, especially, this training is far more diversified than here, always being colored if not determined by the prevalent industry of the region and more specialised and helped out by evening and even Sunday classes in the school buildings, and by the still strong apprentice system. Froebelian influence in manual training reaches through the eight school years and is in some respects better than ours in lower grades, but is very rarely coeducational, girls' work of sewing, knitting, crocheting, weaving, etc., not being considered manual training. There are now over 1,500 schools and workshops in Germany where manual training is taught; twenty-five of these are independent schools. The work really began in 1875 with v. Kass, and is promoted by the great Society for Boys' Handwork. Much stress is laid on paper and pasteboard work in lower grades, under the influence of Kurufa of Darmstadt. Many objects for illustrating science are made, and one course embraces the Seyner water-wheel.[2]

In France it is made more effective by the equal salaries of teachers everywhere, thus securing better instruction in the country. Adolescence is the golden period for acquiring the skill that comes by practice, so essential in the struggle for survival. In general this kind of motor education is least of all free, but subservient to the tool, machine, process, finished product, or end in view; and to these health and development are subordinated, so that they tend to be ever more narrow and special. The standard here is maximal efficiency of the capacities that earn. It may favor bad habitual attitudes, muscular development of but one part, excessive large or small muscles, involve too much time or effort, unhealthful conditions, etc., but it has the great advantage of utility, which is the mainspring of all industry. In a very few departments and places this training has felt the influence of the arts and crafts movement and has been faintly touched with the inspiration of beauty. While such courses give those who follow them marked advantage over those who do not, they are chiefly utilitarian and do little to mature or unfold the physical powers, and may involve arrest or degeneration.

Where not one but several or many professes are taught, the case is far better. Of all work-schools, a good farm is probably the best for motor development. This is due to its great variety of occupations, healthful conditions, and the incalculable phyletic reënforcement from immemorial times. I have computed some three-score industries[3] as the census now classifies them; that were more or less generally known and practiced sixty years ago in a little township, which not only in this but in other respects has many features of an ideal educational environment for adolescent boys, combining as it does not only physical and industrial, but civil and religious elements in wise proportions and with pedagogic objectivity, and representing the ideal of such a state of intelligent citizen voters as was contemplated by the framers of our Constitution.

Contrast this life with that of a "hand" in a modern shoe factory, who does all day but one of the eighty-one stages or processes from a tanned hide to a finished shoe, or of a man in a shirt shop who is one of thirty-nine, each of whom does as piece-work a single step requiring great exactness, speed, and skill, and who never knows how a whole shirt is made, and we shall see that the present beginning of a revival of interest in muscular development comes none too early. So liberal is muscular education of this kind that its work in somewhat primitive form has been restored and copied many features by many educational institutions for adolescents, of the Abbotsholme type and grade, and several others, whose purpose is to train for primitive conditions of colonial life. Thousands of school gardens have also been lately developed for lower grades, which have given a new impetus to the study of nature. Farm training at its best instills love of country, ruralizes taste, borrows some of its ideals from Goethe's pedagogic province, and perhaps even from Gilman's pie-shaped communities, with villages at the center irradiating to farms in all directions. In England, where by the law of primogeniture holdings are large and in few hands, this training has never flourished, as it has greatly in France, where nearly every adult male may own land and a large proportion will come to do so. So of processes. As a student in Germany I took a few lessons each of a bookbinder, a glassblower, a shoemaker, a plumber, and a blacksmith, and here I have learned in a crude way the technique of the gold-beater and old-fashioned broom-maker, etc., none of which come amiss in the laboratory; and I am proud that I can still mow and keep my scythe sharp, chop, plow, milk, churn, make cheese and soap, braid a palm-leaf hat complete, knit, spin and even "put in a piece" in an old-fashioned hand loom, and weave frocking. But thus pride bows low before the pupils of our best institutions for negroes, Indians, and juvenile delinquents, whose training is often in more than a score of industries and who to-day in my judgment receive the best training in the land, if judged by the annual growth in mind, morals, health, physique, ability, and knowledge, all taken together. Instead of seeking soft, ready-made places near home, such education impels to the frontier, to strike out new careers, to start at the bottom and rise by merit, beginning so low that every change must be a rise. Wherever youth thus trained are thrown, they land like a cat on all-fours and are armed *cap-à-pie* for the struggle of life. Agriculture, manufacture, and commerce are the bases of national prosperity; and on them all professions, institutions, and even culture, are more and more dependent, while the old ideals of mere study and brain-work are fast becoming obsolete. We really retain only the knowledge we apply. We should get up interest in new processes like that of a naturalist in new species. Those who leave school at any age or stage should be best fitted to take up their life work instead of leaving unfitted for it, aimless and discouraged. Instead of dropping out limp and disheartened, we should train "struggle-for-lifeurs," in Daudet's phrase, and that betimes, so that the young come back to it not too late for securing the best benefits, after having wasted the years best fitted for it in profitless studies or in the hard school of failure. By such methods many of our flabby, undeveloped, anemic, easy-living city youth would be regenerated in body and spirit. Some of the now oldest, richest, and most famous schools of the world were at first established by charity for poor boys who worked their way, and such institutions have an undreamed-of future. No others so well fit for a life of respectable and successful muscle work, and perhaps this should be central for all at this stage. This diversity of training develops the muscular activities rendered necessary by man's early development, which were so largely concerned with food, shelter, clothing, making and selling commodities necessary for life, comfort and safety. The natural state of man is not war, hot peace; and perhaps Dawson[4] is right in thinking that three-fourths of man's physical activities in the past have gone into such vocations. Industry has determined the nature and trend of muscular development; and youth, who have pets, till the soil, build, manufacture, use tools, and master elementary processes and skills, are most truly repeating the history of the race. This, too, lays the best foundation for intellectual careers. The study of pure science, as well as its higher technology, follows rather than precedes this. In the largest sense this is the order of nature, from fundamental and generalized to finer accessory and specialized organs and functions; and such a sequence best weeds out and subordinates automatisms. The age of stress in most of these kinds of training is that of most rapid increment of muscular power, as we have seen in the middle and later teens rather than childhood, as some recent methods have mistakenly assumed; and this prepolytechnic work, wherever and in whatever degree it is possible, is a better adjunct of secondary courses than manual training, the sad fact being that, according to the best estimates, only a fraction of one per cent of those who need this training in this country are now receiving it.

[Footnote 1: The Place of Industrial and Technical Training in Public Education. Technology Review, January, 1902, vol. 4, pp. 10-37.]

[Footnote 2: See an article by Dr. H.E. Kock, Education, December, 1902, vol. 23, pp. 193-203.]

[Footnote 3: See my Boy Life in a Massachusetts Country Town Forty Years Ago. Pedagogical Seminary, June, 1906, vol. 13, pp. 192-207.]

[Footnote 4: The Muscular Activities Rendered Necessary by Man's Early Environment, American Physical Education Review, June, 1902, vol. 7, pp. 80-85.]

CHAPTER IV - MANUAL TRAINING AND SLOYD

History of the movement—Its philosophy—The value of hand training in the development of the brain and its significance in the making of man—A grammar of our many industries hard—The best we do can reach but few—Very great defects in our manual training methods which do not base on science and make nothing salable—The Leipzig system—Sloyd is hypermethodic—These crude peasant industries can never satisfy educational needs—The gospel of work, William Morris and the arts and crafts movement—Its spirit desirable—The magic effects of a brief period of intense work—The natural development of the drawing instinct in the child.

Manual training has many origins; but in its now most widely accepted form it came to us more than a generation ago from Moscow, and has its best representation here in our new and often magnificent manual-training high schools and in many courses in other public schools. This work meets the growing demand of the country for a more practical education, a demand which often greatly exceeds the accommodations. The philosophy, if such it may be called, that underlies the movement, is simple, forcible, and sound, and not unlike Pestalozzi's *"keine Kentnisse ohne Fertigkeiten,"* [No knowledge without skill] in that it lessens the interval between thinking and doing; helps to give control, dexterity, and skill an industrial trend to taste; interests many not successful in ordinary school; tends to the better appreciation of good, honest work; imparts new zest for some studies; adds somewhat to the average length of the school period; gives a sense of capacity and effectiveness, and is a useful preparation for a number of vocations. These claims are all well founded, and this work is a valuable addition to the pedagogic agencies of any country or state. As man excels the higher anthropoids perhaps almost as much in hand power as in mind, and since the manual areas of the brain are wide near the psychic zones, and the cortical centers are thus directly developed, the hand is a potent instrument in opening the intellect as well as in training sense and will. It is no reproach to these schools that, full as they are, they provide for but an insignificant fraction of the nearly sixteen millions or twenty per cent of the young people of the country between fifteen and twenty-four.

When we turn to the needs of these pupils, the errors and limitations of the method are painful to contemplate. The work is essentially manual and offers little for the legs, where most of the muscular tissues of the body lie, those which respond most to training and are now most in danger of degeneration at this age; the back and trunk also are little trained. Consideration of proportion and bilateral asymmetry are practically ignored. Almost in proportion as these schools have multiplied, the rage for uniformity, together with motives of economy and administrative efficiency on account of overcrowding, have made them rigid and inflexible, on the principle that as the line lengthens the stake must be strengthened. This is a double misfortune; for the courses were not sufficiently considered at first and the plastic stage of adaptation was too short, while the methods of industry have undergone vast changes since they were given shape. There are now between three and four hundred occupations in the census, more than half of these involving manual work, so that never perhaps was there so great a pedagogic problem as to make these natural developments into conscious art, to extract what may be called basal types. This requires an effort not without analogy to Aristotle's attempt to extract from the topics of the marketplace the underlying categories eternally conditioning all thought, or to construct a grammar of speech. Hardly an attempt worthy the name, not even the very inadequate one of a committee, has been made in this field to study the conditions and to meet them. Like Froebel's gifts and occupations, deemed by their author the very roots of human occupations in infant form, the processes selected are underived and find their justification rather in their logical sequence and coherence than in being true norms of work. If these latter be attainable at all, it is not likely that they will fit so snugly in a brief curriculum, so that its simplicity is suspicious. The wards of the keys that lock the secrets of nature and human life are more intricate and mazy. As H.T. Bailey well puts it in substance, a master in any art-craft must have a fourfold equipment: 1. Ability to grasp an idea and embody it. 2. Power to utilize all nerve, and a wide repertory of methods, devices, recipes, discoveries, machines, etc. 3. Knowledge of the history of the craft. 4. Skill in technical processes. American schools emphasize chiefly only the last.

The actual result is thus a course rich in details representing wood and iron chiefly, and mostly ignoring other materials; the part of the course treating of the former, wooden in its teachings and distinctly tending to make joiners, carpenters, and cabinet-makers; that of the latter, iron in its rigidity and an excellent school for smiths, mechanics, and machinists. These courses are not liberal because they hardly touch science, which is rapidly becoming the real basis of every industry. Almost nothing that can be called scientific knowledge is required or even much favored, save some geometrical and mechanical drawing and its implicates. These schools instinctively fear and repudiate plain and direct utility, or suspect its educational value or repute in the community because of this strong bias toward a few trades. This tendency also they even fear, less often because unfortunately trade-unions in this country sometimes jealously suspect it and might vote down supplies, than because the teachers in these schools were generally trained in older scholastic and even classic methods and matter. Industry is everywhere and always for the sake of the product, and to cut loose from this as if it were a contamination is a fatal mistake. To focus on process only, with no reference to the object made, is here an almost tragic case of the sacrifice of content to form, which in all history has been the chief stigma of degeneration in education. Man is a tool-using animal; but tools are always only a means to an end, the latter prompting even their invention. Hence a course in tool manipulation only, with persistent refusal to consider the product lest features of trade-schools be introduced, has made most of our manual-training high schools ghastly, hollow, artificial institutions. Instead of making in the lower grades certain toys which are masterpieces of mechanical simplification, as tops and kites, and introducing such processes as glass-making and photography, and in higher grades making simple scientific apparatus more generic than machines, to open the great principles of the material universe, all is sacrificed to supernormalized method.

As in all hypermethodic schemes, the thought side is feeble. There is no control of the work of these schools by the higher technical institutions such as the college exercises over the high school, so that few of them do work that fits for advanced training or is thought best by technical faculties. In most of its current narrow forms, manual training will prove to be historically, as it is educationally, extemporized and tentative, and will soon be superseded by broader methods and be forgotten and obsolete, or cited only as a low point of departure from which future progress will loom up.

Indeed in more progressive centers, many new departures are now in the experimental stage. Goetze at Leipzig, as a result of long and original studies and trials, has developed courses in which pasteboard work and modeling are made of equal rank with wood and iron, and he has connected them even with the kindergarten below. In general the whole industrial life of our day is being slowly explored in the quest of new educational elements; and rubber, lead, glass, textiles, metallurgical operations, agriculture, every tool and many machines, etc., are sure to contribute their choicest pedagogical factors to the final result. In every detail the prime consideration should be the nature and needs of the youthful body and will at each age, their hygiene and fullest development; and next, the closest connection with science at every point should do the same for the intellect. Each operation and each tool—the saw, knife, plane, screw, hammer, chisel, draw-shave, sandpaper, lathe—will be studied with reference to its orthopedic value, bilateral asymmetry, the muscles it develops, and the attitudes and motor habits it favors; and uniformity, which in France often requires classes to saw, strike, plane up, down, right, left, all together, upon count and command, will give place to individuality.

Sloyd has certain special features and claims. The word means skilful, deft. The movement was organised in Sweden a quarter of a century ago as an effort to prevent the extinction by machinery of peasant home industry during the long winter night. Home sloyd was installed in an institution of its own for training teachers at Nääs. It works in wood only, with little machinery, and is best developed for children of from eleven to fifteen. It no longer aims to make artisans; but its manipulations are meant to be developmental, to teach both sexes not only to be useful but self-active and self-respecting, and to revere exactness as a form of truthfulness. It assumes that all and especially the motor-minded can really understand only what they make, and that one can work like a peasant and think like a philosopher. It aims to produce wholes rather than parts like the Russian system, and to be so essentially educational that, as a leading exponent says, its best effects would be conserved if the hands were cut off. This change of its original utilitarianism from the lower to the liberal motor development of the middle and upper classes and from the land where it originated to another, has not eliminated the dominant marks of its origin in its models, the Penates of the sloyd household, the unique features of which persist like a national school of art, despite transplantation and transformation.[1]

Sloyd at its best tries to correlate several series, viz., exercises, tools, drawing, and models. Each must be progressive, so that every new step in each series involves a new and next developmental step in all the others, and all together, it is claimed, fit the order and degree of development of each power appealed to in the child. Yet there has been hardly an attempt to justify either the physiological or the psychological reason of a single step in any of these series, and the coördination of the series even with each other, to say nothing of their adaptation to the stages of the child's development. This, if as pat and complete as is urged, would indeed constitute on the whole a paragon of all the harmony, beauty, totality in variety, etc., which make it so magnificent in the admirer's eyes. But the "45 tools, 72 exercises, 31 models, 15 of which are joints," all learned by teachers in one school year of daily work and by pupils in four years, are overmethodic; and such correlation is impossible in so many series at once. Every dual order, even of work and unfoldment of powers, is hard enough, since the fall lost us Eden; and woodwork, could it be upon that of the tree of knowledge itself, incompatible with enjoying its fruit. Although a philosopher may see the whole universe in its smallest part, all his theory can not reproduce educational wholes from fragments of it. The real merits of sloyd have caused its enthusiastic leaders to magnify its scope and claims far beyond their modest bounds; and although its field covers the great transition from childhood to youth, one searches in vain both its literature and practise for the slightest recognition of the new motives and methods that puberty suggests. Especially in its partially acclimatized forms to American conditions, it is all adult and almost scholastic; and as the most elaborate machinery may sometimes be run by a poor power-wheel, if the stream be swift and copious enough, so the mighty rent that sets toward motor education would give it some degree of success were it worse and less economic of pedagogic momentum than it is. It holds singularly aloof from other methods of efferent training and resists coördination with them, and its provisions for other than hand development are slight. It will be one of the last to accept its true but modest place as contributing certain few but precious elements in the greater synthesis that impends. Indian industries, basketry, pottery, bead, leather, bows and arrows, bark, etc., which our civilization is making lost arts by forcing the white man's industries upon red men at reservation schools and elsewhere, need only a small part of the systemization that Swedish peasant work has received to develop even greater educational values; and the same is true of the indigenous household work of the old New England farm, the real worth and possibilities of which are only now, and perhaps too late, beginning to be seen by a few educators.

This brings us to the arts and crafts movement, originating with Carlyle's gospel of work and Ruskin's medievalism, developed by William Morris and his disciples at the Red House, checked awhile by the ridicule of the comic opera "Patience," and lately revived in some of its features by Cobden-Sanderson, and of late to some extent in various centers in this country. Its ideal was to restore the day of the seven ancient guilds and of Hans Sachs, the poet cobbler, when conscience and beauty inspired work, and the hand did what machines only imitate and vulgarize. In the past, which this school of motor culture harks back to, work, for which our degenerate age lacks even respect, was indeed praise. Refined men and women have remembered these early days, when their race was in its prime, as a lost paradise which they would regain by designing and even weaving tapestries and muslins; experimenting in vats with dyes to rival Tyrian purple; printing and binding by hand books that surpass the best of the Aldine, and Elzevirs; carving in old oak; hammering brass; forging locks, irons, and candlesticks; becoming artists in burned wood and leather; seeking old effects of simplicity and solidity in furniture and decoration, as well as architecture, stained glass, and to some extent in dress and manners; and all this toil and moil was *ad majorem gloriam hominis* [To the greater glory of man] in a new socialistic state, where the artist, and even the artisan, should take his rightful place above the man who merely knows. The day of the mere professor, who deals in knowledge, is gone; and the day of the doer, who creates, has come. The brain and the hand, too long divorced and each weak and mean without the other; use and beauty, each alone vulgar; letters and labor, each soulless without the other, are henceforth to be one and inseparable; and this union will lift man to a higher level. The workman in his apron and paper hat, inspired by the new socialism and the old spirit of chivalry as revived by Scott, revering Wagner's revival of the old *Deutschenthum* that was to conquer *Christenthum*, or Tennyson's Arthurian cycle—this was its ideal; even as the Jews rekindled their loyalty to the ancient traditions of their race and made their Bible under Ezra; as we begin to revere the day of the farmer-citizen, who made our institutions, or as some of us would revive his vanishing industrial life for the red man.

Although this movement was by older men and women and had in it something of the longing regret of senescence for days that are no more, it shows us the glory which invests racial adolescence when it is recalled in maturity, the time when the soul can best appreciate the value of its creations and its possibilities, and really lives again in its glamour and finds in it its greatest inspiration. Hence it has its lessons for us here. A touch, but not too much of it, should be felt in all manual education, which is just as capable of idealism as literary education. This gives soul, interest, content, beauty, taste. If not a polyphrastic philosophy seeking to dignify the occupation of the workshop by a pretentious Volapük of reasons and abstract theories, we have here the pregnant suggestion of a psychological quarry of motives and spirit opened and ready to be worked. Thus the best forces from the past should be turned on to shape and reinforce the best tendencies of the present. The writings of the above gospelers of work not only could and should, but will be used to inspire manual-training high schools, sloyd and even some of the less scholastic industrial courses; but each is incomplete without the other. These books and those that breathe their spirit should be the mental workshop of all who do tool, lathe, and forge work; who design and draw patterns, carve or mold; or of those who study how to shape matter for human uses, and whose aim is to obtain diplomas or certificates of fitness to teach all such things. The muse of art and even of music will have some voice in the great synthesis which is to gather up the scattered, hence ineffective, elements of secondary motor training, in forms which shall represent all the needs of adolescents in the order and proportion that nature and growth stages indicate, drawing, with this end supreme, upon all the resources that history and reform offer to our selection. All this can never make work become play. Indeed it will and should make work harder and more unlike play and of another genus, because the former is thus given its own proper soul and leads its own distinct, but richer, and more abounding life.

I must not close this section without brief mention of two important studies that have supplied each a new and important determination concerning laws of work peculiar to adolescence.

The main telegraphic line requires a speed of over seventy letters per minute of all whom they will employ. As a sending rate this is not very difficult and is often attained after two months' practise. This standard for a receiving rate is harder and later, and inquiry at schools where it is taught shows that about seventy-five per cent of those who begin the study fail to reach this speed and so are not employed. Bryan and Harter[2] explained the rate of improvement in both sending and receiving, with results represented for one typical subject in the curve on the following page.

From the first, sending improves most rapidly and crosses the deadline a few months before the receiving rate, which may fall short. Curves 1 and 2 represent the same student. I have added line 3 to illustrate the three-fourths who fail. Receiving is far less pleasant than sending, and years of daily practise at ordinary rates will not bring a man to his maximum rate; he remains on the low plateau with no progress beyond a certain point. If forced by stress of work, danger of being dropped, or by will power to make a prolonged and intense effort, he breaks through his hidebound rate and permanently attains a faster pace. This is true at each step, and every advance seems to cost even more intensive effort than the former one. At length, for those who go on, the rate of receiving, which is a more complex process, exceeds that of sending; and the curves of the above figure would cross if prolonged. The expert receives so much faster than he sends that abbreviated codes are used, and he may take eighty to eighty-five words a minute on a typewriter in correct form.

The motor curve seems to asymptotically approach a perhaps physiological limit, which the receiving curve does not suggest. This seems a special case of a general though not yet explained law. In learning a foreign language, speaking is first and easiest, and hearing takes a late but often sudden start to independence. Perhaps this holds of every ability. To Bryan this suggests as a hierarchy of habits, the plateau of little or no improvement, meaning that lower order habits are approaching their maximum but are not yet automatic enough to leave the attention free to attack higher order habits. The second ascent from drudgery to freedom, which comes through automatism, is often as sudden as the first ascent. One stroke of attention comes to do what once took many. To attain such effective speed is not dependent on reaction time. This shooting together of units distinguishes the master from the man, the genius from the hack. In many, if not all, skills where expertness is sought, there is a long discouraging level, and then for the best a sudden ascent, as if here, too, as we have reason to think in the growth of both the body as a whole and in that of its parts, nature does make leaps and attains her ends by alternate rests and rushes. Youth lives along on a low level of interest and accomplishment and then starts onward, is transformed, converted; the hard becomes easy; the old life sinks to a lower stratum; and a new and higher order, perhaps a higher brain level and functions, is evolved. The practical implication here of the necessity of hard concentrative effort as a condition of advancement is re-enforced by a quotation from Senator Stanford on the effect of early and rather intensive work at not too long periods in training colts for racing. Let-ups are especially dangerous. He says, "It is the supreme effort that develops." This, I may add, suggests what is developed elsewhere, that truly spontaneous attention is conditioned by spontaneous muscle tension, which is a function of growth, and that muscles are thus organs of the mind; and also that even voluntary attention is motivated by the same nisus of development even in its most adult form, and that the products of science, invention, discovery, as well as the association plexus of all that was originally determined in the form of consciousness, are made by rhythmic alternation of attack, as it moves from point to point creating diversions and recurrence.

The other study, although quite independent, is part a special application and illustration of the same principle.

At the age of four or five, when they can do little more than scribble, children's chief interest in pictures is as finished products; but in the second period, which Lange calls that of artistic illusion, the child sees in his own work not merely what it represents, but an image of fancy back of it. This, then, is the golden period for the development of power to create artistically. The child loves to draw everything with the pleasure chiefly in the act, and he cares little for the finished picture. He draws out of his own head, and not from copy before his eye. Anything and everything is attempted in bold lines in this golden age of drawing. If he followed the teacher, looked carefully and drew what he saw, he would be abashed at his production. Indians, conflagrations, games, brownies, trains, pageants, battles—everything is graphically portrayed; but only the little artist himself sees the full meaning of his lines. Criticism or drawing strictly after nature breaks this charm, since it gives place to mechanical reproduction in which the child has little interest. Thus awakens him from his dream to a realization that he can not draw, and from ten to fifteen his power of perceiving things steadily increases and he makes almost no progress in drawing. Adolescence arouses the creative faculty and the desire and ability to draw are checked and decline after thirteen or fourteen. The curve is the plateau which Barnes has described. The child has measured his own productions upon the object they reproduced and found them wanting, is discouraged and dislikes drawing. From twelve on, Barnes found drawing more and more distasteful; and this, too, Lukens found to be the opinion of our art teachers. The pupils may draw very properly and improve in technique, but the interest is gone. This is the condition in which most men remain all their lives. Their power to appreciate steadily increases. Only a few gifted adolescents about this age begin a to develop a new zest in production, rivaling that of the period from five to ten, when their satisfaction is again chiefly in creation. These are the artists whose active powers dominate.

Lukens[3] finds in his studies of drawing, that in what he calls his fourth period of artistic development, there are those "who during adolescence experience a rebirth of creative power." Zest in creation then often becomes a stronger incentive to work than any pleasure or profit to be derived from the finished product, so that in this the propitious conditions of the first golden age of childhood are repeated and the deepest satisfaction is again found in the work itself. At about fourteen or fifteen, which is the transition period, nascent faculties sometimes develop very rapidly. Lukens[4] draws the interesting curve shown on the following page.

The reciprocity between the power to produce and that to appreciate, roughly represented in the above curve, likely is true also in the domain of music, and may be, perhaps, a general law of development. Certain it is that the adolescent power to apperceive and appreciate never so far outstrips his power to produce or reproduce as about midway in the teens. Now impressions sink deepest. The greatest artists are usually those who paint later, when the expressive powers are developed, what they have felt most deeply and known best at this age, and not those who in the late twenties, or still later, have gone to new environments and sought to depict them. All young people draw best those objects they love most, and their proficiency should be some test of the contents of their minds. They must put their own consciousness into a picture. At the dawn of this stage of appreciation the esthetic tastes should be stimulated by exposure to, and instructed in feeling for, the subject-matter of masterpieces; and instruction in technique, detail, criticism, and learned discrimination of schools of painting should be given intermittently. Art should not now be for art's sake, but for the sake of feeling and character, life, and conduct; it should be adjunct to morals, history, and literature; and in all, edification should be the goal; and personal interest, and not that of the teacher, should be the guide. Insistence on production should be eased, and the receptive imagination, now so hungry, should be fed and reinforced by story and all other accessories. By such a curriculum, potential creativeness, if it exists, will surely be evoked in its own good time. It will, at first, attempt no commonplace drawing-master themes, but will essay the highest that the imagination can bode forth. It may be crude and lame in execution, but it will be lofty, perhaps grand; and if it is original in consciousness, it will be in effect. Most creative painters before twenty have grappled with the greatest scenes in literature or turning points in history, representations of the loftiest truths, embodiments of the most inspiring ideals. None who deserve the name of artist copy anything now, and least of all with objective fidelity to nature; and the teacher that represses or criticizes this first point of genius, or who can not pardon the grave faults of technique inevitable at this age when ambition ought to be too great for power, is not an educator but a repressor, a pedagogic Philistine committing, like so many of his calling in other fields, the unpardonable sin against budding promise, always at this age so easily blighted. Just as the child of six or seven should be encouraged in his strong instinct to draw the most complex scenes of his daily life, so now the inner life should find graphic utterance in all its intricacy up to the full limit of unrepressed courage. For the great majority, on the other hand, who only appreciate and will never create, the mind, if it have its rights, will be stored with the best images and sentiments of art; for at this time they are best remembered and sink deepest into heart and life. Now, although the hand may refuse, the fancy paints the world in brightest hues and fairest forms; and such an opportunity for infecting the soul with vaccine of ideality, hope, optimism, and courage in adversity, will never come again. I believe that in few departments are current educational theories and practises so hard on youth of superior gifts, just at the age when all become geniuses for a season, very brief for most, prolonged for some, and permanent for the best. We do not know how to teach to, see, hear, and feel when the sense centers are most indelibly impressible, and to give relative rest to the hand during the years when its power of accuracy is abated and when all that is good is idealized furthest, and confidence in ability to produce is at its lowest ebb.

Finally, our divorce between industrial and manual training is abnormal, and higher technical education is the chief sufferer. Professor Thurston, of Cornell, who has lately returned from a tour of inspection abroad, reported that to equal Germany we now need: "1. Twenty technical universities, having in their schools of engineering 50 instructors and 500 students each. 2. Two thousand technical high schools or manual-training schools, each having not less than 200 students and 10 instructors." If we have elementary trade-schools, this would mean technical high schools enough to accommodate 700,000 students, served by 20,000 teachers. With the strong economic arguments in this direction we are not here concerned; but that there are tendencies to unfit youth for life by educational method and matter shown in strong relief from this standpoint, we shall point out in a later chapter.

[Footnote 1: This I have elsewhere tried to show in detail. Criticisms of High School Physics and Manual Training and Mechanic Arts in High Schools. Pedagogical Seminary, June, 1902, vol. 9, pp. 193-204.]

[Footnote 2: Studies in the Physiology and Psychology of the Telegraphic Language. Psychological Review, January, 1897, vol. 4, pp. 27-53, and July, 1899, vol. 6, pp. 344-375.]

[Footnote 3: A Study of Children's Drawings in the Early Years. Pedagogical Seminary, October, 1896, vol. 4, pp. 79-101. See also Drawing in the Early Years, Proceedings of the National Educational Association, 1899, pp. 946-953. Das Kind als Künstler, von C. Götze. Hamburg, 1898. The Genetic *vs.* the Logical Order in Drawing, by F. Burk. Pedagogical Seminary, September, 1902, vol. 9, pp. 296-323.]

[Footnote 4: Die Entwickelungsstufen beim Zeichnen. Die Kinderfehler, September, 1897, vol. 2, pp. 166-179.]

CHAPTER V - GYMNASTICS

The story of Jahn and the Turners—The enthusiasm which this movement generated in Germany—The ideal of bringing out latent powers—The concept of more perfect voluntary control—Swedish gymnastics—Doing everything possible for the body as a machine—Liberal physical culture—Ling's orthogenic scheme of economic postures and movements and correcting defects—The ideal of symmetry and prescribing exercises to bring the body to a standard—Lamentable lack of correlation between these four systems—Illustrations of the great good that a systematic training can effect—Athletic records—Greek physical training.

Under the term gymnastics, literally naked exercises, we here include those denuded of all utilities or ulterior ends save those of physical culture. This is essentially modern and was unknown in antiquity, where training was for games, for war, etc. Several ideals underlie this movement, which although closely related are distinct and as yet by no means entirely harmonized. These may be described as follows:

A. One aim of Jahn, more developed by Spiess, and their successors, was to do everything physically possible for the body as a mechanism. Many postures and attitudes are assumed and many movements made that are never called for in life. Some of these are so novel that a great variety of new apparatus had to be devised to bring them out; and Jahn invented many new names, some of them without etymologies, to designate the repertory of his discoveries and inventions that extended the range of motor life. Common movements, industries, and even games, train only a limited number of muscles, activities, and coördinations, and leave more or less unused groups and combinations, so that many latent possibilities slumber, and powers slowly lapse through disuse. Not only must these be rescued, but the new nascent possibilities of modern progressive man must be addressed and developed. Even the common things that the average untrained youth can not do are legion, and each of these should be a new incentive to the trainer as he realizes how very far below their motor possibilities meet men live. The man of the future may, and even must, do things impossible in the past and acquire new motor variations not given by heredity. Our somatic frame and its powers must therefore be carefully studied, inventoried, and assessed afresh, and a kind and amount of exercise required that is exactly proportioned, not perhaps to the size but to the capability of each voluntary muscle. Thus only can we have a truly humanistic physical development, analogous to the training of all the powers of the mind in a broad, truly liberal, and non-professional or non-vocational educational curriculum. The body will thus have its rightful share in the pedagogic traditions and inspirations of the renaissance. Thus only can we have a true scale of standardised culture values for efferent processes; and from this we can measure the degrees of departure, both in the direction of excess and defect, of each form of work, motor habit; and even play. Many modern Epigoni in the wake of this great ideal, where its momentum was early spent, feeling that new activities might be discovered with virtues hitherto undreamed of, have almost made fetiches of special disciplines, both developmental and corrective, that are pictured and landed in scores of manuals. Others have had expectations no less excessive in the opposite direction and have argued that the greatest possible variety of movements best developed the greatest total of motor energy. Jahn especially thus made gymnastics a special art and inspired great enthusiasm of humanity, and the songs of his pupils were of a better race of man and a greater and united fatherland. It was this feature that made his work unique in the world, and his disciples are fond of reminding us of the fact that it was just about one generation of men after the acme of influence of his system that, in 1870, Germany showed herself the greatest military power since ancient Rome, and took the acknowledged leadership of the world both in education and science.

These theorizations even in their extreme forms have been not only highly suggestive but have brought great and new enthusiasms and ideals into the educational world that admirably fit adolescence. The motive of bringing out latent, decaying, or even new powers, skills, knacks, and feats, is full of inspiration. Patriotism is aroused, for thus the country can be better served; thus the German Fatherland was to be restored and unified after the dark days that followed the humiliation of Jena. Now the ideals of religion are invoked that the soul may have a better and regenerated somatic organism with which to serve Jesus and the Church. Exercise is made a form of praise to God and of service to man, and these motives are reënforced by those of the new hygiene which strives for a new wholeness-holiness, and would purify the body as the temple of the Holy Ghost. Thus in Young Men's Christian Association training schools and gymnasiums the gospel of Christianity is preached anew and seeks to bring salvation to man's physical frame, which the still lingering effects of asceticism have caused to be too long neglected in its progressive degeneration. As the Greek games were in honor of the gods, so now the body is trained to better glorify God; and regimen, chastity, and temperance are given a new momentum. The physical salvation thus wrought will be, when adequately written, one of the most splendid chapters in the modern history of Christianity. Military ideals have been revived in cult and song to hearten the warfare against evil within and without. Strength is prayed for as well as worked for, and consecrated to the highest uses. Last but not least, power thus developed over a large surface may be applied to athletic contests in the field, and victories here are valuable as fore-gleams of how sweet the glory of achievements in higher moral and spiritual tasks will taste later.

The dangers and sources of error in this ideal of all-sided training are, alas, only too obvious, although they only qualify its paramount good. First, it is impossible thus to measure the quanta of training needed so as rightly to assign to each its modicum and best modality of training. Indeed no method of doing this has ever been attempted, but the assessments have been arbitrary and conjectural, probably right in some and wrong in other respects, with no adequate criterion or test for either save only empirical experience. Secondly, heredity, which lays its heavy ictus upon some neglected forms of activity and fails of all support for others, has been ignored. As we shall see later, one of the best norms here is phyletic emphasis, and what lacks this must at best be feeble; and if new powers are unfolding, their growth must be very slow and they must be nurtured as tender buds for generations. Thirdly, too little regard is had for the vast differences in individuals, most of whom need much personal prescription.

B. In practise the above ideal is never isolated from others. Perhaps the most closely associated with it is that of increased volitional control. Man is largely a creature of habit, and many of his activities are more or less automatic reflexes from the stimuli of his environment. Every new power of controlling these by the will frees man from slavery and widens the field of freedom. To acquire the power of doing all with consciousness and volition mentalizes the body, gives control over to higher brain levels, and develops them by rescuing activities from the dominance of lower centers. Thus *mens agitat molem*. [Footnote: Mind rules the body.] This end is favored by the Swedish *commando* exercises, which require great alertness of attention to translate instantly a verbal order into an act and also, although in somewhat less degree, by quick imitation of a leader. The stimulus of music and rhythm are excluded because thought to interfere with this end. A somewhat sophisticated form of this goal is sought by several Delsartian schemes of relaxation, decomposition, and recomposition of movements. To do all things with consciousness and to encroach on the field of instinct involves new and more vivid sense impressions, the range of which is increased directly as that of motion, the more closely it approaches the focus of attention. By thus analyzing settled and established coördinations, their elements are set free and may be organized into new combinations, so that the former is the first stage toward becoming a virtuoso with new special skills. This is the road to inner secrets or intellectual rules of professional and expert successes, such as older athletes often rely upon when their strength begins to wane. Every untrained automatism must be domesticated, and every striated muscle capable of direct muscular control must be dominated by volition. Thus tensions and incipient contractures that drain off energy can be relaxed by fiat. Sandow's "muscle dance," the differentiation of movements of the right and left hand — one, e.g., writing a French madrigal while the other is drawing a picture of a country dance, or each playing tunes of disparate rhythm and character simultaneously on the piano — controlling heart rate, moving the ears, crying, laughing, blushing, moving the bowels, etc., at will, feats of inhibition of reflexes, stunts of all kinds, proficiency with many tools, deftness in sports — these altogether would mark the extremes in this direction.

This, too, has its inspiration for youth. To be a universal adept like Hippias suggests Diderot and the encyclopedists in the intellectual realm. To do all with consciousness is a means to both remedial and expert ends. Motor life often needs to be made over to a greater or less extent; and that possibilities of vastly greater accomplishments exist than are at present realized, is undoubted, even in manners and morals, which are both at root only motor habits. Indeed consciousness itself is largely and perhaps wholly corrective in its very essence and origin. Thus life is adjusted to new environments; and if the Platonic postulate be correct, that untaught virtues that come by nature and instinct are no virtues, but must be made products of reflection and reason, the sphere and need of this principle is great indeed. But this implies a distrust of physical human nature as deep-seated and radical as that of Calvinism for the unregenerate heart, against which modern common sense, so often the best muse of both psychophysics and pedagogy, protests. Individual prescription is here as imperative as it is difficult. Wonders that now seem to be most incredible, both of hurt and help, can undoubtedly be wrought, but analysis should always be for the sake of synthesis and never be beyond its need and assured completion. No thoughtful student fully informed of the facts and tentatives in this field can doubt that here lies one of the most promising fields of future development, full of far-reaching and rich results for those, as yet far too few, experts in physical training, who have philosophic minds, command the facts of modern psychology, and whom the world awaits now as never before.

C. Another yet closely correlated ideal is that of economic postures and movements. The system of Ling is less orthopedic than orthogenic, although he sought primarily to correct bad attitudes and perverted growth. Starting from the respiratory and proceeding to the muscular system, he and his immediate pupils were content to refer to the ill-shapen bodies of most men about them. One of their important aims was to relax the flexor and tone up the extensor muscles and to open the human form into postures as opposite as possible to those of the embryo, which it tends so persistently to approximate in sitting, and in fatigue and collapse attitudes generally. The head must balance on the cervical vertebra and not call upon the muscles of the neck to keep it from rolling off; the weight of the shoulders must be thrown back off the thorax; the spine be erect to allow the abdomen free action; the joints of the thigh extended; the hand and arm supinated, etc. Bones must relieve muscles and nerves. Thus an erect, self-respecting carriage must be given, and the unfortunate association, so difficult to overcome, between effort and an involuted posture must be broken up. This means economy and a great saving of vital energy. Extensor action goes with expansive, flexor with depressive states of mind; hence courage, buoyancy, hope, are favored and handicaps removed. All that is done with great effort causes wide irradiation of tensions to the other half of the body and also sympathetic activities in those not involved; the law of maximal ease and minimal expenditure of energy must be always striven for, and the interests of the viscera never lost sight of. This involves educating weak and neglected muscles, and like the next ideal, often shades over by almost imperceptible gradation into the passive movements by the Zander machines. Realizing that certain activities are sufficiently or too much emphasized in ordinary life, stress is laid upon those which are complemental to them, so that there is no pretense of taking charge of the totality of motor processes, the intention being principally to supplement deficiencies, to insure men against being warped, distorted, or deformed by their work in life, to compensate specialties and perform more exactly what recreation to some extent aims at.

This wholesome but less inspiring endeavor, which combats one of the greatest evils that under modern civilization threatens man's physical weal, is in some respects as easy and practical as it is useful. The great majority of city bred men, as well as all students, are prone to deleterious effects from too much sitting; and indeed there is anatomical evidence in the structure of the tissues, and especially the blood-vessels of the groins, that, at his best, man is not yet entirely adjusted to the upright position. So a method that straightens knees, hips, spine, and shoulders, or combats the school-desk attitude, is a most salutary contribution to a great and growing need. In the very act of stretching, and perhaps yawning, for which much is to be said, nature itself suggests such correctives and preventives. To save men from being victims of their occupations is often to add a better and larger half to their motor development. The danger of the system, which now best represents this ideal, is inflexibility and overscholastic treatment. It needs a great range of individual variations if it would do more than increase circulation, respiration, and health, or the normal functions of internal organs and fundamental physiological activities. To clothe the frame with honest muscles that are faithful servants of the will adds not only strength, more active habits and efficiency, but health; and in its material installation this system is financially economic. Personal faults and shortcomings are constantly pointed out where this work is best represented, and it has a distinct advantage in inciting an acquaintance with physiology and inviting the larger fields of medical knowledge.

D. The fourth gymnastic aim is symmetry and correct proportions. Anthropometry and average girths and dimensions, strength, etc., of the parts of the body are first charted in percentile grades; and each individual is referred to the apparatus and exercises best fitted to correct weaknesses and subnormalities. The norms here followed are not the canons of Greek art, but those established by the measurement of the largest numbers properly grouped by age, weight, height, etc. Young men are found to differ very widely. Some can lift 1,000 pounds, and some not 100; some can lift their weight between twenty and forty times, and some not once; some are most deficient in legs, others in shoulders, arms, backs, chests. By photography, tape, and scales, each is interested in his own bodily condition and incited to overcome his greatest defects; and those best endowed by nature to attain ideal dimensions and make new records are encouraged along these lines. Thus this ideal is also largely though not exclusively remedial.

This system can arouse youth to the greatest pitch of zest in watching their own rapidly multiplying curves of growth in dimensions and capacities, in plotting curves that record their own increment in girths, lifts, and other tests, and in observing the effects of sleep, food, correct and incorrect living upon a system so exquisitely responsive to all these influences as are the muscles. To learn to know and grade excellence and defect, to be known for the list of things one can do and to have a record, or to realize what we lack of power to break best records, even to know that we are strengthening some point where heredity has left us with some shortage and perhaps danger, the realization of all this may bring the first real and deep feeling for growth that may become a passion later in things of the soul. Growth always has its selfish aspects, and to be constantly passing our own examination in this respect is a new and perhaps sometimes too self-conscious endeavor of our young college barbarians; but it is on the whole a healthful regulative, and this form of the struggle toward perfection and escape from the handicap of birth will later move upward to the intellectual and moral plane. To kindle a sense of physical beauty of form in every part, such as a sculptor has, may be to start youth on the lowest round of the Platonic ladder that leads up to the vision of ideal beauty of soul, if his ideal be not excess of brawn, or mere brute strength, but the true proportion represented by the classic or mean temperance balanced like justice between all extremes. Hard, patient, regular work, with the right dosage for this self-cultural end, has thus at the same time a unique moral effect.

The dangers of this system are also obvious. Nature's intent can not be too far thwarted; and as in mental training the question is always pertinent, so here we may ask whether it be not best in all cases to some extent, and in some cases almost exclusively, to develop in the direction in which we most excel, to emphasize physical individuality and even idiosyncrasy, rather than to strive for monotonous uniformity. Weaknesses and parts that lag behind are the most easily overworked to the point of reaction and perhaps permanent injury. Again, work for curative purposes lacks the exuberance of free sports: it is not inspiring to make up areas; and therapeutic exercises imposed like a sentence for the shortcomings of our forebears bring a whiff of the atmosphere of the hospital, if not of the prison, into the gymnasium.

These four ideals, while so closely interrelated, are as yet far from harmonized. Swedish, Turner, Sargent, and American systems are each, most unfortunately, still too blind to the others' merits and too conscious of the others' shortcomings. To some extent they are prevented from getting together by narrow devotion to a single cult, aided sometimes by a pecuniary interest in the sale of their own apparatus and books or in the training of teachers according to one set of rubrics. The real elephant is neither a fan, a rope, a tree nor a log, as the blind men in the fable contended, each thinking the part he had touched to be the whole. This inability of leaders to combine causes uncertainty and lack of confidence in, and of enthusiastic support for, any system on the part of the public. Even the radically different needs of the sexes have failed of recognition from the same partisanship. All together represent only a fraction of the nature and needs of youth. The world now demands what this country has never had, a man who, knowing the human body, gymnastic history, and the various great athletic traditions of the past, shall study anew the whole motor field, as a few great leaders early in the last century tried to do; who shall gather and correlate the literature and experiences of the past and present with a deep sense of responsibility to the future; who shall examine martial training with all the inspirations, warnings, and new demands; and who shall know how to revive the inspiration of the past animated by the same spirit as the Turners, who were almost inflamed by referring back to the hardy life of the early Teutons and trying to reproduce its best features; who shall catch the spirit of, and make due connections with, popular sports past and present, study both industry and education to compensate their debilitating effects, and be himself animated by a great ethical and humanistic hope and faith in a better future. Such a man, if he ever walks the earth, will be the idol of youth, will know their physical secrets, will come almost as a savior to the bodies of men, and will, like Jahn, feel his calling and work sacred, and his institution a temple in which every physical act will be for the sake of the soul. The world of adolescence, especially that part which sits in closed spaces conning books, groans and travails all the more grievously and yearningly, because unconsciously, waiting for a redeemer for its body. Till he appears, our culture must remain for most a little hollow, falsetto, and handicapped by school-bred diseases. The modern gymnasium performs its chief service during adolescence and is one of the most beneficent agencies of which not a few, but every youth, should make large use. Its spirit should be instinct with euphoria, where the joy of being alive reaches a point of high, although not quite its highest, intensity. While the stimulus of rivalry and even of records is not excluded, and social feelings may be appealed to by unison exercises and by the club spirit, and while competitions, tournaments, and the artificial motives of prizes and exhibitions may be invoked, the culture is in fact largely individual. And yet in this country the annual *Turnerfest* brings 4,000 or 5,000 men from all parts of the Union, who sometimes all deploy and go through some of the standard exercises together under one leader. Instead of training a few athletes, the real problem now presented is how to raise the general level of vitality so that children and youth may be fitted to stand the strain of modern civilization, resist zymotic diseases, and overcome the deleterious influences of city life. The almost immediate effects of systematic training are surprising and would hardly be inferred from the annual increments tabled earlier in this chapter. Sandow was a rather weakly boy and ascribes his development chiefly to systematic training.

We have space but for two reports believed to be typical. Enebuske reports on the effects of seven months' training on young women averaging 22.3 years. The figures are based on the 50 percentile column.

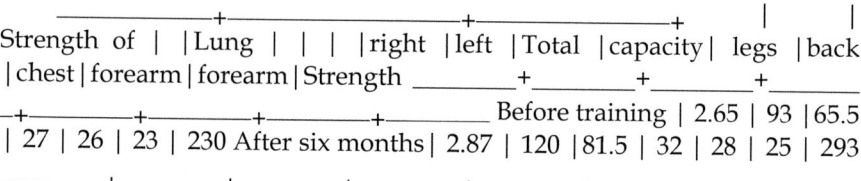

By comparing records of what he deems standard normal growth with that of 188 naval cadets from sixteen to twenty-one, who had special and systematic training, just after the period of most rapid growth in height, Beyer concluded that the effect of four years of this added a little over an inch of stature, and that this gain as greatest at the beginning. This increase was greatest for the youngest cadets. He found also a marked increase in weight, nearly the same for each year from seventeen to twenty one. This he thought more easily influenced by exercise than height. A high vital index ratio of lung capacity to weight is a very important attribute of good training. Beyer[1] found, however, that the addition of lung area gained by exercise did not keep up with the increase thus caused in muscular substance, and that the vital index always became smaller in those who had gained weight and strength by special physical training. How much gain in weight is desirable beyond the point where the lung capacity increases at an equal rate is unknown. If such measurements were applied to the different gymnastic systems, we might be able to compare their efficiency, which would be a great desideratum in view of the unfortunate rivalry between them. Total strength, too, can be greatly increased. Beyer thinks that from sixteen to twenty-one it may exceed the average or normal increment fivefold, and he adds, "I firmly believe that the now so wonderful performances of most of our strong men are well within the reach of the majority of healthy men, if such performances were a serious enough part of their ambition to make them do the exercises necessary to develop them." Power of the organs to respond to good training by increased strength probably reaches well into middle life.

It is not encouraging to learn that, according to a recent writer,[2] we now have seventy times as many physicians in proportion to the general population as there are physical directors, even for the school population alone considered. We have twice as many physicians per population as Great Britain, four times a many as Germany, or 2 physicians, 1.8 ministers, 1.4 lawyers per thousand of the general population; while even if all male teachers of physical training taught only males of the military age, we should have but 0.05 of a teacher per thousand, or if the school population alone be considered, 20 teachers per million pupils. Hence, it is inferred that the need of wise and classified teachers in this field is at present greater than in any other. But fortunately while spontaneous, unsystematic exercise in a well-equipped modern gymnasium may in rare cases do harm, so far from sharing the prejudice often felt for it by professional trainers, we believe that free access to it without control or direction is unquestionably a boon to youth. Even if its use be sporadic and occasional, as it is likely to be with equal opportunity for out-of-door exercises and especially sports, practise is sometimes hygienic almost inversely to its amount, while even lameness from initial excess has its lessons, and the sense of manifoldness of inferiorities brought home by experiences gives a wholesome self-knowledge and stimulus.

In this country more than elsewhere, especially in high school and college, gymnasium work has been brought into healthful connection with field sports and record competitions for both teams and individuals who aspire to championship. This has given the former a healthful stimulus although it is felt only by a picked few. Scores of records have been established for running, walking, hurdling, throwing, putting, swimming, rowing, skating, etc., each for various shorter and longer distances and under manifold conditions, and for both amateurs and professionals, who are easily accessible. These, in general, show a slow but steady advance in this country since 1876, when athletics were established here. In that year there was not a single world's best record held by an American amateur, and high-school boys of to-day could in most, though not in all lines, have won the American championship twenty-five years ago. Of course, in a strict sense, intercollegiate contests do not show the real advance in athletics, because it is not necessary for a man in order to win a championship to do his best; but they do show general improvement.

We select for our purpose a few of those records longest kept. Not dependent on external conditions like boat-racing, or on improved apparatus like bicycling, we have interesting data of a very different order for physical measurements. These down to present writing—July, 1906—are as follows: For the 100-yard dash, every annual record from 1876 to 1895 is 10 or 11 seconds, or between these, save in 1890, where Owen's record of 9-4/5 seconds still stands. In the 220-yard run there is slight improvement since 1877, but here the record of 1896 (Wefers, 21-1/5 seconds) has not been surpassed. In the quarter-mile run, the beet record was in 1900 (Long, 47 seconds). The half-mile record, which still stands, was made in 1895 (Kilpatrick, 1 minute 52-2/5 seconds); the mile run in 1895 (Conneff, 4 minutes 15-3/5 seconds). The running broad jump shows a very steady improvement, with the best record in 1900 (Prinstein, 24 feet 7-1/4 inches). The running high jump shows improvement, but less, with the record of 1895 still standing (Sweeney, 6 feet 5-5/8 inches). The record for pole vaulting, corrected to November, 1905, is 12 feet 132/100 inches (Dole); for throwing the 16-pound hammer head, 100 feet 5 inches (Queckberner); for putting the 16-pound shot, 49 feet 6 inches (Coe, 1905); the standing high jump, 5 feet 5-1/2 inches (Ewry); for the running high jump, 6 feet 5-5/8 inches (Sweeney). We also find that if we extend our purview to include all kinds of records for physical achievement, that not a few of the amateur records for activities involving strength combined with rapid rhythm movement are held by young men of twenty or even less.

In putting the 16-pound shot under uniform conditions the record has improved since the early years nearly 10 feet (Coe, 49 feet 6 inches, best at present writing, 1906). Pole vaulting shows a very marked advance culminating in 1904 (Dole, 12 feet 132/100 inches). Most marked of all perhaps is the great advance in throwing the 16-pound hammer. Beginning between 70 and 80 feet in the early years, the record is now 172 feet 11 inches (Flanagan, 1904). The two-mile bicycle race also shows marked gain, partly, of course, due to improvement in the wheel, the early records being nearly 7 minutes, and the best being 2 minutes 19 seconds (McLean, 1903). Some of these are world records, and more exceed professional records.[3] These, of course, no more indicate general improvement than the steady reduction of time in horse-racing suggests betterment in horses generally.

In Panhellenic games as well as at present, athleticism in its manifold forms was one of the most characteristic expressions of adolescent nature and needs. Not a single time or distance record of antiquity has been preserved, although Grasberger[4] and other writers would have us believe that in those that are comparable, ancient youthful champions greatly excelled ours, especially in leaping and running. While we are far from cultivating mere strength, our training is very one-sided from the Greek norm of unity or of the ideals that develop the body only for the salve of the soul. While gymnastics in our sense, with apparatus, exercises, and measurements independently of games was unknown, the ideal and motive were as different from ours as was its method. Nothing, so far as is known, was done for correcting the ravages of work, or for overcoming hereditary defects; and until athletics degenerated there were Do exercises for the sole purpose of developing muscle.

On the whole, while modern gymnastics has done more for the trunk, shoulders, and arms than for the legs, it is now too selfish and ego-centric, deficient on the side of psychic impulsion, and but little subordinated to ethical or intellectual development. Yet it does a great physical service to all who cultivate it, and is a safeguard of virtue and temperance. Its need is radical revision and coordination of various cults and theories in the light of the latest psycho-physiological science.

Gymnastics allies itself to biometric work. The present academic zeal for physical development is in great need of closer affiliation with anthropometry. This important and growing department will be represented in the ideal gymnasium of the future—First, by courses, if not by a chair, devoted to the apparatus of measurements of human proportions and symmetry, with a kinesological cabinet where young men are instructed in the elements of auscultation, the use of calipers, the sphygmograph, spirometer, plethysmograph, kinesometer to plot graphic curves, compute average errors, and tables of percentile grades and in statistical methods, etc. Second, anatomy, especially of muscles, bones, heart, and skin, will be taught, and also their physiology, with stress upon myology, the effects of exercise on the flow of blood and lymph, not excluding the development of the upright position, and all that it involves and implies. Third, hygiene will be prominent and comprehensive enough to cover all that pertains to body-keeping, regimen, sleep, connecting with school and domestic and public hygiene—all on the basis of modern as distinct from the archaic physiology of Ling, who, it is sufficient to remember, died in 1839, before this science was recreated, and the persistence of whose concepts are an anomalous survival to-day. Mechanico-therapeutics, the purpose and service of each chief kind of apparatus and exercise, the value of work on stall bars with chest weights, of chinning, use of the quarter-staff, somersaults, rings, clubs, dumb-bells, work with straight and flexed knees on machinery, etc., will be taught. Fourth, the history of gymnastics from the time of its highest development in Greece to the present is full of interest and has a very high and not yet developed culture value for youth. This department, both in its practical and theoretical side, should have its full share of prizes and scholarships to stimulate the seventy to seventy-five per cent of students who are now unaffected by the influence of athletics. By these methods the motivation of gymnastics, which now in large measure goes to waste in enthusiasm, could be utilised to aid the greatly needed intellectualization of those exercises which in their nature are more akin to work than play. Indeed, Gutsmuths's first definition of athletics was "work under the garb of youthful pleasure." So to develop these courses that they could chiefly, if not entirely, satisfy the requirements for the A.B. degree, would coordinate the work of the now isolated curriculum of the training-schools with that of the college and thus broaden the sphere of the latter; but besides its culture value, which I hold very high, such a step would prepare for the new, important, and, as we have seen, very inadequately manned profession of physical trainers. This has, moreover, great but yet latent and even unsuspected capacities for the morals of our academic youth. Grote states that among the ancient Greeks one-half of all education as devoted to the body, and Galton urges that they as much excelled us as we do the African negro. They held that if physical perfection was cultivated, moral and mental excellence would follow; and that, without this, national culture rests on an insecure basis. In our day there are many new reasons to believe that the best nations of the future will be those which give most intelligent care to the body.

[Footnote 1: See H.G. Beyer. The Influence of Exercise on Growth. American Physical Education Review, September-December, 1896, vol. I, pp. 76-87.]

[Footnote 2: J.H. McCurdy, Physical Training as a Profession. Association Seminar, March, 1902, vol. 10, pp. 11-24.]

[Footnote 3: These records are taken from the World Almanac, 1906, and Olympic Games of 1906 at Athens. Edited by J.E. Sullivan, Commissioner from the United States to the Olympic Games. Spalding's Athletic Library, New York, July, 1906.]

[Footnote 4: O.H. Jaeger, Die Gymnastik der Hellenen. Heitz, Stuttgart 1881. L. Grasberger's great standard work, Erziehung und Unterricht im klassischen Alterthum. Würzburg, 1864-81, 3 vols.]

* * * * *

CHAPTER VI - PLAY, SPORTS, AND GAMES

The view of Groos partial and a better explanation of play proposed as rehearsing ancestral activities—The glory of Greek physical training, its ideals and results—The first spontaneous movements of infancy as keys to the past—Necessity of developing basal powers before those that are later and peculiar to the individual—Plays that interest due to their antiquity—Play with dolls—Play distinguished by age—Play preferences of children and their reasons—The profound significance of rhythm—The value of dancing and also its significance, history, and the desirability of re-introducing it—Fighting—Boxing—Wrestling—Bushido—Foot-ball—Military ideals—Showing off—Cold baths—Hill climbing—The playground movement—The psychology of play—Its relation to work.

Play, sports, and games constitute a more varied, far older, and more popular field. Here a very different spirit of joy and gladness rules. Artifacts often enter but can not survive unless based upon pretty purely hereditary momentum. Thus our first problem is to seek both the motor tendencies and the psychic motives bequeathed to us from the past. The view of Groos that play is practise for future adult activities is very partial, superficial, and perverse. It ignores the past where lie the keys to all play activities. True play never practises what is phyletically new; and this, industrial life often calls for. It exercises many atavistic and rudimentary functions, a number of which will abort before maturity, but which live themselves out in play like the tadpole's tail, that must be both developed and used as a stimulus to the growth of legs which will otherwise never mature. In place of this mistaken and misleading view, I regard play as the motor habits and spirit of the past of the race, persisting in the present, as rudimentary functions sometimes of and always akin to rudimentary organs. The best index and guide to the stated activities of adults in past ages is found in the instinctive, untaught, and non-imitative plays of children which are the most spontaneous and exact expressions of their motor needs. The young grow up into the same forms of motor activity, as did generations that have long preceded them, only to a limited extent; and if the form of every human occupation were to change to-day, play would be unaffected save in some of its superficial imitative forms. It would develop the motor capacities, impulses, and fundamental forms of our past heritage, and the transformation of these into later acquired adult forms is progressively later. In play every mood and movement is instinct with heredity. Thus we rehearse the activities of our ancestors, back we know not how far, and repeat their life work in summative and adumbrated ways. It is reminiscent albeit unconsciously, of our line of descent; and each is the key to the other. The psycho-motive impulses that prompt it are the forms in which our forebears have transmitted to us their habitual activities. Thus stage by stage we reënact their lives. Once in the phylon many of these activities were elaborated in the life and death struggle for existence. Now the elements and combinations oldest in the muscle history of the race are rerepresented earliest in the individual, and those later follow in order. This is why the heart of youth goes out into play as into nothing else, as if in it man remembered a lost paradise. This is why, unlike gymnastics, play has as much soul as body, and also why it so makes for unity of body and soul that the proverb "Man is whole only when he plays" suggests that the purest plays are those that enlist both alike. To address the body predominantly strengthens unduly the fleshy elements, and to overemphasize the soul causes weakness and automatisms. Thus understood, play is the ideal type of exercise for the young, most favorable for growth, and most self-regulating in both kind and amount. For its forms the pulse of adolescent enthusiasm beats highest. It is unconstrained and free to follow any outer or inner impulse. The zest of it vents and satisfies the strong passion of youth for intense erethic and perhaps orgiastic states, gives an exaltation of self-feeling so craved that with no vicarious outlet it often impels to drink, and best of all realizes the watchword of the Turners, *frisch, frei, fröhlich, fromm* [Fresh, free, jovial, pious.].

Ancient Greece, the history and literature of which owe their perennial charm for all later ages to the fact that they represent the eternal adolescence of the world, best illustrates what this enthusiasm means for youth. Jäger and Guildersleeve, and yet better Grasberger, would have us believe that the Panhellenic and especially the Olympic games combined many of the best features of a modern prize exhibition, a camp-meeting, fair, Derby day, a Wagner festival, a meeting of the British Association, a country cattle show, intercollegiate games, and medieval tournament; that they were the "acme of festive life" and drew all who loved gold and glory, and that night and death never seemed so black as by contrast with their splendor. The deeds of the young athletes were ascribed to the inspiration of the gods, whose abodes they lit up with glory; and in doing them honor these discordant states found a bond of unity. The victor was crowned with a simple spray of laurel; cities vied with each other for the honor of having given him birth, their walls were taken down for his entry and immediately rebuilt; sculptors, for whom the five ancient games were schools of posture, competed in the representation of his form; poets gave him a pedigree reaching back to the gods, and Pindar, who sang that only he is great who is great with his hands and feet, raised his victory to symbolize the eternal prevalence of good over evil. The best body implied the best mind; and even Plato, to whom tradition gives not only one of the fairest souls, but a body remarkable for both strength and beauty, and for whom weakness was perilously near to wickedness, and ugliness to sin, argues that education must be so conducted that the body can be safely entrusted to the care of the soul and suggests, what later became a slogan of a more degenerate gladiatorial athleticism, that to be well and strong is to be a philosopher— *valare est philosophari*. The Greeks could hardly conceive bodily apart from psychic education, and physical was for the sake of mental training. A sane, whole mind could hardly reside in an unsound body upon the integrity of which it was dependent. Knowledge for its own sake, from this standpoint, is a dangerous superstition, for what frees the mind is disastrous if it does not give self-control; better ignorance than knowledge that does not develop a motor side. Body culture is ultimately only for the sake of the mind and soul, for body is only its other ego. Not only is all muscle culture at the same time brain-building, but a book-worm with soft hands, tender feet, and tough rump from much sitting, or an anemic girl prodigy, "in the morning hectic, in the evening electric," is a monster. Play at its best is only a school of ethics. It gives not only strength but courage and confidence, tends to simplify life and habits, gives energy, decision, and promptness to the will, brings consolation and peace of mind in evil days, is a resource in trouble and brings out individuality.

How the ideals of physical preformed those of moral and mental training in the land and day of Socrates is seen in the identification of knowledge and virtue, "*Kennen und Können*." [To know and to have the power to do] Only an extreme and one-sided intellectualism separates them and assumes that it is easy to know and hard to do. From the ethical standpoint, philosophy, and indeed all knowledge, is the art of being and doing good, conduct is the only real subject of knowledge, and there is no science but morals. He is the best man, says Xenophon, who is always studying how to improve, and he is the happiest who feels that he is improving. Life is a skill, an art like a handicraft, and true knowledge a form of will. Good moral and physical development are more than analogous; and where intelligence is separated from action the former becomes mystic, abstract, and desiccated, and the latter formal routine. Thus mere conscience and psychological integrity and righteousness are allied and mutually inspiring.

Not only play, which is the purest expression of motor heredity, but work and all exercise owe most of whatever pleasure they bring to the past. The first influence of all right exercise for those in health is feeling of well-being and exhilaration. This is one chief source of the strange enthusiasm felt for many special forms of activity, and the feeling is so strong that it animates many forms of it that are hygienically unfit. To act vigorously from a full store of energy gives a reflex of pleasure that is sometimes a passion and may fairly intoxicate. Animals must move or cease growing and die. While to be weak is to be miserable, to feel strong is a joy and glory. It gives a sense of superiority, dignity, endurance, courage, confidence, enterprise, power, personal validity, virility, and virtue in the etymological sense of that noble word. To be active, agile, strong, is especially the glory of young men. Our nature and history have so disposed our frame that thus all physiological and psychic processes are stimulated, products of decomposition are washed out by oxygenation and elimination, the best reaction of all the ganglionic and sympathetic activities is accused, and vegetative processes are normalized. Activity may exalt the spirit almost to the point of ecstasy, and the physical pleasure of it diffuse, irradiate, and mitigate the sexual stress just at the age when its premature localization is most deleterious. Just enough at the proper time and rate contributes to permanent elasticity of mood and disposition, gives moral self-control, rouses a love of freedom with all that that great word means, and favors all higher human aspirations.

In all these modes of developing our efferent powers, we conceive that the race comes very close to the individual youth, and that ancestral momenta animate motor neurons and muscles and preside over most of the combinations. Some of the elements speak with a still small voice raucous with age. The first spontaneous movements of infancy are hieroglyphs, to most of which we have as yet no good key. Many elements are so impacted and felted together that we can not analyze them. Many are extinct and many perhaps made but once and only hint things we can not apprehend. Later the rehearsals are fuller, and their significance more intelligible, and in boyhood and youth the correspondences are plain to all who have eyes to see. Pleasure is always exactly proportional to the directness and force of the current of heredity, and in play we feel most fully and intensely ancestral joys. The pain of toil died with our forebears; its vestiges in our play give pure delight. Its variety prompts to diversity that enlarges our life. Primitive men and animals played, and that too has left its traces in us. Some urge that work was evolved or degenerated from play; but the play field broadens with succeeding generations youth is prolonged, for play is always and everywhere the best synonym of youth. All are young at play and only in play, and the best possible characterization of old age is the absence of the soul and body of play. Only senile and overspecialized tissues of brain, heart, and muscles know it not.

Gulick[1] has urged that what makes certain exercises more interesting than others is to be found in the phylon. The power to throw with accuracy and speed was once pivotal for survival, and non-throwers were eliminated. Those who could throw unusually well best overcame enemies, killed game, and sheltered family. The nervous and muscular systems are organized with certain definite tendencies and have back of them a racial setting. So running and dodging with speed and endurance, and hitting with a club, were also basal to hunting and fighting. Now that the need of these is leas urgent for utilitarian purposes, they are still necessary for perfecting the organism. This makes, for instance, baseball racially familiar, because it represents activities that were once and for a long time necessary for survival. We inherit tendencies of muscular coördination that have been of great racial utility. The best athletic sports and games a composed of these racially old elements, so that phylogenetic muscular history is of great importance. Why is it, this writer asks, that a city man so loves to sit all day and fish! It is because this interest dates back to time immemorial. We are the sons of fishermen, and early life was by the water's side, and this is our food supply. This explains why certain exercises are more interesting than others. It is because they touch and revive the deep basic emotions of the race. Thus we see that play is not doing things to be useful later, but it is rehearsing racial history. Plays and games change only in their external form, but the underlying neuro-muscular activities, and also the psychic content of them, are the same. Just as psychic states must be lived out up through the grades, so the physical activities most be played off, each in its own time.

The best exercise for the young should thus be more directed to develop the basal powers old to the race than those peculiar to the individual, and it should enforce those psycho-neural and muscular forms which race habit has banded down rather than insist upon those arbitrarily designed to develop our ideas of symmetry regardless of heredity. The best guide to the former is *interest*, zest, and spontaneity. Hereditary moment, really determine, too, the order in which nerve centers come into function. The oldest, racial parts come first, and those which are higher and represent volition come in much later.[2] As Hughlings Jackson has well shown, speech uses most of the same organs as does eating, but those concerned with the former are controlled from a higher level of nerve-cells. By right mastication, deglutition, etc., we are thus developing speech organs. Thus not only the kind but the time of forms and degrees of exercise is best prescribed by heredity. All growth is more or less rhythmic. There are seasons of rapid increment followed by rest and then perhaps succeeded by a period of augmentation, and this may occur several times. Roberts's fifth parliamentary report shows that systematic gymnastics, which, if applied at the right age, produce such immediate and often surprising development of lung capacity, utterly fail with boys of twelve, because this nascent period has not yet come. Donaldson showed that if the eyelid of a young kitten be forced open prematurely at birth and stimulated with light, medullation was premature and imperfect; so, too, if proper exercise is deferred too long, we know that little result is achieved. The sequence in which the maturation of levels, nerve areas, and bundles of fibers develop may be, as Flechsig thinks, causal; or, according to Cajal, energy, originally employed in growth by cell division, later passes to fiber extension and the development of latent cells; or as in young children, the nascent period of finger movements may stimulate that of the thumb which comes later, and the independent movement of the two eyes, their subsequent coördination, and so on to perhaps a third and yet higher level. Thus exercise ought to develop nature's first intention and fulfil the law of nascent periods, or else not only no good but great harm may be done. Hence every determination of these periods is of great practical as well as scientific importance. The following are the chief attempts yet made to fix them, which show the significance of adolescence.

The doll curve reaches its point of highest intensity between eight and nine,[3] and it is nearly ended at fifteen, although it may persist. Children can give no better reason why they stop playing with dolls than because other things are liked better, or they are too old, ashamed, love real babies, etc. The Roman girl, when ripe for marriage, hung up her childhood doll as a votive offering to Venus. Mrs. Carlyle, who was compelled to stop, made sumptuous dresses and a four-post bed, and made her doll die upon a funeral pyre like Dido, after speaking her last farewell and stabbing herself with a penknife by way of Tyrian sword. At thirteen or fourteen it is more distinctly realized that dolls are not real, because they have no inner life or feeling, yet many continue to play with them with great pleasure, in secret, till well on in the teens or twenties. Occasionally single women or married women with no children, and in rare cases even those who have children, play dolls all their lives. Gales's[4] student concluded that the girls who played with dolls up to or into pubescent years were usually those who had the fewest number, that they played with them in the most realistic manner, kept them because actually most fond of them, and were likely to be more scientific, steady, and less sentimental than those who dropped them early. But the instinct that "dollifies" new or most unfit things is gone, as also the subtle points of contact between doll play and idolatry. Before puberty dolls are more likely to be adults; after puberty they are almost always children or babies. There is no longer a struggle between doubt and reality in the doll cosmos, no more abandon to the doll illusion; but where it lingers it is a more atavistic rudiment, and just as at the height of the fever dolls are only in small part representatives of future children, the saying that the first child is the last doll is probably false. Nor are doll and child comparable to first and second dentition, and it is doubtful if children who play with dolls as children with too great abandonment are those who make the best mothers later, or if it has any value as a preliminary practise of motherhood. The number of motor activities that are both inspired and unified by this form of play and that can always be given wholesome direction is almost incredible, and has been too long neglected both by psychologists and teachers. Few purer types of the rehearsal by the individual of the history of the race can probably be found even though we can not yet analyze the many elements involved and assign to each its phyletic correlate.

In an interesting paper Dr. Gulick[5] divides play into three childish periods, separated by the ages three and seven, and attempts to characterize the plays of early adolescence from twelve to seventeen and of later adolescence from seventeen to twenty-three. Of the first two periods he says, children before seven rarely play games spontaneously, but often do so under the stimulus of older persons. From seven to twelve, games are almost exclusively individualistic and competitive, but in early adolescence "two elements predominate—first, the plays are predominantly team games, in which the individual is more or less sacrificed for the whole, in which there is obedience to a captain, in which there is coöperation among a number for a given end, in which play has a program and an end. The second characteristic of the period is with reference to its plays, and there seems to be all of savage out-of-door life—hunting, fishing, stealing, swimming, rowing, sailing, fighting, hero-worship, adventure, love of animals, etc. This characteristic obtains more with boys than with girls." "The plays of adolescence are socialistic, demanding the heathen virtues of courage, endurance, self-control, bravery, loyalty, enthusiasm."

Croswell[6] found that among 2,000 children familiar with 700 kinds of amusements, those involving physical exercises predominated over all others, and that "at every age after the eighth year they were represented as almost two to one and in the sixteenth year rose among boys as four to one." The age of the greatest number of different amusements is from ten to eleven, nearly fifteen being mentioned, but for the next eight or nine years there is a steady decline of number, and progressive specialisation occurs. The games of chase, which are suggestive on the recapitulation theory, rise from eleven per cent in boys of six to nineteen per cent at nine, but soon after decline, and at sixteen have fallen to less than four per cent. Toys and original make-believe games decline still earlier, while ball rises steadily and rapidly to eighteen, and card and table games rise very steadily from ten to fifteen in girls, but the increment is much less in boys. "A third or more of all the amusements of boys just entering their teens are games of contest — games in which the end is in one way or another to gain an advantage one's fellows, in which the interest is n the struggle between peers." "As children approach the teens, a tendency arises that is well expressed by one of the girls who no longer makes playthings but things that are useful." Parents and society must, therefore, provide the most favorable conditions for the kind of amusement fitting at each age. As the child grows older, society plays a larger rôle in all the child's amusements, and from the thirteenth year "amusements take on a decidedly coöperative and competitive character, and efforts are ore and more confined to the accomplishments of some definite aim. The course for this period will concentrate the effort upon fewer lines," and more time will be devoted to each. The desire for mastery is now at its height. The instinct is to maintain one's self independently and ask no odds. At fourteen, especially, the impulse is, in manual training, to make something and perhaps to coöperate.

McGhee[7] collected the play preferences of 15,718 children, and found a very steady decline in running plays among girls from nine to eighteen, but a far more rapid rise in plays of chance from eleven to fifteen, and a very rapid rise from sixteen to eighteen. From eleven onward with the most marked fall before fourteen, there was a distinct decline in imitative games for girls and a slower one for boys. Games involving rivalry increased rapidly among boys from eleven to sixteen and still more rapidly among girls, their percentage of preference even exceeding that of boys at eighteen, when it reached nearly seventy per cent. With adolescence, specialization upon a few plays was markedly increased in the teens among boys, whereas with girls in general there were a large number of plays which were popular with none preëminent. Even at this age the principle of organization in games so strong with boys is very slight with girls. Puberty showed the greatest increase of interest among pubescent girls for croquet, and among boys for swimming, although baseball and football, the most favored for boys, rose rapidly. Although the author does not state it, it would seem from his data that plays peculiar to the different seasons were most marked among boys, in part, at least, because their activities are more out of doors.

Ferrero and others have shown that the more intense activities of primitive people tend to be rhythmic and with strongly automatic features. No form of activity is more universal than the dance, which is not only intense but may express chiefly in terms of fundamental movements, stripped of their accessory finish and detail, every important act, vocation, sentiment, or event in the life of man in language so universal and symbolic that music and poetry themselves seem to have arisen out of it. Before it became specialized much labor was cast in rhythmic form and often accompanied by time-marking and even tone to secure the stimulus of concert on both economic and social principles. In the dark background of history there is now much evidence that at some point, play, art, and work were not divorced. They all may have sprung from rhythmic movement which is so deep-seated in biology because it secures most joy of life with least expense. By it Eros of old ordered chaos, and by its judicious use the human soul is cadenced to great efforts toward high ideals. The many work-songs to secure concerted action in lifting, pulling, stepping, the use of flail, lever, saw, ax, hammer, hoe, loom, etc., show that areas and thesis represent flexion and extension, that accent originated in the acme of muscular stress, as well as how rhythm eases work and also makes it social. Most of the old work-canticles are lost, and machines have made work more serial, while rhythms are obscured or imposed from without so as to limit the freedom they used to express. Now all basal, central, or strength movements tend to be oscillatory, automatically repetitive, or rhythmic like savage music, as if the waves of the primeval sea whence we came still beat in them, just as all fine peripheral and late movements tend to be serial, special, vastly complex, end diversified. It is thus natural that during the period of greatest strength increment in muscular development, the rhythmic function of nearly all fundamental movements should be strongly accentuated. At the dawn of this age boys love marching; and, as our returns show, there is a very remarkable rise in the passion for beating time, jigging, double shuffling, rhythmic clapping, etc. The more prominent the factor of repetition the more automatic and the less strenuous is the hard and new effort of constant psychic adjustment and attention. College yells, cheers, rowing, marching, processions, bicycling, running, tug-of-war, calisthenics and class gymnastics with counting, and especially with music, horseback riding, etc., are rhythmic; tennis, baseball and football, basketball, golf, polo, etc., are less rhythmic, but are concerted and intense. These latter emphasise the conflict factor, best brought out in fencing, boxing, and wrestling, and lay more stress on the psychic elements of attention and skill. The effect of musical accompaniment, which the Swedish system wrongly rejects, is to make the exercises more fundamental and automatic, and to proportionately diminish the conscious effort and relieve the neuro-muscular mechanism involved in fine movements.

Adolescence is the golden period of nascency for rhythm. Before this change many children have a very imperfect sense of it, and even those who march, sing, play, or read poetry with correct and overemphasised time marking, experience a great broadening of the horizon of consciousness, and a marked, and, for mental power and scope, all-conditioning increase in the carrying power of attention and the sentence-sense. The soul now feels the beauty of cadences, good ascension, and the symmetry of well-developed periods—and all, as I am convinced, because this is the springtime of the strength movements which are predominantly rhythmic. Not only does music start in time marking, the drum being the oldest instrument, but quantity long took precedence of sense and form of content, both melody and words coming later. Even rhythmic tapping or beating of the foot (whence the poetic feet of prosody and meter thus later imposed monotonous prose to make poetry) exhilarates, makes glad the soul and inspires it to attack, gives compulsion and a sense of unity. The psychology of rhythm shows its basal value in cadencing the soul. We can not conceive what war, love, and religion would be without it. The old adage that "the parent of prose is poetry, the parent of poetry is music, the parent of music is rhythm, and the parent of rhythm is God" seems borne out not only in history, but by the nature of thought and attention that does not move in a continuum, but flies and perches alternately, or on stepping-stones and as if influenced by the tempo of the leg swinging as a compound pendulum.

Dancing is one of the best expressions of pure play and of the motor needs of youth. Perhaps it is the most liberal of all forms of motor education. Schopenhauer thought it the apex of physiological irritability and that it made animal life most vividly conscious of its existence and most exultant in exhibiting it. In very ancient times China ritualised it in the spring and made it a large part of the education of boys after the age of thirteen. Neale thinks it was originally circular or orbicular worship, which he deems oldest. In Japan, in the priestly Salic College of ancient Rome, in Egypt, in the Greek Apollo cult, it was a form of worship. St. Basil advised it; St. Gregory introduced it into religious services. The early Christian bishops, called præsuls, led the sacred dance around the altar; and only in 692, and again in 1617, was it forbidden in church. Neale and others have shown how the choral processionals with all the added charm of vestment and intonation have had far more to do in Christianizing many low tribes, who could not understand the language of the church, than has preaching. Savages are nearly all great dancers, imitating every animal they know, dancing out their own legends, with ritual sometimes so exacting that error means death. The character of people is often learned from their dances, and Molière says the destiny of nations depends on them. The gayest dancers are often among the most downtrodden and unhappy people. Some mysteries can be revealed only in them, as holy passion-plays. If we consider the history of secular dances, we find that some of them, when first invented or in vogue, evoked the greatest enthusiasm. One writer says that the polka so delighted France and England that statesmen forgot politics. The spirit of the old Polish aristocracy still lives in the polonaise. The gipsy dances have inspired a new school of music. The Greek drama grew out of the evolution of the tragic chorus. National dances like the hornpipe and reel of Scotland, the *Reihen*, of Germany, the *rondes* of France, the Spanish tarantella and *chaconne*, the strathspey from the Spey Valley, the Irish jig, etc., express racial traits. Instead of the former vast repertory, the stately pavone, the graceful and dignified saraband, the wild *salterrelle*, the bourrée with song and strong rhythm, the light and skippy bolero, the courtly bayedere, the dramatic plugge, gavotte, and other peasant dances in costume, the fast and furious fandango, weapon and military dances; in place of the pristine power to express love, mourning, justice, penalty, fear, anger, consolation, divine service, symbolic and philosophical conceptions, and every industry or characteristic act of life in pantomime and gesture, we have in the dance of the modern ballroom only a degenerate relict, with at best but a very insignificant culture value, and too often stained with bad associations. This is most unfortunate for youth, and for their sake a work of rescue and revival is greatly needed; for it is perhaps, not excepting even music, the completest language of the emotions and can be made one of the best schools of sentiment and even will, inculcating good states of mind and exorcising bad ones as few other agencies have power to do. Right dancing can cadence the very soul, give nervous poise and control, bring harmony between basal and finer muscles, and also between feeling and intellect, body and mind. It can serve both as an awakener and a test of intelligence, predispose the heart against vice, and turn the springs of character toward virtue. That its present decadent forms, for those too devitalized to dance aright, can be demoralizing, we know in this day too well, although even questionable dances may sometimes work off vicious propensities in ways more harmless than those in which they would otherwise find vent. Its utilization for and influence on the insane would be another interesting chapter.

Very interesting scientifically and suggestive practically is another correspondence which I believe to be new, between the mode of spontaneous activity in youth and that of labor in the early history of the race. One of the most marked distinctions between savage and civilized races is in the longer rhythm of work and relaxation. The former are idle and lazy for days, weeks, and perhaps months, and then put forth intense and prolonged effort in dance, hunt, warfare, migration, or construction, sometimes dispensing with sleep and manifesting remarkable endurance. As civilization and specialization advance, hours become regular. The cultured man is less desultory in all his habits, from eating and sleeping to performing social and religious duties, although he may put forth no more aggregate energy in a year than the savage. Women are schooled to regular work long before men, and the difficulty of imposing civilization upon low races is compared by Bücher[8] to that of training a eat to work when harnessed to a dog-cart. It is not dread of fatigue but of the monotony of method makes them hate labor. The effort of savages is more intense and their periods of rest more prolonged and inert. Darwin thinks all vital function bred to go in periods, as vertebrates are descended from tidal ascidian.[9] There is indeed much that suggests some other irregular rhythm more or less independent of day and night, and perhaps sexual in its nature, but not lunar, and for males. This mode of life not only preceded the industrial and commercial period of which regularity is a prime condition, but it lasted indefinitely longer than the latter has yet existed; during this early time great exertion, sometimes to the point of utter exhaustion and collapse, alternated with seasons of almost vegetative existence. We see abundant traces of this psychosis in the muscle habits of adolescents, and, I think, in student and particularly in college life, which can enforce regularity only to a limited extent. This is not reversion, but partly expression of the nature and perhaps the needs of this stage of immaturity, and partly the same instinct of revolt against uniformity imposed from without, which rob life of variety and extinguish the spirit of adventure and untrammeled freedom, and make the savage hard to break to the harness of civilization. The hunger for fatigue, too, can become a veritable passion and is quite distinct from either the impulse for activity for its own sake or the desire of achievement. To shout and put forth the utmost possible strength in crude ways is erethic intoxication at a stage when every tissue can become erectile and seems, like the crying of infants, to have a legitimate function in causing tension and flushing, enlarging the caliber of blood vessels, and forcing the blood perhaps even to the point of extravasation to irrigate newly growing fibers, cells, and organs which atrophy if not thus fed. When maturity is complete this need abates. If this be correct, the phenomenon of second breath, so characteristic of adolescence, and one factor in the inebriate's propensity, is ontogenetic expression of a rhythm trait of a long racial period. Youth needs overexertion to compensate for underexertion, to undersleep in order to offset oversleep at times. This seems to be nature's provision to expand in all directions its possibilities of the body and soul in this plastic period when, without this occasional excess, powers would atrophy or suffer arrest for want of use, or larger possibilities world not be realized without this regimen peculiar to nascent periods. This is treated more fully elsewhere.

Perhaps next to dancing in phyletic motivation come personal conflicts, such as wrestling, fighting, boxing, dueling, and in some sense, hunting. The animal world is full of struggle for survival, and primitive warfare is a wager of battle, of personal combat of foes contesting eye to eye and hand to hand, where victory of one is the defeat and perhaps death of the other, and where life is often staked against life. In its more brutal forms we see one of the most degrading of all the aspects of human nature. Burk[10] has shown how the most bestial of these instincts survive and crop out irresistibly in boyhood, where fights are often engaged in with desperate abandon. Noses are bitten, ears torn, sensitive places kicked, hair pulled, arms twisted, the head stamped on and pounded on stones, fingers twisted, and hoodlums sometimes deliberately try to strangle, gouge out an eye, pull off an ear, pull out the tongue, break teeth, nose, or bones, or dislocate jaws or other joints, wring the neck, bite off a lip, and torture in utterly nameless ways. In unrestrained anger, man becomes a demon in love with the blood of his victim. The face is distorted, and there are yells, oaths, animal snorts and grunts, cries, and then exultant laughter at pain, and each is bruised, dirty, disheveled and panting with exhaustion. For coarser natures, the spectacle of such conflicts has an intense attraction, while some morbid souls are scarred by a distinct phobia for everything suggestive of even lower degrees of opposition. These instincts, more or less developed in boyhood, are repressed in normal cases before strength and skill are sufficiently developed to inflict serious bodily injury, while without the reductives that orthogenetic growth brings they become criminal. Repulsive as are these grosser and animal manifestations of anger, its impulsion can not and should not be eliminated, but its expression transformed and directed toward evils that need all its antagonism. To be angry aright is a good part of moral education, and non-resistance under all provocations is unmanly, craven, and cowardly.[11] An able-bodied young man, who can not fight physically, can hardly have a high and true sense of honor, and is generally a milksop, a lady-boy, or sneak. He lacks virility, his masculinity does not ring true, his honesty can not be sound to the core. Hence, instead of eradicating this instinct, one of the great problems of physical and moral pedagogy is rightly to temper and direct it.

Sparta sedulously cultivated it in boys; and in the great English schools, where for generations it has been more or less tacitly recognized, it is regulated by custom, and their literature and traditions abound in illustrations of its man-making and often transforming influence in ways well appreciated by Hughes and Arnold. It makes against degeneration, the essential feature of which is weakening of will and loss of honor. Real virtue requires enemies, and women and effeminate and old men want placid, comfortable peace, while a real man rejoices in noble strife which sanctifies all great causes, casts out fear, and is the chief school of courage. Bad as is overpugnacity, a scrapping boy is better than one who funks a fight, and I have no patience with the sentimentality that would here "pour out the child with the bath," but would have every healthy boy taught boxing at adolescence if not before. The prize-ring is degrading and brutal, but in lieu of better illustrations of the spirit of personal contest I would interest a certain class of boys in it and try to devise modes of pedagogic utilization of the immense store of interest it generates. Like dancing it should be rescued from its evil associations, and its educational force put to do moral work, even though it be by way of individual prescriptions for specific defects of character. At its best, it is indeed a manly art, a superb school for quickness of eye and hand, decision, force of will, and self-control. The moment this is lost stinging punishment follows. Hence it is the surest of all cures for excessive irascibility and has been found to have a most beneficent effect upon a peevish or unmanly disposition. It has no mean theoretic side, of rules, kinds of blow and counters, arts of drawing out and tiring an opponent, hindering but not injuring him, defensive and offensive tactics, etc., and it addresses chiefly the fundamental muscles in both training and conflict. I do not underestimate the many and great difficulties of proper purgation, but I know from both personal practise and observation that they are not unconquerable.

This form of personal conflict is better than dueling even in its comparatively harmless German student form, although this has been warmly defended by Jacob Grimm, Bismarck, and Treitschke, while Paulsen, Professor of Philosophy and Pedagogy, and Schrempf, of Theology, have pronounced it but a slight evil, and several Americans have thought it better than hazing, which it makes impossible. The dark side of dueling is seen in the hypertrophied sense of honor which under the code of the corps becomes an intricate and fantastic thing, prompting, according to Ziegler,[12] a club of sixteen students to fight over two hundred duels in four weeks in Jena early in this century. It is prone to degenerate to an artificial etiquette demanding satisfaction for slight and unintended offenses. Although this professor who had his own face scarred on the *mensur*, pleaded for a student court of honor, with power to brand acts as infamous and even to expel students, on the ground that honor had grown more inward, the traditions in favor of dueling were too strong. The duel had a religious romantic origin as revealing God's judgment, and means that the victim of an insult is ready to stake body, or even life, and this is still its ideal side. Anachronism as it now is and degenerating readily to sport or spectacle, overpunishing what is often mere awkwardness or ignorance, it still impresses a certain sense of responsibility for conduct and gives some physical training, slight and specialized though it be. The code is conventional, drawn directly from old French military life, and is not true to the line that separates real honor from dishonor, deliberate insult that wounds normal self-respect from injury fancied by oversensitiveness or feigned by arrogance; so that in its present form it is not the best safeguard of the sacred shrine of personality against invasion of ifs rights. If, as is claimed, it is some diversion from or fortification against corrosive sensuality, it has generally allied itself with excessive beer-drinking. Fencing, while an art susceptible of high development and valuable for both pose and poise, and requiring great quickness of eye, arm, and wrist, is unilateral and robbed of the vest of inflicting real pain on an antagonist.

Bushido,[13] which means military-knightly ways, designates the Japanese conception of honor in behavior and in fighting. The youth is inspired by the ideal of Tom Brown "to leave behind him the name of a fellow who never bullied a little boy or turned his back on a big one." It expresses the race ideal of justice, patriotism, and the duty of living aright and dying nobly. It means also sympathy, pity, and love, for only the bravest can be the tenderest, and those most in love are most daring, and it includes politeness and the art of poetry. Honor is a sense of personal dignity and worth, so the *bushi* is truthful without an oath. At the tender age of five the *samurai* is given a real sword, and this gives self-respect and responsibility. At fifteen, two sharp and artistic ones, long and short, are given him, which must be his companions for life. They were made by a smith whose shop is a sanctuary and who begins his work with prayer. They have the finest hilts and scabbards, and are besung as invested with a charm or spell, and symbolic of loyalty and self-control, for they must never be drawn lightly. He is taught fencing, archery, horsemanship, tactics, the spear, ethics and literature, anatomy, for offence and defense; he must be indifferent to money, hold his life cheap beside honor, and die if it is gone. This chivalry is called the soul of Japan, and if it fades life is vulgarised. It is a code of ethics and physical training.

Football is a magnificent game if played on honor. An English tennis champion was lately playing a rubber game with the American champion. They were even and near the end when the American made a bad fluke which would have lost this country its championship. The English player, scorning to win on an accident, intentionally made a similar mistake that the best man might win. The chief evil of modern American football which now threatens its suppression in some colleges is the lust to win at any price, and results in tricks and secret practise. These sneaky methods impair the sentiment of honor which is the best and most potent of all the moral safeguards of youth, so that a young man can not be a true gentleman on the gridiron. This ethical degeneration is far worse than all the braises, sprains, broken bones and even deaths it causes.

Wrestling is a form of personal encounter which in antiquity reached a high development, and which, although now more known and practised as athletics of the body than of the soul, has certain special disciplinary capacities in its various forms. It represents the most primitive type of the struggle of unarmed and unprotected man with man. Purged of its barbarities, and in its Greco-Roman form and properly subject to rules, it cultivates more kinds of movements than any other form—for limbs, trunk, neck, hand, foot, and all in the upright and in every prone position. It, too, has its manual of feints, holds, tricks, and specialties, and calls out wariness, quickness, strength, and shiftiness. Victory need involve no cruelty or even pain to the vanquished. The very closeness of body to body, emphasizing flexor rather than extensor arm muscles, imparts to it a peculiar tone, gives it a vast variety of possible activities, developing many alternatives at every stage, and tempts to many undiscovered forms of permanent mayhem. Its struggle is usually longer and less interrupted by pauses than pugilism, and its situations and conclusions often develop slowly, so that all in all, its character among contests is unique. As a school of posture for art, its varieties are extremely manifold and by no means developed, for it contains every kind of emphasis of every part and calls out every muscle group and attitude of the human body; hence its training is most generic and least specialized, and victories have been won by very many kinds of excellence.

Perhaps nothing is more opposed to the idea of a gentleman than the *sæva animi tempestas* [Fierce tempest of the soul] of anger. A testy, quarrelsome, mucky humor is antisocial, and an outburst of rage is repulsive. Even non-resistance, turning the other cheek, has its victories and may be a method of moral combat. A strong temper well controlled and kept in leash makes a kinetic character; but in view of bullying, unfair play, cruel injustice to the weak and defenseless, of outrageous wrong that the law can not reach, patience and forbearance may cease to be virtues, and summary redress may have a distinct advantage to the ethical nature of man and to social order, and the strenuous soul must fight or grow stagnant or flabby. If too repressed, righteous indignation may turn to sourness and sulks, and the disposition be spoiled. Hence the relief and exhilaration of an outbreak that often clears the psychic atmosphere like a thunderstorm, and gives the "peace that passeth understanding" so often dilated on by our correspondents. Rather than the abject fear of making enemies whatever the provocation, I would praise those whose best title of honor is the kind of enemies they make. Better even an occasional nose dented by a fist, a broken bone, a rapier-scarred face, or even sometimes the sacrifice of the life of one of our best academic youth than stagnation, general cynicism and censoriousness, bodily and psychic cowardice, and moral corruption, if this indeed be, as it sometimes is, its real alternative.

So closely are love and war connected that not only is individual pugnacity greatly increased at the period of sexual maturity, when animals acquire or develop horns, fangs, claws, spurs, and weapons of offense and defense, but a new spirit of organization arises which makes teams possible or more permanent. Football, baseball, cricket, etc., and even boating can become schools of mental and moral training. First, the rules of the game are often intricate, and to master and observe them effectively is no mean training for the mind controlling the body. These are steadily being revised and improved, and the reasons for each detail of construction and conduct of the game require experience and insight into human nature. Then the subordination of each member to the whole and to a leader cultivates the social and coöperative instincts, while the honor of the school, college, or city, which each team represents, is confided to each and all. Group loyalty in Anglo-Saxon games, which shows such a marked increment in coördination and self-subordination at the dawn of puberty as to constitute a distinct change in the character of sports at this age, can be so utilized as to develop a spirit of service and devotion not only to town, country, and race, but to God and the church. Self must be merged and a sportsmanlike spirit cultivated that prefers defeat to tricks and secret practise, and a clean game to the applause of rooters and fans, intent only on victory, however won. The long, hard fight against professionalism that brings in husky muckers, who by every rule of true courtesy and chivalry belong outside academic circles, scrapping and underhand advantages, is a sad comment on the character and spirit of these games, and eliminates the best of their educational advantages. The necessity of intervention, which has imposed such great burdens on faculties and brought so much friction with the frenzy of scholastic sentiment in the hot stage of seasonal enthusiasms, when fanned to a white heat by the excessive interest of friends and patrons and the injurious exploitation of the press, bears sad testimony to the strength and persistence of warlike instincts from our heredity. But even thus the good far predominates. The elective system has destroyed the class games, and our institutions have no units like the English colleges to be pitted against each other, and so colleges grow, an ever smaller percentage of students obtain the benefit of practise on the teams, while electioneering methods often place second-best men in place of the best. But both students and teachers are slowly learning wisdom in the dear school of experience. On the whole, there is less license in "breaking training" and in celebrating victories, and even at their worst, good probably predominates, while the progress of recent years bids us hope.

Finally, military ideals and methods of psycho-physical education are helpful regulations of the appetite for combat, and on the whole more wholesome and robust than those which are merely esthetic. Marching in step gives proper and uniform movement of legs, arms, and carriage of body; the manual of arms, with evolution and involution of figures in the ranks, gives each a corporate feeling of membership, and involves care of personal appearance and accouterments, while the uniform levels social distinction in dress. For the French and Italian and especially the German and Russian adolescent of the lower classes, the two or three years of compulsory military service is often compared to an academic course, and the army is called, not without some justification, the poor man's university. It gives severe drill, strict discipline, good and regular hours, plain but wholesome fare and out-of-door exercise, exposure, travel, habits of neatness, many useful knacks and devices, tournaments and mimic or play battles; these, apart from its other functions, make this system a great promoter of national health and intelligence. Naval schools for midshipmen, who serve before the mast, schools on board ship that visit a wide curriculum of ports each year, cavalry schools, where each boy is given a horse to care for, study and train, artillery courses and even an army drill-master in an academy, or uniform, and a few exterior features of soldierly life, all give a distinct character to the spirit of any institution. The very fancy of being in any sense a soldier opens up a new range of interests too seldom utilized; and tactics, army life and service, military history, battles, patriotism, the flag, and duties to country, should always erect a new standard of honor. Youth should embrace every opportunity that offers in this line, and instruction should greatly increase the intellectual opportunities created by every interest in warfare. It would be easy to create pregnant courses on how soldiers down the course of history have lived, thought, felt, fought, and died, how great battles were won and what causes triumphed in them, and to generalize many of the best things taught in detail in the best schools of war in different grades and lands.

A subtle but potent intersexual influence is among the strongest factors of all adolescent sport. Male birds and beasts show off their charms of beauty and accomplishment in many a liturgy of love antics in the presence of the female. This instinct seems somehow continuous with the growth of ornaments in the mating season. Song, tumbling, balking, mock fights, etc., are forms of animal courtship. The boy who turns cartwheels past the home of the girl of his fancy, is brilliant, brave, witty, erect, strong in her presence, and elsewhere dull and commonplace enough, illustrates the same principle. The true cake-walk as seen in the South is perhaps the purest expression of this impulse to courtship antics seen in man, but its irradiations are many and pervasive. The presence of the fair sex gives tonicity to youth's muscles and tension to his arteries to a degree of which he is rarely conscious. Defeat in all contests is more humiliating and victory more glorious thereby. Each sex is constantly passing the examination of the other, and each judges the other by standards different from its own. Alas for the young people who are not different with the other sex from what they are with their own!—and some are transformed into different beings. Achievement proclaims ability to support, defend, bring credit and even fame to the object of future choice, and no good point is lost. Physical force and skill, and above all, victory and glory, make a hero and invest him with a romantic glamour, which, even though concealed by conventionality or etiquette, is profoundly felt and makes the winner more or less irresistible. The applause of men and of mates is sweet and even intoxicating, but that of ladies is ravishing. By universal acclaim the fair belong to the brave, strong, and victorious. This stimulus is wholesome and refining. As is shown later, a bashful youth often selects a maiden onlooker and is sometimes quite unconsciously dominated in his every movement by a sense of her presence, stranger and apparently unnoticed though she be, although in the intellectual work of coeducation girls are most influenced thus. In athletics this motive makes for refinement and good form. The ideal knight, however fierce and terrible, must not be brutal, but show capacity for fine feeling, tenderness, magnanimity, and forbearance. Evolutionists tell us that woman has domesticated and educated savage man and taught him all his virtues by exercising her royal prerogative of selecting in her mate just those qualities that pleased her for transmission to future generations and eliminating others distasteful to her. If so, she is still engaged in this work as much as ever, and in his dull, slow way man feels that her presence enforces her standards, abhorrent though it would be to him to compromise in one iota his masculinity. Most plays and games in which both sexes participate have some of the advantages with some of the disadvantages of coeducation. Where both are partners rather than antagonists, there is less eviration. A gallant man would do his best to help, but his worst not to beat a lady. Thus, in general, the latter performs her best in her true rule of sympathetic spectator rather than as fellow player, and is now an important factor in the physical education of adolescents.

How pervasive this femininity is, which is slowly transforming our schools, is strikingly seen in the church. Gulick holds that the reason why only some seven per cent of the young men of the country are in the churches, while most members and workers are women, is that the qualities demanded are the feminine ones of love, rest, prayer, trust, desire for fortitude to endure, a sense of atonement—traits not involving ideals that most stir young men. The church has not yet learned to appeal to the more virile qualities. Fielding Hall[14] asks why Christ and Buddha alone of great religious teachers were rejected by their own race and accepted elsewhere. He answers that these mild beliefs of peace, nonresistance, and submission, rejected by virile warrior races, Jews and ancient Hindus, were adopted where women were free and led in these matters. Confucianism, Mohammedanism, etc., are virile, and so indigenous, and in such forms of faith and worship women have small place. This again suggests how the sex that rules the heart controls men.

Too much can hardly be said in favor of cold baths and swimming at this age. Marro[15] quotes Father Kneipp, and almost rivals his hydrotherapeutic enthusiasm. Cold bathing sends the blood inward partly by the cold which contracts the capillaries of the skin and tissue immediately underlying it, and partly by the pressure of the water over all the dermal surface, quickens the activity of kidneys, lungs, and digestive apparatus, and the reactive glow is the best possible tonic for dermal circulation. It is the best of all gymnastics for the nonstriated or involuntary muscles and for the heart and blood vessels. This and the removal of the products of excretion preserve all the important dermal functions which are so easily and so often impaired in modern life, lessen the liability to skin diseases, promote freshness of complexion; and the moral effects of plunging into cold and supporting the body in deep water is not inconsiderable in strengthening a spirit of hardihood and reducing overtenderness to sensory discomforts. The exercise of swimming is unique in that nearly all the movements and combinations are such as are rarely used otherwise, and are perhaps in a sense ancestral and liberal rather than directly preparatory for future avocations. Its stimulus for heart and lungs is, by general consent of all writers upon the subject, most wholesome and beneficial. Nothing so directly or quickly reduces to the lowest point the plethora of the sex organs. The very absence of clothes and running on the beach is exhilarating and gives a sense of freedom. Where practicable it is well to dispense with bathing suits, even the scantiest. The warm bath tub is enfeebling and degenerative, despite the cold spray later, while the free swim in cold water is most invigorating.

Happily, city officials, teachers, and sanitarians are now slowly realizing the great improvement in health and temper that comes from bathing and are establishing beach and surf, spray, floating and plunge summer baths and swimming pools; often providing instruction even in swimming in clothes, undressing in the water, treading water, and rescue work, free as well as fee days, bathing suits, and, in London, places for nude bathing after dark; establishing time and distance standards with certificates and even prizes; annexing toboggan slides, swings, etc., realizing that in both the preference of youth and in healthful and moral effects, probably nothing outranks this form of exercise. Such is its strange fascination that, according to one comprehensive census, the passion to get to the water outranks all other causes of truancy, and plays an important part in the motivation of runaways. In the immense public establishment near San Francisco, provided by private munificence, there are accommodations for all kinds of bathing in hot and cold and in various degrees of fresh and salt water, in closed spaces and in the open sea, for small children and adults, with many appliances and instructors, all in one great covered arena with seats in an amphitheater for two thousand spectators, and many adjuncts and accessories. So elsewhere the presence of visitors is now often invited and provided for. Sometimes wash-houses and public laundries are annexed. Open hours and longer evenings and seasons are being prolonged.

Prominent among the favorite games of early puberty and the years just before are those that involve passive motion and falling, like swinging in its many forms, including the May-pole and single rope varieties. Mr. Lee reports that children wait late in the evening and in cold weather for a turn at a park swing. Psychologically allied to these are wheeling and skating. Places for the latter are now often provided by the fire department, which in many cities floods hundreds of empty lots. Ponds are cleared of snow and horse-plowed, perhaps by the park commission, which often provides lights and perhaps ices the walks and streets for coasting, erects shelters, and devises space economy for as many diamonds, bleachers, etc., as possible. Games of hitting, striking, and throwing balls and other objects, hockey, tennis, all the courts of which are usually crowded, golf and croquet, and sometimes fives, cricket, bowling, quoits, curling, etc., have great "thumogenic" or emotional power.

Leg exercise has perhaps a higher value than that of any other part. Man is by definition an upright being, but only after a long apprenticeship. [16] Thus the hand was freed from the necessity of locomotion and made the servant of the mind. Locomotion overcomes the tendency to sedentary habits in modern schools and life, and helps the mind to helpful action, so that a peripatetic philosophy is more normal than that of the easy chair and the study lamp. Hill-climbing is unexcelled as a stimulus at once of heart, lungs, and blood. If Hippocrates is right, inspiration is possible only on a mountain-top. Walking, running, dancing, skating, coasting are also alterative and regulative of sex, and there is a deep and close though not yet fully explained reciprocity between the two. Arm work is relatively too prominent a feature in gymnasia. Those who lead excessively sedentary lives are prone to be turbulent and extreme in both passion and opinion, as witness the oft-adduced revolutionary disposition of cobblers.

The play problem is now fairly open and is vast in its relation to many other things. Roof playgrounds, recreation piers, schoolyards and even school-buildings, open before and after school hours; excursions and outings of many kinds and with many purposes, which seem to distinctly augment growth; occupation during the long vacation when, beginning with spring, most juvenile crime is committed; theatricals, which according to some police testimony lessen the number of juvenile delinquents; boys' clubs with more or less self-government of the George Junior Republic and other types, treated in another chapter; nature-study; the distinctly different needs and propensities of both good and evil in different nationalities; the advantages of playground fences and exclusion, their disciplinary worth, and their value as resting places; the liability that "the boy without a playground will become the father without a job"; the relation of play and its slow transition to manual and industrial education at the savage age when a boy abhors all regular occupation; the necessity of exciting interest, not by what is done for boys, but by what they do; the adjustment of play to sex; the determination of the proper average age of maximal zest in and good from sandbox, ring-toss, bean-bag, shuffle-board, peg top, charity, funeral play, prisoner's base, hill-dill; the value and right use of apparatus, and of rabbits, pigeons, bees, and a small menagerie in the playground; tan-bark, clay, the proper alternation of excessive freedom, that often turns boys stale through the summer, with regulated activities; the disciplined "work of play" and sedentary games; the value of the washboard rubbing and of the hand and knee exercise of scrubbing, which a late writer would restore for all girls with clever and Greek-named play apparatus; as well as digging, shoveling, tamping, pick-chopping, and hod-carrying exercises in the form of games for boys; the relations of women's clubs, parents' clubs, citizens' leagues and unions, etc., to all this work—such are the practical problems.

The playground movement encounters its chief obstacles in the most crowded and slum districts, where its greatest value and success was expected for boys in the early teens, who without supervision are prone to commit abuses upon property and upon younger children,[17] and are so disorderly as to make the place a nuisance, and who resent the "fathering" of the police, without, at least, the minimum control of a system of permits and exclusions. If hoodlums play at all, they become infatuated with baseball and football, especially punting; they do not take kindly to the soft large ball of the Hall House or the Civic League, and prefer at first scrub games with individual self-exhibition to organized teams. Lee sees the "arboreal instincts of our progenitors" in the very strong propensity of boys from ten to fourteen to climb in any form; to use traveling rings, generally occupied constantly to their fullest extent; to jump from steps and catch a swinging trapeze; to go up a ladder and slide down poles; to use horizontal and parallel bars. The city boy has plenty of daring at this age, but does not know what he can do and needs more supervision than the country youth. The young tough is commonly present, and though admired and copied by younger boys, it is, perhaps, as often for his heroic as for his bad traits.

Dr. Sargent and others have well pointed out that athletics afford a wealth of new and profitable topics for discussion and enthusiasm which helps against the triviality and mental vacuity into which the intercourse of students is prone to lapse. It prompts to discussion of diet and regimen. It gives a new standard of honor. For a member of a team to break training would bring reprobation and ostracism, for he is set apart to win fame for his class or college. It supplies a splendid motive against all errors and vices that weaken or corrupt the body. It is a wholesome vent for the reckless courage that would otherwise go to disorder or riotous excess. It supplies new and advantageous topics for compositions and for terse, vigorous, and idiomatic theme-writing, is a great aid to discipline, teaches respect for deeds rather than words or promises, lays instructors under the necessity of being more interesting, that their work be not jejune or dull by contrast; again the business side of managing great contests has been an admirable school for training young men to conduct great and difficult financial operations, sometimes involving $100,000 or more, and has thus prepared some for successful careers. It furnishes now the closest of all links between high school and college, reduces the number of those physically unfit for college, and should give education generally a more real and vigorous ideal. Its obvious dangers are distraction from study and overestimation of the value of victory, especially in the artificial glamours which the press and the popular furor give to great games; unsportsmanlike secret tricks and methods, over-emphasis of combative and too stalwart impulses, and a disposition to carry things by storm, by rush-line tactics; friction with faculties, and censure or neglect of instructors who take unpopular sides on hot questions; action toward license after games, spasmodic excitement culminating in excessive strain for body and mind, with alternations of reaction; "beefiness"; overdevelopment of the physical side of life, and, in some cases, premature features of senility in later life, undergrowth of the accessory motor parts and powers, and erethic diathesis that makes steady and continued mental toil seem monotonous, dull, and boresome.

The propensity to codify sports, to standardize the weight and size of their implements, and to reduce them to what Spencer calls regimentation, is a outcrop of uniformitarianism that works against that individuation which is one of the chief advantages of free play. This, to be sure, has developed old-fashioned rounders to modern baseball, and this is well, but it is seen in the elaborate Draconian laws, diplomacy, judicial and legislative procedures, concerning "eligibility, transfer, and even sale of players." In some games international conformity is gravely discussed. Even where there is no tyranny and oppression, good form is steadily hampering nature and the free play of personality. Togs and targets, balls and bats, rackets and oars are graded or numbered, weighed, and measured, and every emergency is legislated on and judged by an autocratic martinet, jealous of every prerogative and conscious of his dignity. All this separates games from the majority and makes for specialism and professionalism. Not only this, but men are coming to be sized up for hereditary fitness in each point and for each sport. Runners, sprinters, and jumpers,[18] we are told, on the basis of many careful measurements, must be tall, with slender bodies, narrow but deep chests, longer legs than the average for their height, the lower leg being especially long, with small calf, ankle, and feet, small arms, narrow hips, with great power of thoracic inflation, and thighs of small girth. Every player must be studied by trainers for ever finer individual adjustments. His dosage of work must be kept well within the limits of his vitality, and be carefully adjusted to his recuperative power. His personal nascent periods must be noted, and initial embarrassment carefully weeded out.

The field of play is as wide as life and its varieties far outnumber those of industries and occupations in the census. Plays and games differ in seasons, sex, and age. McGhee[19] has shown on the basis of some 8,000 children, that running plays are pretty constant for boys from six to seventeen, but that girls are always far behind boys and run steadily less from eight to eighteen. In games of choice, boys showed a slight rise at sixteen and seventeen, and girls a rapid increase at eleven and a still more rapid one after sixteen. In games of imitation girls excel and show a marked, as boys do a slight, pubescent fall. In those games involving rivalry boys at first greatly excel girls, but are overtaken by the latter in the eighteenth year, both showing marked pubescent increment. Girls have the largest number of plays and specialise on a few less than boys, and most of these plays are of the unorganized kinds. Johnson[20] selected from a far larger number 440 plays and games and arranged the best of them in a course by school grades, from the first to the eighth, inclusive, and also according to their educational value as teaching observation, reading and spelling, language, arithmetic, geography, history, and biography, physical training, and specifically as training legs, hand, arm, back, waist, abdominal muscles, chest, etc. Most of our best games are very old and, Johnson thinks, have deteriorated. But children are imitative and not inventive in their games, and easily learn new ones. Since the Berlin Play Congress in 1894 the sentiment has grown that these are of national importance and are preferable to gymnastics both for soul and body. Hence we have play-schools, teachers, yards, and courses, both for their own value and also to turn on the play impulse to aid in the drudgery of school work. Several have thought that a well-rounded, liberal education could be given by plays and games alone on the principle that there is no profit where there is no pleasure or true euphoria.

Play is motor poetry. Too early distinction between play and work should not be taught. Education perhaps should really begin with directing childish sports aright. Froebel thought it the purest and most spiritual activity of childhood, the germinal leaves of all later life. Schooling that lacks recreation favors dulness, for play makes the mind alert and its joy helps all anabolic activities. Says Brinton, "the measure of value of work is the amount of play there is in it, and the measure of value of play is the amount of work there is in it." Johnson adds that "it is doubtful if a great man ever accomplished his life work without having reached a play interest in it." Sully[21] deplores the increase of "agolasts" or "non-laughers" in our times in merry old England[22] every one played games; and laughter, their natural accompaniment, abounded. Queen Elizabeth's maids of honor played tag with hilarity, but the spirit of play with full abandon seems taking its departure from our overworked, serious, and tons, age. To requote Stevenson with variation, as *laborari*, [To labor] so *ludere, et joculari orare sunt.* [To play and to jest are to pray] Laughter itself, as Kühne long ago showed, is one of the most precious forms of exercise, relieving the arteries of their tension.[23]

The antithesis between play and work is generally wrongly conceived, for the difference is essentially in the degree of strength of the psycho-physic motivations. The young often do their hardest work in play. With interest, the most repellent tasks become pure sport, as in the case Johnson reports of a man who wanted a pile of stone thrown into a ditch and, by kindling a fire in the ditch and pretending the stones were buckets of water, the heavy and long-shirked job was done by tired boys with shouting and enthusiasm. Play, from one aspect of it, is superfluous energy over and above what is necessary to digest, breathe, keep the heart and organic processes going; and most children who can not play, if they have opportunity, can neither study nor work without overdrawing their resources of vitality.

Bible psychology conceives the fall of man as the necessity of doing things without zest, and this is not only ever repeated but now greatly emphasized when youth leaves the sheltered paradise of play to grind in the mills of modern industrial civilization. The curse is overcome only by those who come to love their tasks and redeem their toil again to play. Play, hardly less than work, can be to utter exhaustion; and because it draws upon older stores and strata of psycho-physic impulsion its exhaustion may even more completely drain our kinetic resources, if it is too abandoned or prolonged. Play can do just as hard and painful tasks as work, for what we love is done with whole and undivided personality. Work, as too often conceived, is all body and no soul, and makes for duality and not totality. Its constraint is external, mechanical, or it works by fear and not love. Not effort but zestless endeavor is the tragedy of life. Interest and play are one and inseparable as body and soul. Duty itself is not adequately conceived and felt if it is not pleasure, and is generally too feeble and fitful in the young to awaken much energy or duration of action. Play is from within from congenital hereditary impulsion. It is the best of all methods of organizing instincts. Its cathartic or purgative function regulates irritability, which may otherwise be drained or vented in wrong directions, exactly as Breuer[24] shows psychic traumata may, if overtense, result in "hysterical convulsions." It is also the best form of self-expression; and its advantage is variability, following the impulsion of the idle, perhaps hyperemic, and overnourished centers most ready to act. It involves play illusion and is the great agent of unity and totalization of body and soul, while its social function develops solidarity and unison of action between individuals. The dances, feasts, and games of primitive people, wherein they rehearse hunting and war and act and dance out their legends, bring individuals and tribes together.[25] Work is menial, cheerless, grinding, regular, and requires more precision and accuracy and, because attended with less ease and pleasure and economy of movement, is more liable to produce erratic habits. Antagonistic as the forms often are, it may be that, as Carr says, we may sometimes so suffuse work with the play spirit, and *vice versa*, that the present distinction between work and play will vanish, the transition will be less tragic and the activities of youth will be slowly systematised into a whole that better fits his nature and needs; or, if not this, we may at least find the true proportion and system between drudgery and recreation.

The worst product of striving to do things with defective psychic impulsion is fatigue in its common forms, which slows down the pace, multiplies errors and inaccuracies, and develops slovenly habits, ennui, flitting will specters, velleities and caprices, and neurasthenic symptoms generally. It brings restlessness, and a tendency to many little heterogeneous, smattering efforts that weaken the will and leave the mind like a piece of well-used blotting paper, covered with traces and nothing legible. All beginnings are easy, and only as we leave the early stages of proficiency behind and press on in either physical or mental culture and encounter difficulties, do individual differences and the tendency of weak will, to change and turn to something else increase. Perhaps the greatest disparity between men is the power to make a long concentrative, persevering effort, for *In der Beschränkung zeigt sich der Meister* [The master shows himself in limitation]. Now no kind or line of culture is complete till it issues in motor habits, and makes a well-knit soul texture that admits concentration series in many directions and that can bring all its resources to bear at any point. The brain unorganized by training has, to recur to Richter's well-worn aphorism, saltpeter, sulfur, and charcoal, or all the ingredients of gunpowder, but never makes a grain of it because they never get together. Thus willed action is the language of complete men and the goal of education. When things are mechanized by right habituation, there is still further gain; for not only is the mind freed for further and higher work, but this deepest stratum of motor association is a plexus that determines not only conduct and character, but even beliefs. The person who deliberates is lost, if the intellect that doubts and weighs alternatives is less completely organised than habits. All will culture is intensive and should safeguard us against the chance influence of life and the insidious danger of great ideas in small and feeble minds. Now fatigue, personal and perhaps racial, is just what arrests in the incomplete and mere memory or noetic stage. It makes weak bodies that command, and not strong ones that obey. It divorces knowing and doing, *Kennen* and *Können*, a separation which the Greeks could not conceive because for them knowledge ended in skill or was exemplified in precepts and proverbs that were so clear cut that the pain of violating them was poignant. Ideas must be long worked over till life speaks as with the rifle and not with the shotgun, and still less with the water hose. The purest thought, if true, is only action repressed to be ripened to more practical form. Not only do muscles come before mind, will before intelligence, and sound ideas rest on a motor basis, but all really useless knowledge tends to be eliminated as error or superstition. The roots of play lie close to those of creative imagination and idealism.

The opposite extreme is the factitious and superficial motivation of fear, prizes, examinations, artificial and immediate rewards and penalties, which can only tattoo the mind and body with conventional patterns pricked in, but which lead an unreal life in the soul because they have no depth of soil in nature or heredity. However precious and coherent in themselves, all subject-matters thus organized are mere lugs, crimps, and frills. All such culture is spurious, unreal, and parasitic. It may make a scholastic or sophistic mind, but a worm is at the root and, with a dim sense of the vanity of all knowledge that does not become a rule of life, some form of pessimism is sure to supervene in every serious soul. With age a civilization accumulates such impedimenta, traditional flotsam and jetsam, and race fatigue proceeds with equal step with its increasing volume. Immediate utilities are better, but yet not so much better than acquisitions that have no other than a school or examination value. If, as Ruskin says, all true work is praise, all true play is love and prayer. Instil into a boy's soul learning which he sees and feels not to have the highest worth and which can not become a part of his active life and increase it, and his freshness, spontaneity, and the fountains of play slowly run dry in him, and his youth fades to early desiccation. The instincts, feelings, intuitions, the work of which is always play, are superseded by method, grind, and education by instruction which is only an effort to repair the defects of heredity, for which, at its best, it is vulgar, pinchbeck substitute. The best play is true genius, which always comes thus into the world, and has this way of doing its work, and all the contents of the memory pouches is luggage to be carried rather than the vital strength that carries burdens. Grosswell says that children are young because they play, and not *vice versa*; and he might have added, men grow old because they stop playing, and not conversely, for play is, at bottom, growth, and at the top of the intellectual scale it is the eternal type of research from sheer love of truth. Home, school, church, state, civilization, are measured in one supreme scale of values, viz., whether and how, for they aid in bringing youth to its fullest maturity. Even vice, crime, and decline are often only arrest or backsliding or reversion. National and racial decline beginning in eliminating one by one the last and highest styles of development of body and mind, mental stimulus of excessive dosage lowers general nutrition. A psychologist that turns his back on mere subtleties and goes to work in a life of service has here a great opportunity, and should not forget, as Horace Mann said, "that for all that grows, one former is worth one hundred reformers."

[Footnote 1: Interest in Relation to Muscular Exercise. American Physical Education Review, June, 1902, vol. 7, pp. 57-65.]

[Footnote 2: The Influence of Exercise upon Growth by Frederic Burk. American Physical Education Review, December, 1899, vol. 4, pp. 340-349.]

[Footnote 3: A Study of Dolls, by G. Stanley Hall and A.C. Ellis. Pedagogical Seminary, December, 1896, vol. 4, pp. 129-175.]

[Footnote 4: Studies in Imagination, by Lilian H. Chalmers. Pedagogical Seminary, April, 1900, vol. 7, pp. 111-123.]

[Footnote 5: Some Psychical Aspects of Physical Exercise. Popular Science Monthly, October, 1898, vol. 53, pp. 703-805.]

[Footnote 6: Amusements of Worcester School Children. Pedagogical Seminary, September, 1899, vol. 6, pp. 314-371.]

[Footnote 7: A Study in the Play Life of Some South Carolina Children. Pedagogical Seminary, December, 1900, vol. 7, pp. 439-478.]

[Footnote 8: Arbeit und Rythmus. Trubner, Leipzig, 1896.]

[Footnote 9: Descent of Man. D. Appleton and Co., 1872, vol. 1, chap. vi, p. 204 *et seq*]

[Footnote 10: Teasing and Bullying. Pedagogical Seminary, April, 1897, vol. 4, pp. 336-371.]

[Footnote 11: See my Study of Anger. American Journal of Psychology, July, 1899, vol. 10, pp. 516-591.]

[Footnote 12: Der deutsche Student am Ende des 19 Jahrhunderts, 6th ed., Göschen, Leipzig, 1896. See also H. P. Shelden: History and Pedagogy of American Student Societies, New York, 1901, p. 31 *et seq*.]

[Footnote 13: Bushido: The Soul of Japan. An exposition of Japanese thought, by Inazo Nitobé. New York, 1905, pp. 203 *et seq*.]

[Footnote 14: The Hearts of Men. Macmillan, 1901, chap. xxii.]

[Footnote 15: La Puberté. Schleicher Frères, éditeurs, Paris, 1902.]

[Footnote 16: See A.W. Trettien. Creeping and Walking. American Journal of Psychology, October, 1900, vol. 12, pp. 1-57.]

[Footnote 17: Constructive and Preventive Philanthropy, by Joseph Lee. Macmillan, New York, 1902, chaps. x and xi.]

[Footnote 18: C.O. Bernies. Physical Characteristics of the Runner and Jumper. American Physical Education Review, September, 1900, vol. 5, pp. 235-245.]

[Footnote 19: A Study in the Play Life of some South Carolina Children. Pedagogical Seminary, December, 1900, vol. 7, pp. 459-478.]

[Footnote 20: Education by Plays and Games. Pedagogical Seminary, October, 1894, vol. 3, pp. 97-133.]

[Footnote 21: An Essay on Laughter. Longmans, Green and Co., London, 1902, p. 427 *et seq.*]

[Footnote 22: See Brand's Popular Antiquities of Great Britain, 3 Vols., London, 1883.]

[Footnote 23: Psychology of Tickling, Laughing, and the Comic, by G. Stanley Hall and Arthur Allin. American Journal of Psychology, October, 1897, vol. 9, pp. 1-41.]

[Footnote 24: I. Breuer and S. Freud. Studien über Hysterie. F. Deuticke, Wien, 1895. See especially p. 177 *et seq.*]

[Footnote 25: See a valuable discussion by H. A. Carr. The Survival Values of Play, Investigations of the Department of Psychology and Education of the University of Colorado, Arthur Allin, Ph.D., Editor, November, 1902, vol. 1, pp. 3-47]

* * * * *

CHAPTER VII - FAULTS, LIES, AND CRIMES

Classifications of children's faults — Peculiar children — Real faults as distinguished from interference with the teacher's ease — Truancy, its nature and effects — The genesis of crime — The lie, its classes and relations to imagination — Predatory activities — Gangs — Causes of crime — The effects of stories of crime — Temibility — Juvenile crime and its treatment.

Siegert[1] groups children of problematical nature into the following sixteen classes: the sad, the extremely good or bad, star-gazers, scatter-brains, apathetic, misanthropic, doubters and investigators, reverent, critical, executive, stupid and clownish, naive, funny, anamnesic, disposed to learn, and *blasé*; patience, foresight, and self-control, he thinks, are chiefly needed.

A unique and interesting study was undertaken by Közle[2] by collecting and studying thirty German writers on pedagogical subjects since Pestalozzi, and cataloguing all the words they use describing the faults of children. In all, this gave 914 faults, far more in number than their virtues. These were classified as native and of external origin, acute and chronic, egoistic and altruistic, greed, perverted honor, self-will, falsity, laziness, frivolity, distraction, precocity, timidity, envy and malevolence, ingratitude, quarrelsomeness, cruelty, superstition; and the latter fifteen were settled on as resultant groups, and the authors who describe them best are quoted.

Bohannon[3] on the basis of *questionnaire* returns classified peculiar children as heavy, tall, short, small, strong, weak, deft, agile, clumsy, beautiful, ugly, deformed, birthmarked, keen and precocious, defective in sense, mind, and speech, nervous, clean, dainty, dirty, orderly, obedient, disobedient, disorderly, teasing, buoyant, buffoon, cruel, selfish, generous, sympathetic, inquisitive, lying, ill-tempered, silent, dignified, frank, loquacious, courageous, timid, whining, spoiled, gluttonous and only child.

Marro[4] tabulated the conduct of 3,012 boys in gymnasial and lyceal classes in Italy from eleven to eighteen years of age (see table given above). Conduct was marked as good, bad, and indifferent, according to the teacher's estimate, and was good at eighteen in 74 per cent of the cases; at eleven in

70 per cent; at seventeen in 69 per cent; and at fourteen in only 58 per cent. In positively bad conduct, the age of fifteen led, thirteen and fourteen were but little better, while it improved at sixteen, seventeen, and eighteen. In general, conduct was good at eleven; declined at twelve and thirteen; said, to its worst at fourteen; and then improved in yearly increments that did not differ much, and at seventeen was nearly as good as at eleven, and at eighteen four points better.

He computed also the following percentage table of the causes of punishments in certain Italian schools for girls and boys near pubescent ages:

	Boys	Girls
Quarrels and blows	53.90	17.4
Laziness, negligence	1.80	21.3
Untidiness	10.70	24.7
Improper language	.41	14.6
Indecent acts and words	1.00	.24
Refusal to work	.82	1.26
Various offenses against discipline	19.00	19.9
Truancy	9.60	.0
Plots to run away	1.70	.0
Running away	.72	.0

Mr. Sears[5] reports in percentages statistics of the punishments received by a thousand children for the following offenses: Disorder, 17-1/3; disobedience, 16; carelessness, 13-1/3; running away, 12-2/3; quarreling, 10; tardiness, 6-2/3; rudeness, 6; fighting, 5-1/3; lying, 4; stealing, 1; miscellaneous, 7-1/3. He names a long list of punishable offenses, such as malice, swearing, obscenity, bullying, lying, cheating, untidiness, insolence, insult, conspiracy, disobedience, obstinacy, rudeness, noisiness, ridicule; injury to books, building, or other property; and analyzes at length the kinds of punishment, modes of making it fit the offense and the nature of the child, the discipline of consequences, lapse of time between the offense and its punishment, the principle of slight but sure tasks as penalties, etc.

Triplett[6] attempted a census of faults and defeats named by the teacher. Here inattention by far led all others. Defects of sense and speech, carelessness, indifference, lack of honor and of self-restraint, laziness, dreamy listlessness, nervousness, mental incapacity, lack of consideration for others, vanity, affectation, disobedience, untruthfulness, grumbling, etc., follow. Inattention to a degree that makes some children at the mercy of their environment and all its changes, and their mental life one perpetual distraction, is a fault which teachers, of course, naturally observe. Children's views of their own faults and those of other children lay a very different emphasis. Here fighting, bullying, and teasing lead all others; then come stealing, bad manners, lying, disobedience, truancy, cruelty to animals, untidiness, selfishness, etc. Parents' view of this subject Triplett found still different. Here wilfulness and obstinacy led all others with teasing, quarreling, dislike of application and effort, and many others following. The vast number of faults mentioned contrasts very strikingly with the seven deadly sins.

In a suggestive statistical study on the relations of the conduct of children to the weather, Dexter[7] found that excessive humidity was most productive of misdemeanors; that when the temperature was between 90 and 100 the probability of bad conduct was increased 300 per cent, when between 80 and 90 it was increased 104 per cent. Abnormal barometric pressure, whether great or small, was found to increase misconduct 50 per cent; abnormal movements of the wind increased it from 20 to 66 per cent; while the time of year and precipitation seemed to have almost no effect. While the effect of weather has been generally recognized by superintendents and teachers and directors of prisons and asylums, and even by banks, which in London do not permit clerks to do the more important bookkeeping during very foggy days, the statistical estimates of its effect in general need larger numbers for more valuable determinations. Temperature is known to have a very distinct effect upon crime, especially suicide and truancy. Workmen do less in bad weather, blood pressure is modified, etc.[8]

In his study of truancy, Kline[9] starts with the assumption that the maximum metabolism is always consciously or unconsciously sought, and that migrations are generally away from the extremes of hot and cold toward an optimum temperature. The curve of truancies and runaways increases in a marked ratio at puberty, which probably represents the age of natural majority among primitive people. Dislike of school, the passion for out-of-door life, and more universal interests in man and nature now arise, so that runaways may be interpreted as an instinctive rebellion against limitations of freedom and unnatural methods of education as well as against poor homes. Hunger is one of its most potent, although often unconscious causes. The habitual environment now begins to seem dull and there is a great increase in impatience at restraint. Sometimes there is a mania for simply going away and enjoying the liberty of nomadic life. Just as good people in foreign parts sometimes allow themselves unwonted liberties, so vagrancy increases crime. The passion to get to and play at or in the water is often strangely dominant. It seems so fine out of doors, especially in the spring, and the woods and fields make it so hard to voluntarily incarcerate oneself in the schoolroom, that pubescent boys and even girls often feel like animals in captivity. They long intensely for the utter abandon of a wilder life, and very characteristic is the frequent discarding of foot and head dress and even garments in the blind instinct to realise again the conditions of primitive man. The manifestations of this impulse, if read aright, are grave arraignments of the lack of adaptability of the child's environment to his disposition and nature, and with home restraints once broken, the liabilities to every crime, especially theft, are enormously increased. The truant, although according to Kline's measurements slightly smaller than the average child, is more energetic and is generally capable of the greatest activity and usefulness in more out-of-door vocations. Truancy is augmented, too, just in proportion as legitimate and interesting physical exercise is denied.

The vagrant, itinerant, vagabond, gadabout, hobo, and tramp, that Riis has made so interesting, is an arrested, degenerate, or perverted being who abhors work; feels that the world owes him a living; and generally has his first real nomad experience in the teens or earlier. It is a chronic illusion of youth that gives "elsewhere" a special charm. In the immediate present things are mean, dulled by wont, and perhaps even nauseating because of familiarity. There must be a change of scene to see the world; man is not sessile but locomotor; and the moment his life becomes migratory all the restraints and responsibilities of settled life vanish. It is possible to steal and pass on undiscovered and unsuspected, and to steal again. The vagabond escapes the control of public sentiment, which normally is an external conscience, and having none of his own within him thus lapses to a feral state. The constraint of city, home, and school is especially irksome, and if to this repulsion is added the attraction of a love of nature and of perpetual change, we have the diathesis of the roadsman already developed. Adolescence is the normal time of emancipation from the parental roof, when youth seeks to set up a home of its own, but the apprentice to life must wander far and long enough to find the best habitat in which to set up for himself. This is the spring season of emigration; and it should be an indispensable part of every life curriculum, just before settlement, to travel far and wide, if resources and inclination permit. But this stage should end in wisely chosen settlement where the young life can be independently developed, and that with more complacency and satisfaction because the place has been wisely chosen on the basis of a wide comparison. The chronic vagrant has simply failed to develop the reductives of this normal stage.

Crime is cryptogamous and flourishes in concealment, so that not only does falsehood facilitate it, but certain types of lies often cause and are caused by it. The beginning of wisdom in treatment is to discriminate between good and bad lies. My own study[10] of the lies of 300 normal children, by a method carefully devised in order to avoid all indelicacy to the childish consciousness, suggested the following distinct species of lies.

It is often a well-marked epoch when the young child first learns that it can imagine and state things that have no objective counterpart in its life, and there is often a weird intoxication when some absurd and monstrous statement is made, while the first sensation of a deliberate break with truth causes a real excitement which is often the birth pang of the imagination. More commonly this is seen in childish play, which owes a part of its charm to self-deception. Children make believe they are animals, doctors, ogres, play school, that they are dead, mimic all they see and hear. Idealising temperaments sometimes prompt children of three or four suddenly to assert that they saw a pig with five ears, apples on a cherry tree, and other Munchausen wonders, which really means merely that they have had a new mental combination independently of experience. Sometimes their fancy is almost visualisation and develops into a kind of mythopeic faculty which spins clever yarns and suggests in a sense, quite as pregnant as Froschmer asserts of all mental activity and of the universe itself, that all their life is imagination. Its control and not its elimination in a Gradgrind age of crass facts is what should be sought in the interests of the highest truthfulness and of the evolution of thought as something above reality, which prepares the way for imaginative literature. The life of Hartley Coleridge,[11] by his brother, is one of many illustrations. He fancied cataract of what he named "jug-force" would burst out in a certain field and flow between populous banks, where an ideal government, long wars, and even a reform in spelling, would prevail, illustrated in a journal devoted to the affairs of this realm — all these developed in his imagination, where they existed with great reality for years. The vividness of this fancy resembles the pseudo-hallucinations of Kandinsky. Two sisters used to say, "Let us play we are sisters," as if this made the relation more real. Cagliostro found adolescent boys particularly apt for training for his exhibition of phrenological impostures, illustrating his thirty-five faculties. "He lied when he confessed he had lied," said a young Sancho Panza, who had believed the wild tales of another boy who later admitted their falsity. Sir James Mackintosh, near puberty, after reading Roman history, used to fancy himself the Emperor of Constantinople, and carried on the administration of the realm for hours at a time. His fancies never quite became convictions, but adolescence is the golden age of this kind of dreamery and reverie which supplements reality and totalizes our faculties, and often gives a special charm to dramatic activities and in morbid cases to simulation and dissimulation. It is a state from which some of the bad, but far more of the good qualities of life and mind arise. These are the noble lies of poetry, art, and idealism, but their pedagogic regime must be wise.

Again with children as with savages, truth depends largely upon personal likes and dislikes. Truth is for friends, and lies are felt to be quite right for enemies. The young often see no wrong in lies their friends wish told, but may collapse and confess when asked if they would have told their mother thus. Boys best keep up complotted lies and are surer to own up if caught than girls. It is harder to cheat in school with a teacher who is liked. Friendships are cemented by confidences and secrets, and when they wane, promises not to tell weaken in their validity. Lies to the priest, and above all to God, are the worst. All this makes special attention to friendships, leaders, and favorites important, and suggests the high value of science for general veracity.

The worst lies, perhaps, are those of selfishness. They ease children over many hard places in life, and are convenient covers for weakness and vice. These lies are, on the whole, judging from our census, most prevalent. They are also most corrupting and hard to correct. All bad habits particularly predispose to the lie of concealment; for those who do wrong are almost certain to have recourse to falsehood, and the sense of meanness thus slowly bred, which may be met by appeals to honor, for so much of which school life is responsible, is often mitigated by the fact that falsehoods are frequently resorted to in moments of danger and excitement, are easily forgotten when it is over, and rarely rankle. These, even more than the pseudomaniac cases mentioned later, grow rankly in those with criminal predispositions.

The lie heroic is often justified as a means of noble ends. Youth has an instinct which is wholesome for viewing moral situations as wholes. Callow casuaists are fond of declaring that it would be a duty to state that their mother was out when she was in, if it would save her life, although they perhaps would not lie to save their own. A doctor, many suggested, might tell an overanxious patient or friend that there was hope, saving his conscience perhaps by reflecting that there was hope, although they had it while he had none. The end at first in such cases may be very noble and the fib or quibble very petty, but worse lies for meaner objects may follow. Youth often describes such situations with exhilaration as if there were a feeling of easement from the monotonous and tedious obligation of rigorous literal veracity, and here mentors are liable to become nervous and err. The youth who really gets interested in the conflict of duties may reverently be referred to the inner lie of his own conscience, the need of keeping which as a private tribunal is now apparent.

Many adolescents become craven literalists and distinctly morbid and pseudophobiac, regarding every deviation from scrupulously literal truth as alike heinous; and many systematized palliatives and casuistic word-splittings, methods of whispering or silently interpolating the words "not," "perhaps," or "I think," sometimes said over hundreds of times to neutralize the guilt of intended or unintended falsehoods, appear in our records as a sad product of bad methods.

Next to the selfish lie for protection—of special psychological interest for adolescent crime—is what we may call pseudomania, seen especially in pathological girls in their teens, who are honeycombed with selfishness and affectation and have a passion for always acting a part, attracting attention, etc. The recent literature of telepathy and hypnotism furnishes many striking examples of this diathesis of impostors of both sexes. It is a strange psychological paradox that some can so deliberately prefer to call black white and find distinct inebriation in flying diametrically in the face of truth and fact. The great impostors, whose entire lives have been a fabric of lies, are cases in point. They find a distinct pleasure not only in the sense of power which their ability to make trouble gives, but in the sense of making truth a lie, and of decreeing things into and out of existence.

Sheldon's interesting statistics show that among the institutional activities of American children,[12] predatory organizations culminate from eleven to fifteen, and are chiefly among boys. These include bands of robbers, clubs for hunting and fishing, play armies, organized fighting bands between separate districts, associations for building forts, etc. This form of association is the typical one for boys of twelve. After this age their interests are gradually transferred to less loosely organized athletic clubs. Sheldon's statistics are as follows:

Age 8 9 10 11 12 13 14 15 16 17 Total No. of predatory 4 5 3 0 7 1 1 3 1 0 25 = Girls societies 4 2 17 31 18 22 (11) 7 1 0 111 = Boys

Innocent though these predatory habits may be in small boys, if they are not naturally and normally reduced at the beginning of the teens and their energy worked off into athletic societies, they become dangerous. "The robber knight, the pirate chief, and the marauder become the real models." The stealing clubs gather edibles and even useless things, the loss of which causes mischief, into some den, cellar, or camp in the woods, where the plunder of their raids is collected. An organized gang of boy pilferers for the purpose of entering stores had a cache, where the stolen goods were brought together. Some of these bands have specialized on electric bells and connections, or golf sticks and balls. Jacob Riis says that on the East Side of New York, every corner has its gang with a program of defiance of law and order, where the young tough who is a coward alone becomes dangerous when he hunts with the pack. He is ambitious to get "pinched" or arrested and to pose as a hero. His vanity may obliterate common fear and custom as his mind becomes inflamed with flash literature and "penny dreadfuls." Sometimes whole neighborhoods are terrorized so that no one dares to testify against the atrocities they commit. Riis even goes so far as to say that "a bare enumeration of the names of the best-known gangs would occupy the pages of this book."[13] The names are sufficiently suggestive — hell's kitchen gang, stable gang, dead men, floaters, rock, pay, hock gang, the soup-house gang, plug uglies, back-alley men, dead beats, cop beaters, and roasters, hell benders, chain gang, sheeny skinners, street cleaners, tough kids, sluggers, wild Indians, cave and cellar men, moonlight howlers, junk club, crook gang, being some I have heard of. Some of the members of these gangs never knew a home, were found perhaps as babies wrapped in newspapers, survivors of the seventy-two dead infants Riis says were picked up on the streets in New York in 1889, or of baby farming. They grow up street arabs, slum waifs, the driftwood of society, its flotsam and jetsam, or plankton, fighting for a warn corner in their resorts or living in crowded tenement-houses that rent for more than a house on Fifth Avenue. Arrant cowards singly, they dare and do anything together. A gang stole a team in East New York and drove down the avenue, shopping to throw in supplies, one member sitting in the back of the wagon and shooting at all who interfered. One gang specialized on stealing baby carriages, depositing their inmates on the sidewalk. Another blew up a grocery store because its owner refused a gift they demanded. Another tried to saw off the head of a Jewish pedler. One member killed another for calling him "no gent." Six murderous assaults were made at one time by these gangs within a single week. One who is caught and does his "bit" or "stretch" is a hero, and when a leader is hanged, as has sometimes happened, he is almost envied for his notoriety. A frequent ideal is to pound a policeman with his own club. The gang federates all nationalities. Property is depreciated and may be ruined if it is frequented by these gangs or becomes their lair or "hang-out." A citizen residing on the Hudson procured a howitzer and pointed it at a boat gang, forbidding them to land on his river frontage. They have their calls, whistles, signs, rally suddenly from no one knows where, and vanish in the alleys, basements, roofs, and corridors they know so well. Their inordinate vanity is well called the slum counterpart of self-esteem, and Riis calls the gang a club run wild. They have their own ideality and a gaudy pinchbeck honor. A young tough, when arrested, wrenched away the policeman's club, dashed into the street, rescued a baby from a runaway, and came back and gave himself up. They batten on the yellowest literature. Those of foreign descent, who come to speak our language better than their parents, early learn to despise them. Gangs emulate each other in hardihood, and this is one cause of epidemics in crime. They passionately love boundless independence, are sometimes very susceptible to good influence if applied with great wisdom and discretion, but easily fall away. What is the true moral antitoxin for this class, or at least what is the safety-valve and how and when to pull it, we are now just beginning to learn, but it is a new specialty in the great work of salvage from the wreckage of city life. In London, where these groups are better organised and yet more numerous, war is often waged between them, weapons are used and murder is not so very infrequent. Normally this instinct passes harmlessly over into associations for physical training, which furnishes a safe outlet for these instincts, until the reductives of maturer years have perfected their work.

The causation of crime, which the cure seeks to remove, is a problem comparable with the origin of sin and evil. First, of course, comes heredity, bad antenatal conditions, bad homes, unhealthful infancy and childhood, overcrowded slums with their promiscuity and squalor, which are always near the border of lawlessness, and perhaps are the chief cause of crime. A large per cent of juvenile offenders, variously estimated, but probably one-tenth of all, are vagrants or without homes, and divorce of parents and illegitimacy seem to be nearly equal as causative agencies. If whatever is physiologically wrong is morally wrong, and whatever is physiologically right is morally right, we have an important ethical suggestion from somatic conditions. There is no doubt that conscious intelligence during a certain early stage of its development tends to deteriorate the strength and infallibility of instinctive processes, so that education is always beset with the danger of interfering with ancestral and congenital tendencies. Its prime object ought to be moralization, but it can not be denied that in conquering ignorance we do not thereby conquer poverty or vice. After the free schools in London were opened there was an increase of juvenile offenders. New kinds of crime, such as forgery, grand larceny, intricate swindling schemes, were doubled, while sneak thieves, drunkards, and pick-pockets decreased, and the proportion of educated criminals was greatly augmented.[14] To collect masses of children and ram them with the same unassimilated facts is not education in this sense, and we ought to confess that youthful crime is an expression of educational failure. Illiterate criminals are more likely to be detected, and also to be condemned, than are educated criminals. Every anthropologist knows that the deepest poverty and ignorance among primitive people are in nowise incompatible with honesty, integrity, and virtue. Indeed there is much reason to suspect that the extremes of wealth and poverty are more productive of crime than ignorance, or even intemperance. Educators have no doubt vastly overestimated the moral efficiency of the three R's and forgotten that character in infancy is all instinct; that in childhood it is slowly made over into habits; while at adolescence more than at any other period of life, it can be cultivated through ideals. The dawn of puberty, although perhaps marked by a certain moral hebetude, is soon followed by a stormy period of great agitation, when the very worst and best impulses in the human soul struggle against each other for its possession, and when there is peculiar proneness to be either very good or very bad. As the agitation slowly subsides, it is found that there has been a renaissance of either the best or the worst elements of the soul, if not indeed of both.

Although pedagogues make vast claims for the moralizing effect of schooling, I cannot find a single criminologist who is satisfied with the modern school, while most bring the severest indictments against it for the blind and ignorant assumption that the three R's or any merely intellectual training can moralize. By nature, children are more or less morally blind, and statistics show that between thirteen and sixteen incorrigibility is between two and three times as great as at any other age. It is almost impossible for adults to realize the irresponsibility and even moral neurasthenia incidental to this stage of development. If we reflect what a girl would do if dressed like a boy and leading his life and exposed to the same moral contagion, or what a boy would do if corseted and compelled to live like a girl, perhaps we can realize that whatever rôle heredity plays, the youth who go wrong are, in the vast majority of cases, victims of circumstances or of immaturity, and deserving of both pity and hope. It was this sentiment that impelled Zarnadelli to reconstruct the criminal law of Italy, in this respect, and it was this sympathy that made Rollet a self-constituted advocate, pleading each morning for the twenty or thirty boys and eight or ten girls arrested every day in Paris.

Those smitten with the institution craze or with any extreme correctionalist views will never solve the problem of criminal youths. First of all, they must be carefully and objectively studied, lived with, and understood as in this country Gulick, Johnson, Forbush and Yoder are doing in different ways, but each with success. Criminaloid youth is more sharply individualized than the common good child, who is less differentiated. Virtue is more uniform and monotonous than sin. There is one right but there are many wrong ways, hence they need to be individually studied by every paidological method, physical and psychic. Keepers, attendants, and even sponsors who have to do with these children should be educators with souls full of fatherhood and motherhood, and they should understand that the darkest criminal propensities are frequently offset by the very best qualities; that juvenile murderers are often very tender-hearted to parents, sisters, children, or pets;[15] they should understand that in the criminal constitution there are precisely the same ingredients, although perhaps differently compounded, accentuated, mutually controlled, etc., by the environment, as in themselves, so that to know all would, in the great majority of cases, be to pardon all; that the home sentiments need emphasis;

that a little less stress of misery to overcome the effects of economic malaise and, above all, a friend, mentor, adviser are needed.

I incline to think that many children would be better and not worse for reading, provided it can be done in tender years, stories like those of Captain Kidd, Jack Sheppard, Dick Turpin, and other gory tales, and perhaps later tales like Eugene Aram, and the ophidian medicated novel, Elsie Venner, etc., on the principle of the Aristotelian catharsis to arouse betimes the higher faculties which develop later, and whose function it is to deplete the bad centers and suppress or inhibit their activity. Again, I believe that judicious and incisive scolding is a moral tonic, which is often greatly needed, and if rightly administered would be extremely effective, because it shows the instinctive reaction of the sane conscience against evil deeds and tendencies. Special pedagogic attention should be given to the sentiment of justice, which is almost the beginning of personal morals in boys; and plays should be chosen and encouraged that hold the beam even, regardless of personal wish and interest. Further yet benevolence and its underlying impulse to do more than justice to our associates; to do good in the world; to give pleasure to those about, and not pain, can be directly cultivated. Truth-telling presents a far harder problem, as we have seen. It is no pedagogical triumph to clip the wings of fancy, but effort should be directed almost solely against the cowardly lies, which cover evil; and the heroism of telling the truth and taking the consequences is another of the elements of the moral sense, so complex, so late in development, and so often permanently crippled. The money sense, by all the many means now used for its development in school, is the surest safeguard against the most common juvenile crime of theft, and much can be taught by precept, example, and moral regimen of the sacredness of property rights. The regularity of school work and its industry is a valuable moralizing agent, but entirely inadequate and insufficient by itself. Educators must face the fact that the ultimate verdict concerning the utility of the school will be determined, as Talleck well says, by its moral efficiency in saving children from personal vice and crime.

Wherever any source of pollution of school communities occurs, it must be at once and effectively detected, and some artificial elements must be introduced into the environment. In other words, there must be a system of moral orthopedics. Garofalo's[16] new term and principle of "temibility" is perhaps of great service. He would thus designate the quantum of evil feared that is sufficient to restrain criminal impulsion. We can not measure guilt or culpability, which may be of all degrees from nothing to infinity perhaps, but we can to some extent scale the effectiveness of restraint, if criminal impulse is not absolutely irresistible. Pain then must be so organised as to follow and measure the offense by as nearly a natural method as possible, while on the other hand the rewards for good conduct must also be more or less accentuated. Thus the problem of criminology for youth can not be based on the principles now recognised for adults. They can not be protective of society only, but must have marked reformatory elements. Solitude[17] which tends to make weak, agitated, and fearful, at this very gregarious age should be enforced with very great discretion. There must be no personal and unmotivated clemency or pardon in such scheme, for, according to the old saw, "Mercy but murders, pardoning those who kill"; nor on the other hand should there be the excessive disregard of personal adjustments, and the uniformitarian, who perhaps celebrated his highest triumph in the old sentence, "Kill all offenders and suspects, for God will know his own," should have no part nor lot here. The philosopher Hartmann has a suggestive article advocating that penal colonies made up of transported criminals should be experimented upon by statesmen in order to put various theories of self-government to a practical test. However this may be, the penologist of youth must face some such problem in the organization of the house of detention, boys' club, farm, reformatory, etc. We must pass beyond the clumsy apparatus of a term sentence., or the devices of a jury, clumsier yet, for this purpose; we must admit the principle of regret, fear, penance, material restoration of damage, and understand the sense in which, for both society and for the individual, it makes no practical difference whether experts think there is some taint of insanity, provided only that irresponsibility is not hopelessly complete.

In few aspects of this theme do conceptions of and practises in regard to adolescence need more radical reconstruction. A mere accident of circumstance often condemns to criminal careers youths capable of the highest service to society, and for a mere brief season of temperamental outbreak or obstreperousness exposes them to all the infamy to which ignorant and cruel public opinion condemns all those who have once been detected on the wrong side of the invisible and arbitrary line of rectitude. The heart of criminal psychology is here; and not only that, but I would conclude with a most earnest personal protest against the current methods of teaching and studying ethics in our academic institutions as a speculative, historical, and abstract thing. Here in the concrete and saliently objective facts of crime it should have its beginning, and have more blood and body in it by getting again close to the hot battle line between vice and virtue, and then only, when balanced and sanified by a rich ballast of facts, can it with advantage slowly work its way over to the larger and higher philosophy of conduct, which, when developed from this basis, will be a radically different thing from the shadowy phantom, schematic speculations of many contemporary moralists, taught in our schools and colleges.

[Footnote 1: Problematische Kindesnaturen. Eine Studie für Schule und Haus. Voigtländer, Leipzig, 1889.]

[Footnote 2: Die pädagogische Pathologie in der Erziehungskunde des 19 Jahrhunderts. Bertelsman, Gütersloh, 1893, p. 494.]

[Footnote 3: Peculiar and Exceptional Children. Pedagogical Seminary, October, 1896, vol. 4, pp. 3-60.]

[Footnote 4: La Puberté. Schleicher Frères, Paris, 1902, p. 72.]

[Footnote 5: Home and School Punishments. Pedagogical Seminary, March, 1899, vol. 6, pp. 159-187.]

[Footnote 6: A Study of the Faults of Children. Pedagogical Seminary, June, 1903, vol. 10, p. 200 *et seq.*]

[Footnote 7: The Child and the Weather, by Edwin G. Dexter. Pedagogical Seminary, April, 1898, vol. 5, pp. 512-522.]

[Footnote 8: Psychic Effects of the Weather, by J.S. Lemon. American Journal of Psychology, January, 1894, vol. 6, pp. 277-279.]

[Footnote 9: Truancy as Related to the Migrating Instinct, by L.W. Kline. Pedagogical Seminary, January, 1898, vol. 5, pp. 381-420.]

[Footnote 10: Children's Lies. American Journal of Psychology, January, 1890, vol. 3, pp. 59-70.]

[Footnote 11: Poems. With memoir by his brother, 2 vols., London, 1851.]

[Footnote 12: American Journal of Psychology, July, 1898, vol. 9, pp. 425-448.]

[Footnote 13: How the Other Half Lives. Scribner's Sons, New York, 1890, p. 229.]

[Footnote 14: The Curse in Education, by Rebecca Harding Davis. North American Review, May, 1899, vol. 168, pp. 609-614.]

[Footnote 15: Holtzendorff: Psychologie des Mordes. C. Pfeiffer, Berlin, 1875]

[Footnote 16: La Criminologie. Paris, Alcan, 1890, p. 332]

[Footnote 17: See its psychology and dangers well pointed out by M.H. Small: Psychical Relations of Society and Solitude. Pedagogical Seminary, April, 1900, vol. 7, pp. 13-69]

* * * * *

CHAPTER VIII - BIOGRAPHIES OF YOUTH

Knightly ideals and honor—Thirty adolescents from Shakespeare—Goethe—C.D. Warner—Aldrich—The fugitive nature of adolescent experience—Extravagance of autobiographies—Stories that attach to great names—Some typical crazes—Illustrations from George Eliot, Edison, Chatterton, Hawthorne, Whittier, Spencer, Huxley, Lyell, Byron, Heine, Napoleon, Darwin, Martineau, Agassiz, Madame Roland, Louisa Alcott, F.H. Burnett, Helen Keller, Marie Bashkirtseff, Mary MacLane, Ada Negri, De Quincey, Stuart Mill, Jefferies, and scores of others.

The knightly ideals and those of secular life generally during the middle ages and later were in striking contrast to the ascetic ideals of the early Christian Church; in some respects they were like those of the Greeks. Honor was the leading ideal, and muscular development and that of the body were held in high respect; so that the spirit of the age fostered conceptions not unlike those of the Japanese Bushido. Where elements of Christianity were combined with this we have the spirit of the pure chivalry of King Arthur and the Knights of the Round Table, which affords perhaps the very best ideals for youth to be found in history, as we shall see more fully later.

In a very interesting paper, entitled "Shakespeare and Adolescence," Dr. M.F. Libby[1] very roughly reckons "seventy-four interesting adolescents among the comedies, forty-six among the tragedies, and nineteen among the histories." He selects "thirty characters who, either on account of direct references to their age, or because of their love-stories, or because they show the emotional and intellectual plasticity of youth, may be regarded as typical adolescents." His list is as follows: Romeo, Juliet, Hamlet, Ophelia, Imogen, Perdita, Arviragus, Guiderius, Palamon, Arcite, Emilia, Ferdinand, Miranda, Isabella, Mariana, Orlando, Rosalind, Biron, Portia, Jessica, Phebe, Katharine, Helena, Viola, Troilus, Cressida, Cassio, Marina, Prince Hal, and Richard of Gloucester. The proof of the youth of these characters, as set forth, is of various kinds, and Libby holds that besides these, the sonnets and poems perhaps show a yet greater, more profound and concentrated knowledge of adolescence. He thinks "Venus and Adonis" a successful attempt to treat sex in a candid, naive way, if it be read as it was meant, as a catharsis of passion, in which is latent a whole philosophy of art. To some extent he also finds the story of the Passionate Pilgrim "replete with the deepest knowledge of the passions of early adolescence" The series culminates in Sonnet 116, which makes love the sole beacon of humanity. It might be said that it is connected by a straight line with the best teachings of Plato, and that here humanity picked up the clue, lost, save with some Italian poets, in the great interval.

In looking over current autobiographies of well-known modern men who deal with their boyhood, one finds curious extremes. On the one hand are those of which Doctor's is a type, where details are dwelt upon at great length with careful and suggestive philosophic reflections. The development of his own tastes, capacities, and his entire adult consciousness was assumed to be due to the incidents of childhood and youth, and especially the latter stage was to him full of the most serious problems essential to his self-knowledge; and in the story of his life he has exploited all available resources of this genetic period of storm and stress more fully perhaps than any other writer. At the other extreme, we have writers like Charles Dudley Warner,[2] a self-made man, whose early life was passed on the farm, and who holds his own boyhood there in greater contempt than perhaps any other reputable writer of such reminiscences. All the incidents are treated not only with seriousness, but with a forced drollery and catchy superficiality which reflect unfavorably at almost every point upon the members of his household, who are caricatured; all the precious associations of early life on a New England farm are not only made absurd, but from beginning to end his book has not a scintilla of instruction or suggestion for those that are interested in child life. Aldrich[3] is better, and we have interesting glimpses of the pet horse and monkeys, of his fighting the boy bully, running way, and falling in love with an older girl whose engagement later blighted his life. Howells,[4] White,[5] Mitter,[6] Grahame,[7] Heidi,[8] and Mrs. Barnett,[9] might perhaps represent increasing grades of merit in this field in this respect.

Yoder,[10] in his interesting study of the boyhood of great men, has called attention to the deplorable carelessness of their biographers concerning the facts and influences of their youth. He advocates the great pedagogic influence of biography, and would restore the high appreciation of it felt by the Bolandists, which Comte's positivist calendar, that renamed all the days of the year from three hundred and sixty-five such accounts in 1849, also sought to revive. Yoder selected fifty great modern biographies, autobiographies preferred, for his study. He found a number of lives whose equipment and momentum have been strikingly due to some devoted aunt, and that give many glimpses of the first polarization of genius in the direction in which fame is later achieved. He holds that, while the great men excelled in memory, imagination is perhaps still more a youthful condition of eminence; magnifies the stimulus of poverty, the fact that elder sons become prominent nearly twice as often as younger ones; and raises the question whether too exuberant physical development does not dull genius and talent.

One striking and cardinal fact never to be forgotten considering its each and every phenomenon and stage is that the experiences of adolescence are extremely transitory and very easily forgotten, so that they are often totally lost to the adult consciousness. Lancaster[11] observes that we are constantly told by adults past thirty that they never had this and that experience, and that those who have had them are abnormal; that they are far more rare than students of childhood assert, etc. He says, "Not a single young person with whom I have had free and open conversation has been free from serious thoughts of suicide," but these are forgotten later. A typical case of many I could gather is that of a lady, not yet in middle life, precise and carefully trained, who, on hearing a lecture on the typical phases of adolescence, declared that she must have been abnormal, for she knew nothing of any of these experiences. Her mother, however, produced her diary, and there she read for the first time since it was written, beginning in the January of her thirteenth year, a long series of resolutions which revealed a course of conduct that brought the color to her face, that she should have found it necessary to pledge not to swear, lie, etc., and which showed conclusively that she had passed through about all the phases described. These phenomena are sometimes very intense and may come late in life, but it is impossible to remember feelings and emotions with definiteness, and these now make up a large part of life. Hence we are prone to look with some incredulity upon the immediate records of the tragic emotions and experiences typical and normal at this time, because development has scored away their traces from the conscious soul.

There is a wall around the town of Boyville, says White,[12] in substance, which is impenetrable when its gates have once shut upon youth. An adult may peer over the wall and try to ape the games inside, but finds it all a mockery and himself banished among the purblind grown-ups. The town of Boyville was old when Nineveh was a hamlet; it is ruled by ancient laws; has its own rulers and idols; and only the dim, unreal noises of the adult world about it have changed.

In exploring such sources we soon see how few writers have given true pictures of the chief traits of this developmental period, which can rarely be ascertained with accuracy. The adult finds it hard to recall the emotional and instinctive life of the teens which is banished without a trace, save as scattered hints may be gathered from diaries, chance experiences, or the recollections of others. But the best observers see but very little of what goes on in the youthful soul, the development of which is very largely subterranean. Only when the feelings erupt in some surprising way is the process manifest. The best of these sources are autobiographies, and of these only few are full of the details of this stage. Just as in the mythic prehistoric stage of many nations there is a body of legendary matter, which often reappears in somewhat different form, so there is a floating plankton-like mass of tradition and storiology that seems to attach to eminence wherever it emerges and is repeated over and over again, concerning the youth of men who later achieve distinction, which biographers often incorporate and attach to the time, place, and person of their heroes.

As Burnham[13] well intimates, many of the literary characterizations of adolescence are so marked by extravagance, and sometimes even by the struggle for literary effects, that they are not always the best documents, although often based on personal experience. Confessionalism is generally overdrawn, distorted, and especially the pains of this age are represented as too keen. Of George Eliot's types of adolescent character, this may best be seen in Maggie Tulliver, with her enthusiastic self-renunciation, with "her volcanic upheavings of imprisoned passions," with her "wide, hopeless yearning for that something, whatever it was, that was greatest and best on this earth," and in Gwendolen, who, from the moment she caught Deronda's eye, was "totally swayed in feeling and action by the presence of a person of the other sex whom she had never seen before." There was "the resolute action from instinct and the setting at defiance of calculation and reason, the want of any definite desire to marry, while all her conduct tended to promote proposals." Exaggeration, although not the perversions of this age often found in adult characterizations, is marked trait of the writings of adolescents, whose conduct meanwhile may appear rational, so that this suggests that consciousness may at this stage serve as a harmless vent for tendencies that would otherwise cause great trouble if turned to practical affairs. If Harmodius and Aristogeiton, the adolescent tyrant slayers of Greece, had been theorists, they might have been harmless on the principle that its analysis tends to dissipate emotion.

Lancaster[14] gathered and glanced over a thousand biographies, from which he selected 200 for careful study, choosing them to show different typical directions of activity. Of these, 120 showed a distinct craze for reading in adolescence; 109 became great lovers of nature; 58 wrote poetry, 58 showed a great and sudden development of energy; 55 showed great eagerness for school; 53 devoted themselves for a season to art and music; 53 became very religious; 51 left home in the teens; 51 showed dominant instincts of leadership; 49 had great longings of many kinds; 46 developed scientific tastes; 41 grew very anxious about the future; 34 developed increased keenness of sensation or at least power of observation; in 32 cases health was better; 31 were passionately altruistic; 23 became idealists; 23 showed powers of invention; 17 were devoted to older friends; 15 would reform society; 7 hated school. These, like many other statistics, have only indicative value, as they are based on numbers that are not large enough and upon returns not always complete.

A few typical instances from Lancaster must here suffice. Savonarola was solitary, pondering, meditating, felt profoundly the evils of the world and need of reform, and at twenty-two spent a whole night planning his career. Shelley during these years was unsocial, much alone, fantastic, wandered much by moonlight communing with stars and moon, was attached to an older man. Beecher was intoxicated with nature, which he declared afterward to have been the inspiration of his life. George Eliot at thirteen had a passion for music and became a clever pianist. At sixteen she was religious, founded societies for the poor and for animals, and had fitting spells of misanthropy. Edison undertook to read the Detroit Free Library through, read fifteen solid feet as the books stand on the shelves, was stopped, and says he has read comparatively little since. Tolstoi found the aspect of things suddenly changed. Nature put on a new appearance. He felt he might commit the most dreadful crimes with no purpose save curiosity and the need of action. The future looked gloomy. He became furiously angry without cause; thought he was lost, hated by everybody, was perhaps not the son of his father, etc. At seventeen he was solitary, musing about immortality, human destiny, feeling death at hand, giving up his studies, fancying himself a great man with new truths for humanity. By and by he took up the old virtuous course of life with fresh power, new resolutions, with the feeling that he had lost much time. He had a deep religious experience at seventeen and wept for joy over his new life. He had a period before twenty when he told desperate lies, for which he could not account, then a passion for music, and later for French novels. Rousseau at this age was discontented, immensely in love, wept often without cause, etc. Keats had a great change at fourteen, wrestling with frequent obscure and profound stirrings of soul, with a sudden hunger for knowledge which consumed his days with fire, and "with passionate longing to drain the cup of experience at a draft." He was "at the morning hour when the whole world turns to gold." "The boy had suddenly become a poet." Chatterton was too proud to eat a gift dinner, though nearly starved, and committed suicide at seventeen for lack of appreciation. John Hunter was dull and hated study, but at twenty his mind awoke as did that of Patrick Henry, who before was a lonely wanderer, sitting idly for hours under the trees. Alexander Murray awoke to life at fifteen and acquired several languages in less than two years. Gifford was distraught for lack of reading, went to sea at thirteen, became a shoemaker, studying algebra late at night, was savagely unsociable, sunk into torpor from which he was roused to do splenetic and vexatious tricks, which alienated his friends. Rittenhouse at fourteen was a plowboy, covering the fences with figures, musing on infinite time and space. Benjamin Thompson was roused to a frenzy for sciences at fifteen; at seventeen walked nine miles daily to attend lectures at Cambridge; and at nineteen married a widow of thirty-three. Franklin had a passion for the sea; at thirteen read poetry all night; wrote verses and sold them on the streets of Boston; doubted everything at fifteen; left home for good at seventeen; started the first public library in Philadelphia before he was twenty-one. Robert Fulton was poor, dreamy, mercurial, devoted to nature, art, and literature. He became a painter of talent, then a poet, and left home at seventeen. Bryant was sickly till fourteen and became permanently well thereafter; was precociously devoted to nature, religion, prayed for poetic genius and wrote Thanatopsis before he was eighteen. Jefferson doted on animals and nature at fourteen, and at seventeen studied fifteen hours a day. Garfield, though living in Ohio, longed for the sea, and ever after this period the sight of a ship gave him a strange thrill. Hawthorne was devoted to the sea and wanted to sail on and on forever and never touch shore again. He would roam through the Maine woods alone; was haunted by the fear that he would die before twenty-five. Peter Cooper left home at seventeen; was passionately altruistic; and at eighteen vowed he would build a place like his New York Institute. Whittier at fourteen found a copy of Burns, which excited him and changed the current of his life. Holmes had a passion for flowers, broke into poetry at fifteen, and had very romantic attachments to certain trees. J. T. Trowbridge learned German, French, and Latin alone before twenty-one; composed poetry at the plow and wrote it out in the evening. Henry followed a rabbit under the Public Library at Albany, found a hole in the floor that admitted him to the shelves, and, unknown to any one, read all the fiction the library contained, then turned to physics, astronomy, and chemistry, and developed a passion for the sciences. He was stage-struck, and became a good amateur actor. H. H. Boyesen was thrilled by nature and by the thought that he was a Norseman. He had several hundred pigeons, rabbits, and other pets; loved to be in the woods at night; on leaving home for school was found with his arms around the neck of a calf to which he was saying good-by. Maxwell, at sixteen, had almost a horror of destroying a leaf, flower, or fly. Jahn found growing in his heart, at this age, an inextinguishable feeling for right and wrong—which later he thought the cause of all his inner weal and outer woe. When Nansen was in his teens he spent weeks at a time alone in the forest, full of longings, courage, altruism, wanted to get away from every one and live like Crusoe. T. B. Reed, at twelve and thirteen, had a passion for reading; ran away at seventeen; painted, acted, and wrote poetry. Cartwright, at sixteen, heard voices from the sky saying, "Look above, thy sins are forgiven thee." Herbert Spencer became an engineer at seventeen, after one idle year. He never went to school, but was a private pupil of his uncle. Sir James Mackintosh grew fond of history at eleven; fancied he was the Emperor of Constantinople; loved solitude at thirteen; wrote poetry at fourteen; and fell in love at seventeen. Thomas Buxton loved dogs, horses, and literature, and combined these while riding on an old horse. At sixteen be fell in love with an older literary woman, which aroused every latent power to do or die, and thereafter he took all the school prizes. Scott began to like poetry at thirteen. Pascal wrote treatises on conic sections at sixteen and invented his arithmetical machine at nineteen. Nelson went to sea at twelve; commanded a boat in peril at fifteen, which at the same age he left to fight a polar bear. Banks, the botanist, was idle and listless till fourteen, could not travel the road marked out for him; when coming home from bathing, he was struck by the beauty of the flowers and at once began his career. Montcalm and Wolfe both distinguished themselves as leaders in battle at sixteen. Lafayette came to America at nineteen, thrilled by our bold strike for liberty. Gustavus Adolphus declared his own majority at seventeen and was soon famous. Ida Lewis rescued four men in a boat at sixteen. Joan of Arc began at thirteen to have the visions which were the later guide of her life.

Mr. Swift has collected interesting biographical material[15] to show that school work is analytic, while life is synthetic, and how the narrowness of the school enclosure prompts many youth in the wayward age to jump fences and seek new and more alluring pastures. According to school standards, many were dull and indolent, but their nature was too large or their ideals too high to be satisfied with it. Wagner at the Nikolaischule at Leipzig was relegated to the third form, having already attained to the second at Dresden, which so embittered him that he lost all taste for philology and, in his own words, "became lazy and slovenly." Priestley never improved by any systematic course of study. W.H. Gibson was very slow and was rebuked for wasting his time in sketching. James Russell Lowell was reprimanded, at first privately and then publicly, in his sophomore year "for general negligence in themes, forensics, and recitations," and finally suspended in 1838 "on account of continued neglect of his college duties." In early life Goldsmith's teacher thought him the dullest boy she had ever taught. His tutor called him ignorant and stupid. Irving says that a lad "whose passions are not strong enough in youth to mislead him from that path of science which his tutors, and not his inclinations, have chalked out, by four or five years' perseverance, will probably obtain every advantage and honor his college can bestow. I would compare the man whose youth has been thus passed in the tranquility of dispassionate prudence, to liquors that never ferment, and, consequently, continue always muddy." Huxley detested writing till past twenty. His schooling was very brief, and he declared that those set over him "cared about as much for his intellectual and moral welfare as if they were baby farmers." Humphry Davy was faithful but showed no talent in school, having "the reputation of being an idle boy, with a gift for making verses, but with no aptitude for studies of a graver sort." Later in life he considered it fortunate that he was left so much to himself. Byron was so poor a scholar that he only stood at the head of the class when, as was the custom, it was inverted, and the bantering master repeatedly said to him, "Now, George, man, let me see how soon you'll be at the foot." Schiller's negligence and lack of alertness called for repeated reproof, and his final school thesis was unsatisfactory. Hegel was a poor scholar, and at the university it was stated "that he was of middling industry and knowledge but especially deficient in philosophy." John Hunter nearly became a cabinetmaker. Lyell had excessive aversion to work. George Combe wondered why he was so inferior to other boys in arithmetic. Heine agreed with the monks that Greek was the invention of the devil. "God knows what misery I suffered with it." He hated French meters, and his teacher vowed he had no soul for poetry. He idled away his time at Bonn, and was "horribly bored" by the "odious, stiff, cut-and-dried tone" of the leathery professors. Humboldt was feeble as a child and "had less facility in his studies than most children." "Until I reached the age of sixteen," he says, "I showed little inclination for scientific pursuits." He was essentially self-taught, and acquired most of his knowledge rather late in life. At nineteen he had never heard of botany. Sheridan was called inferior to many of his schoolfellows. He was remarkable for nothing but idleness and winning manners, and was "not only slovenly in construing, but unusually defective in his Greek grammar." Swift was refused his degree because of "dulness and insufficiency," but given it later as a special favor. Wordsworth was disappointing. General Grant was never above mediocrity, and was dropped as corporal in the junior class and served the last year as a private. W. H. Seward was called "too stupid to learn." Napoleon graduated forty-second in his class. "Who," asks Swift, "were the forty-one above him?" Darwin was singularly incapable of mastering any language. "When he left school," he says, "I was considered by all my masters and by my father as a very ordinary boy, rather below the common standard in intellect. To my deep mortification, my father once said to me, 'You care for nothing but shooting, dogs, and rat-catching, and you will be a disgrace to yourself and to all your family.'" Harriet Martineau was thought very dull. Though a horn musician, she could do absolutely nothing in the presence of her irritable master. She wrote a cramped, untidy scrawl until past twenty. A visit to some very brilliant cousins at the age of sixteen had much to do in arousing her backward nature. At this age J. Pierpont Morgan wrote poetry and was devoted to mathematics. Booker T. Washington, at about thirteen or fourteen (he does not know the date of his birth), felt the new meaning of life and started off on foot to Hampton, five hundred miles away, not knowing even the direction, sleeping under a sidewalk his first night in Richmond. Vittorino da Feltre,[16] according to Dr. Burnham, had a low, tardy development, lingering on a sluggish dead level from ten to fourteen, which to his later unfoldment was as the barren, improving years sometimes called the middle ages, compared with the remainder which followed when a new world-consciousness intensified his personality.

Lancaster's summaries show that of 100 actors, the average age of their first great success was exactly 18 years. Those he chose had taken to the stage of their own accord, for actors are more born than made. Nearly half of them were Irish, the unemotional American stock having furnished far less. Few make their first success on the stage after 22, but from 16 to 20 is the time to expect talent in this line, although there is a second rise in his curve before and still more after 25, representing those whose success is more due to intellect. Taking the average age of 100 novelists when their first story met with public approval, the curve reaches its highest point between 30 and 35. Averaging 53 poets, the age at which most first poems were published falls between 15 and 20. The average age at which first publication showed talent he places at 18, which is in striking contrast with the average age of inventors at time of the first patent, which is 33 years.

A still more striking contrast is that between 100 musicians and 100 professional men. Music is by far the most precocious and instinctive of all talents. The average age when marked talent was first shown is a little less than 10 years, 95 per cent showed rare talent before 16, while the professional men graduated at an average age of 24 years and 11 months, and 10 years must be added to mark the point of recognized success. Of 53 artists, 90 per cent showed talent before 20, the average age being 17.2 years. Of 100 pioneers who made their mark in the Far West, leaving home to seek fortunes near the frontier, the greatest number departed before they were 18. Of 118 scientists, Lancaster estimates that their life interest first began to glow on the average a little before they were 19. In general, those whose success is based on emotional traits antedate by some years those whose renown is more purely in intellectual spheres, and taking all together, the curves of the first class culminate between 18 and 20.

While men devoted to physical science, and their biographers, give us perhaps the least breezy accounts of this seething age, it may be, because they mature late, nearly all show its ferments and its circumnutations, as a few almost random illustrations clearly show:

Tycho Brahe, born in 1596 of illustrious Danish stock, was adopted by an uncle, and entered the University of Copenhagen at thirteen, where multiplication, division, philosophy, and metaphysics were taught. When he was fourteen, an eclipse of the sun occurred, which aroused so much interest that he decided to devote himself to the study of the heavenly bodies. He was able to construct a series of interesting instruments on a progressive scale of size, and finally to erect the great Observatory of Uraniberg on the Island of Hven. Strange to say, his scientific conclusions had for him profound astrological significance. An important new star he declared was "at first like Venus and Jupiter and its effects will therefore first be pleasant; but as it then became like Mars, there will next come a period of wars, seditions, captivity, and death of princes, and destruction of cities, together with dryness and fiery meteors in the air, pestilence, and venomous snakes. Lastly, the star became like Saturn, and thus will finally come a time of want, death, imprisonment, and all kinds of sad things!" He says that "a special use of astronomy is that it enables us to draw conclusions from the movements in the celestial regions as to human fate." He labored on his island twenty years. He was always versifying, and inscribed a poem over the entrance of his underground observatory expressing the astonishment of Urania at finding in the interior of the earth a cavern devoted to the study of the heavens.

Galileo[17] was born in 1564 of a Florentine noble, who was poor. As a youth he became an excellent lutist, then thought of devoting himself to painting, but when he was seventeen studied medicine, and at the University of Pisa fell in love with mathematics.

Isaac Newton,[18] born in 1642, very frail and sickly, solitary, had a very low piece in the class lists of his school; wrote poetry, and at sixteen tried farming. In one of his university examinations in Euclid be did so poorly as to incur special censure. His first incentive to diligent study came from being severely kicked by a high class boy. He then resolved to pass him in studies, and soon rose to the head of the school. He made many ingenious toys and windmills; a carriage, the wheels of which were driven by the hands of the occupants, and a clock which moved by water; curtains, kites, lanterns, etc.; and before he was fourteen fell in love with Miss Storey, several yeas older than himself. He entered Trinity College at Cambridge at eighteen.

William Herschel, born in 1738, at the outbreak of the Seven Years' War, when he was eighteen, was a performer in the regimental band, and after a battle passed a night in a ditch and escaped in disguise, to England, where he eked out a precarious livelihood by teaching music. He supported himself until middle age as an organist. In much of his later work he was greatly aided by his sister Caroline. When he discovered a sixth planet he became famous, and devoted himself exclusively to astronomy, training his only son to follow in his footsteps, and dying in 1822.

Agassiz[19] at twelve had developed a mania for collecting. He memorized Latin names, of which he accumulated "great volumes of MSS.", and "modestly expressed the hope that in time he might be able to give the name of every known animal." At fourteen he revolted at mercantile life, for which he was designed, and issued a manifesto planning to spend four years at a Cermem university, then in Paris, when he could begin to write. Rooks were scarce, and a little later he copied, with the aid of his brother, several large volumes, and had fifty live birds in his room at one time.

At twelve Huxley[20] became an omnivorous reader, and two or three years later devoured Hamilton's Logic and became deeply interested in metaphysics. At fourteen he saw and participated in his first post-mortem examination, was left in a strange state of apathy by it, and dates his life-long dyspepsia to this experience. His training was irregular; he taught himself German with a book in one hand while he made hay with the other; speculated about the basis of matter, soul, and their relations, on radicalism and conservatism; and reproached himself that he did not work and get on enough. At seventeen he attempted a comprehensive classification of human knowledge, and having finished his survey, resolved to master the topics one after another, striking them out from his table with ink as soon us they were done. "May the list soon get black, although at present I shall hardly be able, I am afraid, to spot the paper." Beneath the top skimmings of these years he afterward conceived seething depths working beneath the froth, but could give hardly any account of it. He undertook the practise of pharmacy, etc.

Women with literary gifts perhaps surpass men in their power to reproduce and describe the great but so often evanescent ebullitions of this age; perhaps because their later lives, on account of their more generic nature, depart less from this totalizing period, or because, although it is psychologically shorter than in men, the necessities of earning a livelihood less frequently arrest its full development, and again because they are more emotional, and feeling constitutes the chief psychic ingredient of this stage of life, or they dwell more on subjective states.

Manon Philipon (Madame Roland) was born in 1754. Her father was an engraver in comfortable circumstances. Her earliest enthusiasm was for the Bible and Lives of the Saints, and she had almost a mania for reading books of any kind. In the corner of her father's workshop she would read Plutarch for hours, dream of the past glories of antiquity, and exclaim, weeping, "Why was I not born a Greek?" She desired to emulate the brave men of old.

Books and flowers aroused her to dreams of enthusiasm, romantic sentiment, and lofty aspiration. Finding that the French society afforded no opportunity for heroic living, in her visionary fervor she fell back upon a life of religious mysticism, and Xavier, Loyola, St. Elizabeth, and St. Theresa became her new idols. She longed to follow even to the stake those devout men and women who had borne obloquy, poverty, hunger, thirst, wretchedness, and the agony of a martyr's death for the sake of Jesus. Her capacities for self-sacrifice became perhaps her leading trait, always longing after a grand life like George Eliot's Dorothea Brooke. She was allowed at the age of eleven to enter a convent, where, shunning her companions, she courted solitude apart, under the trees, reading and thinking. Artificial as the atmosphere was here, it no doubt inspired her life with permanent tenderness of feeling and loftiness of purpose, and gave a mystic quality to her imagination. Later she experienced to the full revulsion of thought and experience which comes when doubt reacts upon youthful credulity. It was the age of the encyclopedia, and now she came to doubt her creed and even God and the soul, but clung to the Gospels as the best possible code of morals, and later realized that while her intellect had wandered her heart had remained constant. At seventeen she was, if not the moat beautiful, perhaps the noblest woman in all France, and here the curtain moat drop upon her girlhood. All her traits were, of course, set off by the great life she lived and the yet greater death she died.

Gifted people seem to conserve their youth and to be all the more children, and perhaps especially all the more intensely adolescents, because of their gifts, and it is certainly one of the marks of genius that the plasticity and spontaneity of adolescence persists into maturity. Sometimes even its passions, reveries, and hoydenish freaks continue. In her "Histoire de Ma Vie," it is plain that George Sand inherited at this age an unusual dower of gifts. She composed many and interminable stories, carried on day after day, so that her confidants tried to tease her by asking if the prince had got out of the forest yet, etc. She personated an echo and conversed with it. Her day-dreams and plays were so intense that she often came back from the world of imagination to reality with a shock. She spun a weird zoological romance out of a rustic legend of *la grande bête*.

When her aunt sent her to a convent, she passed a year of rebellion and revolt, and was the leader of *les diables*, or those who refused to be devout, and engaged in all wild pranks. At fifteen she became profoundly interested in the lives of the saints, although ridiculing miracles. She entered one evening the convent church for service, without permission, which was an act of disobedience. The mystery and holy charm of it penetrated her; she forgot everything outward and was left alone, and some mysterious change stole over her. She "breathed an atmosphere of ineffable sweetness" more with the mind than the senses; had a sudden indescribable perturbation; her eyes swam; she was enveloped in a white glimmer, and heard a voice murmur the words written under a convent picture of St. Augustine, *Tolle, lege*, and turned around thinking Mother Alicia spoke, but she was alone. She knew it was an hallucination, but saw that faith had laid hold of her, as she wished, by the heart, and she sobbed and prayed to the unknown God till a nun heard her groaning. At first her ardor impelled her not only to brave the jeers of her madcap club of harum-scarums and tomboys, but she planned to become a nun, until this feverish longing for a recluse life passed, but left her changed.[21]

When she passed from the simple and Catholic faith of her grisette mother to the atmosphere of her cynical grandmother at Nohant, who was a disciple of Voltaire, she found herself in great straits between the profound sentiments inspired by the first communion and the concurrent contempt for this faith, instilled by her grandmother for all those mummeries through which, however, for conventional reasons she was obliged to pass. Her heart was deeply stirred, and yet her head holding all religion to be fiction or metaphor, it occurred to her to invent a story which might be a religion or a religion which might be a story into any degree of belief in which she could lapse at will. The name and the form of her new deity was revealed to her in a dream. He was Corambé, pure as Jesus, beautiful as Gabriel, as graceful as the nymphs and Orpheus, less austere than the Christian God, and as much woman as man, because she could best understand this sex from her love for her mother. He appeared in many aspects of physical and moral beauty; was eloquent, master of all arts, and above all of the magic of musical improvisation; loved as a friend and sister, and at the same time revered as a god; not awful and remote from impeccability, but with the fault of excess of indulgence. She estimated that she composed about a thousand sacred books or songs developing phases of his mundane existence. In each of these he became incarnate man on touching the earth, always in a new group of people who were good, yet suffering martyrdoms from the wicked known only by the effects of their malice. In this "gentle hallucination" she could lose herself in the midst of friends, and turn to her hero deity for comfort. There must be not only sacred books, but a temple and ritual, and in a garden thicket, which no eye could penetrate, in a moss-carpeted chamber she built an altar against a tree-trunk, ornamented with a wreath hung over it. Instead of sacrificing, which seemed barbaric, she proceeded to restore life and liberty to butterflies, lizards, green frogs, and birds, which she put in a box, laid on the altar, and "after having invoked the good genius of liberty and protection," opened it. In these mimic rites and delicious reveries she found the germs of a religion that fitted her heart. From the instant, however, that a boy playmate discovered and entered this sanctuary, "Corambé ceased to dwell in it. The dryads and the cherubim deserted it," and it seemed unreal. The temple was destroyed with great care, and the garlands and shells were buried under the tree.[22]

Louisa Alcott's romantic period opened at fifteen, when she began to write poetry, keep a heart journal, and wander by moonlight, and wished to be the Bettine of Emerson, in whose library she foraged; wrote him letters which were never sent; sat in a tall tree at midnight; left wild flowers on the doorstep of her master; sang Mignon's song under his window; and was refined by her choice of an idol. Her diary was all about herself.

If she looked in the glass at her long hair and well-shaped head, she tried to keep down her vanity; her quick tongue, moodiness, poverty, impossible longings, made every day a battle until she hardly wished to live, only something must be done, and waiting is so hard. She imagined her mind a room in confusion which must be put in order; the useless thought swept out; foolish fancies dusted away; newly furnished with good resolutions. But she was not a good housekeeper; cobwebs got in, and it was hard to rule. She was smitten with a mania for the stage, and spent most of her leisure in writing and acting plays of melodramatic style ad high-strung sentiment, improbable incidents, with no touch of common life or sense of humor, full of concealments and surprises, bright dialogues, and lofty sentiments. She had much dramatic power and loved to transform herself into Hamlet and declaim in mock heroic style. From sixteen to twenty-three was her apprenticeship to life. She taught, wrote for the papers, did housework for pay as a servant, and found sewing a pleasant resource because it was tranquillizing, left her free, and set her thoughts going.

Mrs. Burnett,[23] like most women who record their childhood and adolescent memories, is far more subjective and interesting than most men. In early adolescence she was never alone when with flowers, but loved to "speak to them, to bend down and say caressing things, to stoop and kiss them, to praise them for their pretty ways of looking up at her as into the eyes of a friend and beloved. There were certain little blue violets which always seemed to lift their small faces childishly, as if they were saying, 'Kiss me; don't go by like that.'" She would sit on the porch, elbows on knees and chin on hands, staring upward, sometimes lying on the grass. Heaven was so high and yet she was a part of it and was something even among the stars. It was a weird, updrawn, overwhelming feeling as she stared so fixedly and intently that the earth seemed gone, left far behind. Every hour and moment was a wonderful and beautiful thing. She felt on speaking terms with the rabbits. Something was happening in the leaves which waved and rustled as she passed. Just to walk, sit, lie around out of doors, to loiter, gaze, watch with a heart fresh as a young dryad, following birds, playing hide-and-seek with the brook-these were her halcyon hours.

With the instability of genius, Beth[24] did everything suddenly. When twelve or thirteen, she had grown too big to be carried, pulled or pushed; she suddenly stood still one day, when her mother, commanded her to dress. She had been ruled before by physical force, but her will and that of her mother were now in collision, and the latter realised she could make her do nothing unless by persuasion or moral influence. Being constantly reproved, scolded, and even beaten by her mother, Beth one day impulsively jumped into the sea, and was rescued with difficulty. She had spells of being miserable with no cause. She was well and happy, but would burst into tears suddenly, which seemed often to surprise her. Being very sensitive herself, she was morbidly careful of the feelings of others and incessantly committed grave sins of insincerity without compunction in her effort to spare them. To those who confided in her abilities, praised her, and thought she could do things, her nature expanded, but her mother checked her mental growth over and over, instead of helping her by saying, "Don't try, you can't do it," etc.

Just before the dawn of adolescence she had passed through a long period of abject superstition, largely through the influence of a servant. All the old woman's signs were very dominant in her life. She even invented methods of divination, as, "if the boards do not creak when I walk across the room I shall get through my lessons without trouble." She always preferred to see two rooks together to one and became expert in the black arts. She used to hear strange noises at night for a time, which seemed signs and portents of disaster at sea, fell into the ways of her neighbors, and had more faith in incantations than in doctors' doses. She not only heard voices and very ingeniously described them, but claimed to know what was going to happen and compared her forebodings with the maid. She "got religion" very intensely under the influence of her aunt, grew thin, lost her appetite and sleep, had heartache to think of her friends burning in hell, and tried to save them.

Beth never thought at all of her personal appearance until she overheard a gentleman call her rather nice-looking, when her face flushed and she had a new feeling of surprise and pleasure, and took very clever ways of cross-examining her friends to find if she was handsome. All of a sudden the care of her person became of great importance, and every hint she had heard of was acted on. She aired her bed, brushed her hair glossy, pinched her waist and feet, washed in buttermilk, used a parasol, tortured her natural appetite in every way, put on gloves to do dirty work, etc.

The house always irked her. Once stealing out of the school by night, she was free, stretched herself, drew a long breath, bounded and waved her arms in an ecstasy of liberty, danced around the magnolia, buried her face in the big flowers one after another and bathed it in the dew of the petals, visited every forbidden place, was particularly attracted to the water, enjoyed scratching and making her feet bleed and eating a lot of green fruit. This liberty was most precious and all through a hot summer she kept herself healthy by exercise in the moonlight. This revived her appetite, and she ended these night excursions by a forage in the kitchen. Beth had times when she hungered for solitude and for nature. Sometimes she would shut herself in her room, but more often would rove the fields and woods in ecstasy. Coming home from school, where she had long been, she had to greet the trees and fields almost before she did her parents. She had a great habit of stealing out often by the most dangerous routes over roofs, etc., at night in the moonlight, running and jumping, waving her arms, throwing herself on the ground, rolling over, walling on all-fours, turning somersaults, hugging trees, playing hide-and-seek with the shadow fairy-folk, now playing and feeling fear and running away. She invoked trees, stars, etc.

Beth's first love affair was with a bright, fair-haired, fat-faced boy, who sat near her pew Sundays. They looked at each other once during service, and she felt a glad glow in her chest spread over her, dwelt on his image, smiled, and even the next day felt a new desire to please. She watched for him to pass from school. When he appeared, "had a most delightful thrill shoot through her." The first impulse to fly was conquered; she never thought a boy beautiful before. They often met after dark, wrote; finally she grew tired of him because she could not make him feel deeply, sent him off, called him an idiot, and then soliloquized on the "most dreadful grief of her life." The latter stages of their acquaintance she occasionally used to beat him, but his attraction steadily waned. Once later, as she was suffering from a dull, irresolute feeling due to want of a companion and an object, she met a boy of seventeen, whose face, like her own, brightened as they approached. It was the first appearance of nature's mandate to mate. This friendly glance suffused her whole being with the "glory and vision of love." Religion and young men were her need. They had stolen interviews by night and many an innocent embrace and kiss, and almost died once by being caught. They planned in detail what they would do after they were married, but all was taken for granted without formal vows. Only when criticized did they ever dream of caution and concealment, and then they made elaborate parades of ignoring each other in public and fired their imaginations with thoughts of disguises, masks, etc. This passion was nipped in the bud by the boy's removal from his school.

In preparing for her first communion, an anonymous writer[25] became sober and studious, proposing to model her life on that of each fresh saint and to spend a week in retreat examining her conscience with vengeance. She wanted to revive the custom of public confession and wrote letters of penitence and submission, which she tore up later, finding her mind not "all of a piece." She lay prostrate on her prie-dieu weeping from ecstasy, lying on the rim of heaven held by angels, wanting to die, now bathed in bliss or aching intolerably with spiritual joy, but she was only twelve and her old nature often reasserted itself. Religion at that time became an intense emotion nourished on incense, music, tapers, and a feeling of being tangible. It was rapturous and sensuous. While under its spell, she seemed to float and touch the wings of angels. Here solemn Gregorian chants are sung, so that when one comes back to earth there is a sense of hunger, deception, and self-loathing. Now she came to understand how so many sentimental and virtuous souls sought oblivion in the narcotic of religious excitement. Here, at the age of twelve, youth began and childhood ended with her book.

Pathetic is the account of Helen Keller's effort to understand the meaning of the word "love" in its season.[26]

Is it the sweetness of flowers? she asked. No, said her teacher. Is it the warm sun? Not exactly. It can not be touched, "'but you feel the sweetness that it pours into everything. Without love, you would not be happy or want to play.' The beautiful truth burst upon my mind. I felt that there were invisible lines stretched between my spirit and the spirit of others." This period seems to have came gradually and naturally to this wonderful child, whose life has been perhaps the purest ever lived and one of the sweetest. None has ever loved every aspect of nature accessible to her more passionately, or felt more keenly the charm of nature or of beautiful sentiments. The unhappy Frost King episode has been almost the only cloud upon her life, which unfortunately came at about the dawn of this period, that is perhaps better marked by the great expansion of mind which she experienced at the World's Fair in Chicago in 1893, when she was thirteen. About this time, too, her great ambition of going to college and enjoying all the advantages that other girls did, which, considering her handicap, was one of the greatest human resolutions, was strengthened and deepened. The fresh, spontaneous, and exquisite reactions of this pellucid mind, which felt that each individual could comprehend all the experiences and emotions of the race and that chafed at every pedagogical and technical obstacle between her soul and nature, and the great monuments of literature, show that she has conserved to a remarkable degree, which the world will wish may be permanent, the best impulses of this golden age.

Marie Bashkirtseff,[27] who may be taken as one of the best types of exaggerated adolescent confessionalists, was rich and of noble birth, and began in 1873, at the age of twelve, to write a journal that should be absolutely true and frank, with no pretense, affectation, or concealment. The journal continues until her death, October, 1884, at the age of twenty-three. It may be described as in some sense a feminine counterpart of Rousseau's confessions, but is in some respects a more precious psychological document than any other for the elucidation of the adolescent ferment in an unusually vigorous and gifted soul. Twice I have read it from cover to cover and with growing interest.

At twelve she is passionately in love with a duke, whom she sometimes saw pass, but who had no knowledge of her existence, and builds many air castles about his throwing himself at her feet and of their life together. She prays passionately to see him again, would dazzle him on the stage, would lead a perfect life, develop her voice, and would be an ideal wife. She agonizes before the glass on whether or not she is pretty, and resolves to ask some young man, but prefers to think well of herself even if it is an illusion; constantly modulates over into passionate prayer to God to grant all her wishes; is oppressed with despair; gay and melancholy by turn; believes in God because she prayed Him for a set of croquet and to help her to learn English, both of which He granted. At church some prayers and services seem directly aimed at her; Paris now seems a frightful desert, and she has no motive to avoid carelessness in her appearance. She has freaky and very changeable ideas of arranging the things in her room. When she hears of the duke's marriage she almost throws herself over a bridge, prays God for pardon of her sins, and thinks all is ended; finds it horrible to dissemble her feelings in public; goes through the torture of altering her prayer about the duke. She is disgusted with common people, harrowed by jealousy, envy, deceit and every hideous feeling, yet feels herself frozen in the depth, and moving only on the surface. When her voice improves she welcomes it with tears and feels an all-powerful queen. The man she loves should never speak to another. Her journal she resolves to make the most instructive book that ever was or ever will be written. She esteems herself so great a treasure that no one is worthy of her; pities those who think they can please her; thinks herself a real divinity; prays to the moon to show her in dreams her future husband, and quarrels with her photographs.

In some moods she feels herself beautiful, knows she shall succeed, everything smiles upon her and she is absolutely happy and yet in the next paragraph the fever of life at high pressure palls upon her and things seem asleep and unreal. Her attempts to express her feelings drive her to desperation because words are inadequate. She loves to weep, gives up to despair to think of death, and finds everything transcendently exquisite. She comes to despise men and wonder whether the good are always stupid and the intelligent always false and saturated with baseness, but on the whole believes that some time or other she is destined to meet one true good and great man. Now she is inflated with pride of her ancestry, her gifts, and would subordinate everybody and everything; she would never speak a commonplace word, and then again feels that her life has been a failure and she is destined to be always waiting. She falls on her knees sobbing, praying to God with outstretched hands as if He were in her room; almost vows to make a pilgrimage to Jerusalem one-tenth of the way on foot; to devote her money to good works; lacks the pleasures proper to her age; wonders if she can ever love again. On throwing a bouquet from a window into a crowd in the Corso a young man choked so beautifully a workman who caught it that by that one act of strangling and snatching the bouquet she fell in love. The young man calls and they see each other often. Now she is clad from head to foot in an armor of cold politeness, now vanity and now passion seem uppermost in their meetings. She wonders if a certain amount of sin, like air, is necessary to a man to sustain life. Finally they vow mutual love and Pietro leaves, and she begins to fear that she has cherished illusions or been insulted; is torments at things unsaid or of her spelling in French. She coughs and for three days has a new idea that she is going to die; prays and prostrates herself sixty times, one for each bead in her rosary, touching the floor with her forehead every time; wonders if God takes intentions into account; resolves to read the New Testament, but can not find one and reads Dumas instead. In novel-reading she imagines herself the heroine of every scene; sees her lover and they plan their mode of life together and at last kiss each other, but later she feels humiliated, chilled, doubts if it is real love; studies the color of her lips to see if they have changed; fears that she has compromised herself; has eye symptoms that make her fear blindness. Once on reading the Testament she smiled and clasped her hands, gazed upward, was no longer herself but in ecstasy; she makes many programs for life; is haunted by the phrase "We live but once"; wants to live a dozen lives in one, but feels that she does not live one-fourth of a life; has several spells of solitary illumination. At other times she wishes to be the center of a salon and imagines herself to be so. She soars on poets' wings, but often has hell in her heart; slowly love is vowed henceforth to be a word without meaning to her. Although she suffers from *ennui*, she realizes that women live only from sixteen to forty and cannot bear the thought of losing a moment of her life; criticizes her mother; scorns marriage and child-bearing, which any washerwoman can attain, but pants for glory; now hates, now longs to see new faces; thinks of disguising herself as a poor girl and going out to seek her fortunes; thinks her mad vanity is her devil; that her ambitions are justified by no results; hates moderation in anything, would have intense and constant excitement or absolute repose; at fifteen abandons her idea of the duke but wants an idol, and finally decides to live for fame; studies her shoulders, hips, bust, to gauge her success in life; tries target-shooting, hits every time and feels it to be fateful; at times despises her mother because she is so easily influenced by her; meets another man whose affection for her she thinks might be as reverent as religion and who never profaned the purity of his life by a thought, but finally drops him because the possible disappointment would be unbearable; finds that the more unhappy any one is for love of us the happier we are; wonders why she has weeping spells; wonders what love that people talk so much about really is, and whether she is ever to know. One night, at the age of seventeen, she has a fit of despair which vents itself in moans until arising, she seizes the dining-room clock, rushes out and throws it into the sea, when she becomes happy. "Poor clock!"

    At another time she fears she has used the word love lightly and resolves to no longer invoke God's help, yet in the next line prays Him to let her die as everything is against her, her thoughts are incoherent, she hates herself and everything is contemptible; but she wishes to die peacefully while some one is singing a beautiful air of Verdi. Again she thinks of shaving her head to save the trouble of arranging her hair; is crazed to think that every moment brings her nearer death; to waste a moment of life is infamous, yet she can trust no one; all the freshness of life is gone; few things affect her now; she wonders how in the past she could have acted so foolishly and reasoned so wisely; is proud that no advice in the world could ever keep her from doing anything she wished. She thinks the journal of her former years exaggerated and resolves to be moderate; wants to make others feel as she feels; finds that the only cure for disenchantment with life is devotion to work; fears her face is wearing an anxious look instead of the confident expression which was its chief charm. "Impossible" is a hideous, maddening word; to think of dying like a dog as most people do and leaving nothing behind is a granite wall against which she every instant dashes her head. If she loved a man, every expression of admiration for anything, or anybody else in her presence would be a profanation. Now she thinks the man she loves must never know what it is to be in want of money and must purchase everything he wishes; must weep to see a woman want for anything, and find the door of no palace or club barred to him. Art becomes a great shining light in her life of few pleasures and many griefs, yet she dares hope for nothing.

At eighteen all her caprices are exhausted; she vows and prays in the name of the Father, Son, and Holy Ghost for her wishes. She would like to be a millionaire, get back her voice, obtain the *prix de Rome* under the guise of a man and marry Napoleon IV. On winning a medal for her pictures she does nothing but laugh, cry, and dream of greatness, but the next day is scolded and grows discouraged. She has an immense sense of growth and transformation, so that not a trace of her old nature remains; feels that she has far too much of some things, and far too little of others in her nature; sees defects in her mother's character, whose pertinacity is like a disease; realizes that one of her chief passions is to inspire rather than to feel love; that her temper is profoundly affected by her dress; deplores that her family expect her to achieve greatness rather than give her the stimulus of expecting nothing; declares that she thanks a million thoughts for every word that she writes; is disgusted with and sometimes absolutely hates herself. At one time she coquets with Kant, and wonders if he is right that all things exist only in the imagination; has a passion for such "abracadabrante follies" that seem so learned and logical, but is grieved to feel them to be false; longs to penetrate the intellectual world, to see, learn, and know everything; admires Balzac because he describes so frankly all that he has felt; loves Fleury, who has shown her a wider horizon; still has spells of admiring her dazzling complexion and deploring that she can not go out alone; feels that she is losing her grip on art and also on God, who no longer hears her prayers, and resolves to kill herself if she is not famous at thirty.

At nineteen, and even before, she has spells of feeling inefficient cries, calls on God, feels exhausted; is almost stunned when she hears that the young French prince about whom she has spun romances was killed by the Kaffirs; feels herself growing serious and sensible; despises death; realizes that God is not what she thought, but is perhaps Nature and Life or is perhaps Chance; she thinks out possible pictures she might paint; develops a Platonic friendship for her professor; might marry an old man with twenty-seven millions, but spurns the thought; finds herself growing deaf gradually, and at nineteen finds three grey hairs; has awful remorse for days, when she cannot work and so loses herself in novels and cigarettes;

makes many good resolutions and then commits some folly as if in a dream; has spells of reviewing the past. When the doctor finds a serious lung trouble and commands iodine, cod-liver oil, hot milk, and flannel, she at first scorns death and refuses all, and is delighted at the terror of her friends, but gradually does all that is necessary; feels herself too precocious and doomed; deplores especially that consumption will cost her her good looks; has fits of intense anger alternating with tears; concludes that death is annihilation; realizes the horrible thought that she has a skeleton within her that some time or other will come out; reads the New Testament again and returns to belief in miracle, and prayer to Jesus and the Virgin; distributes one thousand francs to the poor; records the dreamy delusions that flow through her brain at night and the strange sensations by day. Her eye symptoms cause her to fear blindness again; she grows superstitious, believing in signs and fortune-tellers; is strongly impelled to embrace and make up with her mother; at times defies God and death; sees a Spanish bull-fight and gets from it a general impression of human cowardice, but has a strange intoxication with blood and would like to thrust a lance into the neck of every one she meets; coquets a great deal with the thought of marriage; takes up her art and paints a few very successful pictures; tries to grapple with the terrible question, "What is my unbiased opinion concerning myself?" pants chiefly for fame. When the other lung is found diseased the diary becomes sometimes more serious, sometimes more fevered; she is almost racked to find some end in life; shall she marry, or paint? and at last finds much consolation in the visits of Bastien-Lepage, who comes to see her often while he is dying of some gastric trouble. She keeps up occasional and often daily entries in her journal until eleven days before her death, occurring in October, 1884, at the age of twenty-three, and precipitated by a cold incurred while making an open-air sketch.

The confessional outpourings of Mary MacLane[28] constitute a unique and valuable adolescent document, despite the fact that it seems throughout affected and written for effect; however, it well illustrates a real type, although perhaps hardly possible save in this country, and was inspired very likely by the preceding.

She announces at the outset that she is odd, a genius, an extreme egotist; has no conscience; despises her father, "Jim MacLane of selfish memory"; loves scrubbing the floor because it gives her strength and grace of body, although her daily life is an "empty damned weariness." She is a female Napoleon passionately desiring fame; is both a philosopher and a coward; her heart is wooden; although but nineteen, she feels forty; desires happiness even more than fame, for an hour of which she would give up at once fame, money, power, virtue, honor, truth, and genius to the devil, whose coming she awaits. She discusses her portrait, which constitutes the frontispiece; is glad of her good strong body, and still awaits in a wild, frenzied impatience the coming of the devil to take her sacrifice, and to whom she would dedicate her life. She loves but one in all the world, an older "anemone" lady, once her teacher. She ran not distinguish between right and wrong; love is the only thing real which will some day bring joy, but it is agony to wait. "Oh, dame! damn! damn! damn! every living thing in the world!—the universe be damned!" herself included. She is "marvelously deep," but thanks the good devil who has made her without conscience and virtue so that she may take her happiness when it comes. Her soul seeks but blindly, for nothing answers. How her happiness will seethe, quiver, writhe, shine, dance, rush, surge, rage, blare, and wreak with love and light when it comes!

The devil she thinks fascinating and strong, with a will of steel, conventional clothes, whom she periodically falls in love with and would marry, and would love to be tortured by him. She holds imaginary conversations with him. If happiness does not come soon she will commit suicide, and she finds rapture in the thought of death. In Butte, Montana, where she lives, she wanders among the box rustlers, the beer jerkers, biscuit shooters, and plunges out into the sand and barrenness, but finds everything dumb. The six toothbrushes in the bathroom make her wild and profane. She flirts with death at the top of a dark, deep pit, and thinks out the stages of decomposition if she yielded herself to Death, who would dearly love to have her. She confesses herself a thief on several occasions, but comforts herself because the stolen money was given to the poor. Sometimes her "very good legs" carry her out into the country, where she has imaginary love confabs with the devil, but the world is so empty, dreary, and cold, and it is all so hard to bear when one is a woman and nineteen. She has a litany from which she prays in recurrent phrases "Kind devil, deliver me"—as, e.g., from musk, boys with curls, feminine men, wobbly hips, red note-paper, codfish-balls, lisle-thread stockings, the books of A.C. Gunter and Albert Ross, wax flowers, soft old bachelors and widowers, nice young men, tin spoons, false teeth, thin shoes, etc. She does not seem real to herself everything is a blank. Though she doubts everything else, she will keep the one atom of faith in love and the truth that is love and life in her heart. When something shrieks within her, she feels that all her anguish is for nothing and that she is a fool. She is exasperated that people call her peculiar, but confesses that she loves admiration; she can fascinate and charm company if she tries; imagines an admiration for Messalina. She most desires to cultivate badness when there is lead in the sky. "I would live about seven years of judicious badness, and then death if you will." "I long to cultivate the of badness in me." She describes the fascination of making and eating fudge; devotes a chapter to describing how to eat an olive; discusses her figure. "In the front of my shirt-waist there are nine cambric handkerchiefs cunningly distributed." She discusses her foot, her beautiful hair, her hips; describes each of the seventeen little engraved portraits of Napoleon that she keeps, with each of which she falls in love; vows she would give up even her marvelous genius far one dear, bright day free from loneliness. When her skirts need sewing, she simply pins them; this lasts longer, and had she mended them with needle and thread she would have been sensible, which she hates. As she walks over the sand one day she vows that she would like a man to come so be that he was strong and a perfect villain and she would pray him to lead her to what the world calls her ruin. Nothing is of consequence to her except to be rid of unrest and pain. She would be positively and not merely negatively wicked. To poison her soul would rouse her mental power. "Oh, to know just once what it is to be loved!" "I know that I am a genius more than any genius that has lived," yet she often thinks herself a small vile creature for whom no one cares. The world is ineffably dull, heaven has always fooled her, and she is starving for love.

Ada Negri illustrates the other extreme of genuineness and is desperately in earnest.[29] She began to teach school in a squalid, dismal Italian village, and at eighteen to write the poetry that has made her famous. She lived in a dim room back of a stable, up two flights, where the windows were not glass but paper, and where she seems to have been, like her mother, a mill head before she was a teacher. She had never seen a theater, but had read of Duse with enthusiasm; had never seen the sea, mountain, or even a hill, lake, or large city, but she had read of them. After she began to write, friends gave her two dream days in the city. Then she returned, put on her wooden shoes, and began to teach her eighty children to spell. The poetry she writes is from the heart of her own experience.

She craved "the kiss of genius and of light;" but the awful figure of misfortune with its dagger stood by her bed at night. She writes:

"I have no name—my home a hovel damp;
I grew up from the mire;
Wretched and outcast folk my family,
And yet within me burns a flame of fire."

There is always a praying angel and an evil dwarf on either side. The black abyss attracts her yet she is softened by a child's caress. She laughs at the blackest calamities that threaten her, but weeps over thin, wan children without bread. Her whole life goes into song. The boy criminal on the street fascinates her and she would kiss him. She writes of jealousy as a ghost of vengeance. If death comes, she fears "that the haggard doctor will dissect my naked corpse," and pictures herself dying on the operating-table like a stray dog and her well-made body "disgraced by the lustful kiss of the too eager blade" as, "with sinister smile untiring, they tear my bowels out and still gloat over my sold corpse, go on to bare my bones, and veins at will, wrench out my heart," probe vainly for the secrets of hunger and the mystery of pain, until from her "dead breast gurgles a gasp of malediction." Much of her verse is imprecation. "A crimson rain of crying blood dripping from riddled chests" of those slain for liberty falls, on her heart; the sultry factories where "monsters, of steel, huge engines, snort all day," and where the pungent air poisons the blood of the pale weaver girls; the fate of the mason who felt from a high roof and struck the stone flagging, whose funeral she attends, all inspire her to sing occasionally the songs of enfranchised labor. Misery as a drear, toothless ghost visits her, as when gloomy pinions had overspread her dying mother's bed, to wrench with sharp nails all the hope from her breast with which she had defied it. A wretched old man on the street inspires her to sing of what she imagines is his happy though humble prime. There is the song of the pickaxe brandished in revolution when mobs cry "Peace, labor bread," and in mines of industry beneath the earth. She loves the "defeated" in whose house no fire glows, who live in caves and dens, and writes of the mutilation of a woman in the factory machinery. At eighteen years "a loom, two handsome eyes that know no tears, a cotton dress, a love, belong to me." She is inspired by a master of the forge beating a red-hot bar, with his bare neck swelled. He is her demon, her God, and her pride in him is ecstasy. She describes jealousy of two rival women, so intense that they fight and bite, and the pure joy of a guileless, intoxicating, life-begetting first kiss. She longs for infinite stretches of hot, golden sand, over which she would gallop wildly on her steed; anticipates an old age of cap and spectacles; revels in the hurricane, and would rise in and fly and whirl with it adrift far out in the immensity of space. She tells us, "Of genius and light I'm a blithe, millionaire," and elsewhere she longs for the everlasting ice of lofty mountains, the immortal silence of the Alps; sings of her "sad twenty years," "how all, all goes when love is gone and spent." She imagines herself springing into the water which closes over her, while her naked soul, ghostly pale, whirls past through the lonely dale. She imprecates the licentious world of crafty burghers, coquettes, gamblers, well-fed millionaires, cursed geese and serpents that make the cowardly vile world, and whom she would smite in the face with her indignant verse. "Thou crawlest and I soar." She chants the champions of the spade, hammer, pick, though they are ground and bowed with toil, disfigured within, with furrowed brows. She pants for war with outrage and with wrong; questions the abyss for its secret; hears moans and flying shudders; and sees phantoms springing from putrid tombs. The full moon is an old malicious spy, peeping stealthily with evil eye. She is a bird caught in a cursed cage, and prays some one to unlock the door and give her space and light, and let her soar away in ecstasy and glory. Nothing less than infinite space will satisfy her. Even the tempest, the demon, or a malevolent spirit might bear her away on unbridled wings. In one poem she apostrophizes Marie Bashkirtseff as warring with vast genius against unknown powers, but who now is in her coffin among worms, her skull grinning and showing its teeth. She would be possessed by her and thrilled as by an electric current. A dwarf beggar wrings her heart with pity, but she will not be overwhelmed. Though a daring peasant, she will be free and sing out her pæan to the sun, though amid the infernal glow of furnaces, forges, and the ringing noise of hammers and wheels.

Literary men who record their experiences during this stage seem to differ from women in several important respects. First, they write with less abandon. I can recall no male MacLanes. A Bashkirtseff would be less impossible, and a Negri with social reform in her heart is still less so. But men are more prone to characterize their public metamorphoses later in life, when they are a little paled, and perhaps feel less need of confessionalism for that reason. It would, however, be too hazardous to elaborate this distinction too far. Secondly and more clearly, men tend to vent their ephebic calentures more in the field of action. They would break the old moorings of home and strike out new careers, or vent their souls in efforts and dreams of reconstructing the political, industrial, or social world. Their impracticabilities are more often in the field of practical life and remoter from their own immediate surroundings. This is especially true in our practical country, which so far lacks subjective characterizations of this age of eminent literary merit, peculiarly intense as it is here. Thirdly, they erupt in a greater variety of ways, and the many kinds of genius and talent that now often take possession of their lives like fate are more varied and individual. This affords many extreme contrasts, as, e.g., between Trollope's pity for, and Goethe's apotheosis of his youth; Mill's loss of feeling, and Jefferies's unanalytic, passionate outbursts of sentiment; the esthetic ritualism of Symonds, and the progressive religious emancipation of Fielding Hall; the moral and religious supersensitiveness of Oliphant, who was a reincarnation of medieval monkhood, and the riotous storminess of Müller and Ebers; the abnormalities and precocity of De Quincey, and the steady, healthful growth of Patterson; the simultaneity of a fleshly and spiritual love in Keller and Goethe, and the duality of Pater, with his great and tyrannical intensification of sensation for nature and the sequent mysticism and symbolism. In some it is fulminating but episodic, in others gradual and lifelong like the advent of eternal spring. Fourth, in their subjective states women outgrow less in their consciousness, and men depart farther from their youth, in more manifold ways. Lastly, in its religious aspects, the male struggles more with dogma, and his enfranchisement from it is more intellectually belabored. Yet, despite all these differences, the analogies between the sexes are probably yet more numerous, more all-pervasive. All these biographic facts reveal nothing not found in *questionnaire* returns from more ordinary youth, so that for our purposes they are only the latter, writ large because superior minds only utter what all more inwardly feel. The arrangement by nationality which follows gives no yet adequate basis for inference unless it be the above American peculiarity.

In his autobiography from 1785-1803, De Quincey[30] remembered feeling that life was finished and blighted for him at the age of six, up to which time the influence of his sister three years older had brooded over him.

His first remembrance, however, is of a dream of terrific grandeur before he was two, which seemed to indicate that his dream tendencies were constitutional and not due to morphine, but the chill was upon the first glimpse that this was a world of evil. He had been brought up in great seclusion from all knowledge of poverty and oppression in a silent garden with three sisters, but the rumor that a female servant had treated one of them rudely just before her death plunged him into early pessimism. He felt that little Jane would come back certainly in the spring with the roses, and he was glad that his utter misery with the blank anarchy confusion which her death brought could not be completely remembered. He stole into the chamber where her corpse lay, and as he stood, a solemn wind, the saddest he ever heard, that might have swept the fields of mortality for a thousand centuries, blew, and that same hollow Memnonian wind he often had heard since, and it brought back the open summer window and the corpse. A vault above opened into the sky, and he slept and dreamed there, standing by her, he knew not how long; a worm that could not die was at his heart, for this was the holy love between children that could not perish. The funeral was full of darkness and despair for him, and after it he sought solitude, gazed into the heavens to see his sister till he was tired, and realized that he was alone. Thus, before the end of his sixth year, with a mind already adolescent, although with a retarded body, the minor tone of life became dominant and his awakening to it was hard.

As a penniless schoolboy wandering the streets of London at night, he was on familiar and friendly terms of innocent relationship with a number of outcast women. In his misery they were to him simply sisters in calamity, but he found in them humanity, disinterested generosity, courage, and fidelity. One night, after he had walked the streets for weeks with one of these friendless girls who had not completed her sixteenth year, as they sat on the steps of a house, he grew very ill, and had she not rushed to buy from her slender purse cordials and tenderly ministered to and revived him, he would have died. Many years later he used to wander past this house, and he recalled with real tenderness this youthful friendship; he longed again to meet the "noble-minded Ann – –" with whom he had so often conversed familiarly *"more Socratico,"* whose betrayer he had vainly sought to punish, and yearned to hear from her in order to convey to her some authentic message of gratitude, peace, and forgiveness.

His much older brother came home in his thirty-ninth year to die. He had been unmanageable in youth and his genius for mischief was an inspiration, yet he was hostile to everything pusillanimous, haughty, aspiring, ready to fasten a quarrel on his shadow for running before, at first inclined to reduce his boy brother to a fag, but finally before his death became a great influence in his life. Prominent were the fights between De Quincey and another older brother on the one hand, and the factory crowd of boys on the other, a fight incessantly renewed at the close of factory hours, with victory now on one and now on the other side; fought with stones and sticks, where thrice he was taken prisoner, where once one of the factory women kissed him, to the great delight of his heart. He finally invented a kingdom like Hartley Coleridge, called Gom Broon. He thought first that it had no location, but finally because his brother's imaginary realm was north and he wanted wide water between them, his was in the far south. It was only two hundred and seventy miles in circuit, and he was stunned to be told by his brother one day that his own domain swept south for eighty degrees, so that the distance he had relied on vanished. Here, however, he continued to rule for well or ill, raising taxes, keeping an imaginary standing army, fishing herring and selling the product of his fishery for manure, and experiencing how "uneasy lies the head that wears a crown." He worried over his obligations to Gom Broon, and the shadow froze into reality, and although his brother's kingdom Tigrosylvania was larger, his was distinguished for eminent men and a history not to be ashamed of. A friend had read Lord Monboddo's view that men had sprung from apes, and suggested that the inhabitants of Gom Broon had tails, so that the brother told him that his subjects had not emerged from apedom and he must invent arts to eliminate the tails. They must be made to sit down for six hours a day as a beginning. Abdicate he would not, though all his subjects had three tails apiece. They had suffered together. Vain was his brother's suggestion that they have a Roman toga to conceal their ignominious appendages. He was greatly interested in two scrofulous idiots, who finally died, and feared that his subjects were akin to them.

John Stuart Mill's Autobiography presents one of the most remarkable modifications of the later phases of adolescent experience. No boy ever had more diligent and earnest training than his father gave him or responded better. He can not remember when he began to learn Greek, but was told that it was at the age of three. The list of classical authors alone that he read in the original, to say nothing of history, political, scientific, logical, and other works before he was twelve, is perhaps unprecedented in all history. He associated with his father and all his many friends on their own level, but modestly ascribes everything to his environment, insists that in natural gifts he is other below than above par, and declares that everything he did could be done by every boy of average capacity and healthy physical constitution. His father made the Greek virtue of temperance or moderation cardinal, and thought human life "a poor thing at best after the freshness of youth and unsatisfied curiosity had gone by." He scorned "the intense" and had only contempt for strong emotion.

In his teens Mill was an able debater and writer for the quarterlies, and devoted to the propagation of the theories of Bentham, Ricardo, and associationism. From the age of fifteen he had an object in life, viz., to reform the world. This gave him happiness, deep, permanent, and assured for the future, and the idea of struggling to promote utilitarianism seemed an inspiring program for life. But in the autumn of 1826, when he was twenty years of age, he felt into "a dull state of nerves," where he could no longer enjoy and what had produced pleasure seemed insipid; "the state, I should think, in which converts to Methodism usually are when smitten by their first 'conviction of sin.' In this frame of mind it occurred to me to put the question directly to myself; 'Suppose that all your objects in life were realized; that all the changes in institutions and opinions which you are looking forward to could be completely effected at this very instant; would this be a great joy and happiness to you?' And an irrepressible self-consciousness distinctly answered, 'No.' At this my heart sank within me: the whole foundation on which my life was constructed fell down. All my happiness was to have been found in the continual pursuit of this end. The end had ceased to charm, and how could there ever again be any interest in the means? I seemed to have nothing left to live for. At first I hoped that the cloud would pass away of itself, but it did not. A night's sleep, the sovereign remedy for the smaller vexations of life, had no effect on it. I awoke to a renewed consciousness of the woful fact. I carried it with me into all companies, into all occupations. Hardly anything had power to cause me even a few minutes' oblivion of it. For some months the cloud seemed to grow thicker and thicker. The lines in Coleridge's 'Dejection'—I was not then acquainted with them—exactly described my case:

'A grief without a pang, void, dark, and drear,
A drowsy, stifled, unimpassioned grief,
Which finds no natural outlet or relief
In word, or sigh, or tear.'

'In vain I sought relief from my favorite books, those memorials of past nobleness and greatness from which I had always hitherto drawn strength and animation. I read them now without feeling, or with the accustomed feeling minus all its charm; and I became persuaded that my love of mankind, and of excellence for its own sake, had worn itself out. I sought no comfort by speaking to others of what I felt. If I had loved any one sufficiently to make confiding my griefs a necessity, I should not have been in the condition I was. I felt, too, that mine was not an interesting or in anyway respectable distress. There was nothing in it to attract sympathy. Advice, if I had known where to seek it, would have been most precious. The words of Macbeth to the physician often occurred to my thoughts. But there was no one on whom I could build the faintest hope of such assistance. My father, to whom it would have been natural to me to have recourse in any practical difficulties, was the last person to whom, in such a case as this, I looked for help. Everything convinced me that he had no knowledge of any such mental state as I was suffering from, and that even if he could be made to understand it, he was not the physician who could heal it. My education, which was wholly his work, had been conducted without any regard to the possibility of its ending in this result, and I saw no use in giving him the pain of thinking that his plans had failed, when the failure was probably irremediable, and, at all event, beyond the power of his remedies. Of other friends, I had at that time none to whom I had any hope of making my condition intelligible. It was, however, abundantly intelligible to myself, and the more I dwelt upon it the more hopeless it appeared."

He now saw what had hitherto seemed incredible, that the habit of analysis tends to wear away the feelings. He felt "stranded at the commencement of my voyage, with a well-equipped ship and a rudder, but no sail; without any real desire for the ends which I had been so carefully fitted out to work for: no delight in virtue, or the general good, but also just as little in anything else. The fountains of vanity and ambition seemed to have dried up within me as completely as those of benevolence." His vanity had been gratified at too early an age, and, like all premature pleasures, they had caused indifference, until he despaired of creating any fresh association of pleasure with any objects of human dire. Meanwhile, dejected and melancholy as he was through the winter, he went on mechanically with his tasks; thought he found in Coleridge the first description of what he was feeling; feared the idiosyncrasies of his education had made him a being unique and apart. "I asked myself if I could or if I was bound to go on living, when life must be passed in this manner. I generally answered to myself that I did not think I could possibly bear it beyond a year." But within about half that time, in reading a pathetic page of how a mere boy felt that he could save his family and take the place of all they had lost, a vivid conception of the scene came over him and he was moved to tears. From that moment, his burden grew lighter. He saw that his heart was not dead and that he still had some stuff left of which character and happiness are made; and although there were several later lapses, some of which lasted many months, he was never again as miserable as he had been.

These experience left him changed in two respects. He had a new theory of life, having much in common with the anti-consciousness theory of Carlyle. He still held happiness the end of life, but thought it must be aimed at indirectly and taken incidentally. The other change was that for the first time he gave its proper place to internal culture of the individual, especially the training of the feelings which became now cardinal. He relished and felt the power of poetry and art; was profoundly moved by music; fell in love with Wordsworth and with nature, and his later depressions were best relieved by the power of rural beauty, which wrought its charm not because of itself but by the states and feelings it aroused. His ode on the intimations of immortality showed that he also had felt that the first freshness of youthful joy was not lasting, and had sought and found compensation. He had thus come to a very different standpoint from that of his father, who had up to this time formed his mind and life, and developed on this basis his unique individuality.

Jefferies, when eighteen, began his "Story of My Heart,"[31] which he said was an absolutely true confession of the stages of emotion in a soul from which all traces of tradition and learning were erased, and which stood face to face with nature and the unknown.

His heart long seemed dusty and parched for want of feeling, and he frequented a hill, where the pores of his soul opened to a new air. "Lying down on the grass, I spoke in my soul to the earth, the sun, the air and the distant sea.... I desired to have its strength, its mystery and glory. I addressed the sun, desiring the sole equivalent of his light and brilliance, his endurance, and unwearied race. I turned to the blue heaven over, gazing into its depth, inhaling its exquisite color and sweetness. The rich blue of the unobtainable flower of the sky drew my soul toward it, and there it rested, for pure color is the rest of the heart. By all these I prayed. I felt an emotion of the soul beyond all definition; prayer is a puny thing to it." He prayed by the thyme; by the earth; the flowers which he touched; the dust which he let fall through his fingers; was filled with "a rapture, an ecstasy, an inflatus. With this inflatus I prayed.... I hid my face in the grass; I was wholly prostrated; I lost myself in the wrestle.... I see now that what I labored for was soul life, more soul learning." After gazing upward he would turn his face into the grass, shutting out everything with hands each side, till he felt down into the earth and was absorbed in it, whispering deep down to its center. Every natural impression, trees, insects, air, clouds, he used for prayer, "that my soul might be more than the cosmos of life." His "Lyra" prayer was to live a more exalted and intense soul life; enjoy more bodily pleasure and live long and find power to execute his designs. He often tried, but failed for years to write at least a meager account of these experiences. He felt himself immortal just as he felt beauty. He was in eternity already; the supernatural is only the natural misnamed. As he lay face down on the grass, seizing it with both hands, he longed for death, to be burned on a pyre of pine wood on a high hill, to have his ashes scattered wide and broadcast, to be thrown into the space he longed for while living, but he feared that such a luxury of resolution into the elements would be too costly. Thus his naked mind, close against naked mother Nature, wrested from her the conviction of soul, immortality, deity, under conditions as primitive as those of the cave man, and his most repeated prayer was "Give me the deepest soul life."

In other moods he felt the world outré-human, and his mind could by no twist be fitted to the cosmos. Ugly, designless creatures caused him to cease to look for deity in nature, where all happens by chance. He at length concluded there is something higher than soul and above deity, and better than God, for which he searched and labored. He found favorite thinking places, to which he made pilgrimages, where he "felt out into the depths of the ether." His frame could not bear the labor his heart demanded. Work of body was his meat and drink. "Never have I had enough of it. I wearied long before I was satisfied, and weariness did not bring a cessation of desire, the thirst was still there. I rode; I used the ax; I split tree-trunks with wedges; my arms tired, but my spirit remained fresh and chafed against the physical weariness." Had he been indefinitely stronger, he would have longed for more strength. He was often out of doors all day and often half the night; wanted more sunshine; wished the day was sixty hours long; took pleasure in braving the cold so that it should be not life's destroyer but its renewer. Yet he abhorred asceticism. He wrestled with the problem of the origin of his soul and destiny, but could find no solution; revolted at the assertion that all is designed for the best; "a man of intellect and humanity could cause everything to happen in an infinitely superior manner." He discovered that no one ever died of old age, but only of disease; that we do not even know what old age would be like; found that his soul is infinite, but lies in abeyance; that we are murdered by our ancestors and must roll back the tide of death; that a hundredth part of man's labor would suffice for his support; that idleness is no evil; that in the future nine-tenths of the time will be leisure, and to that end he will work with all his heart. "I was not more than eighteen when an inner and esoteric meaning began to come to me from all the visible universe, and indefinable aspirations filled me."

Interesting as is this document, it is impossible to avoid the suspicion that the seventeen years which intervened between the beginning of these experiences and their final record, coupled with the perhaps unconscious tendency toward literary effect, detract more or less from their value as documents of adolescent nature.

Mr. H. Fielding Hall, author of "The Soul of a People," has since written a book[32] in which, beginning with many definitions of Christianity, weighing the opinion of those who think all our advance is made because of, against those who think it in spite of Christianity, he proceeds to give the story of a boy, probably himself, who till twelve was almost entirely reared by women and with children younger than himself.

He was sickly, and believed not in the Old but in the New Testament; in the Sermon on the Mount, which he supposed all accepted and lived by; that war and wealth were bad and learning apt to be a snare; that the ideal life was that of a poor curate, working hard and unhappy. At twelve, he went to a boarding-school, passed from a woman's world into a man's, out of the New Testament into the Old, out of dreams into reality. War was a glorious opportunity, and all followed the British victories, which were announced publicly. Big boys were going to Sandhurst or Woolwich; there were parties; and the school code never turned the other cheek. Wars were God's storms, stirring stagnant natures to new life; wealth was worshiped; certain lies were an honor; knowledge was an extremely desirable thing—all this was at first new and delightful, but extremely wicked. Sunday was the only other Old Testament rule, but was then forgotten. Slowly a repugnance of religion in all its forms arose. He felt his teachers hypocrites; he raised no alarm, "for he was hardly conscious that his anchor had dragged or that he had lost hold" of it forever. At eighteen, he read Darwin and found that if he were right, Genesis was wrong; man had risen, not fallen; if a part was wrong, the whole was. If God made the world, the devil seemed to rule it; prayer can not influence him; the seven days of creation were periods, Heaven knows how long. Why did all profess and no one believe religion? Why is God so stern and yet so partial, and how about the Trinity? Then explanations were given. Heaven grew repulsive, as a place for the poor, the maimed, the stupid, the childish, and those unfit for earth generally.

Faiths came from the East. "The North has originated only Thor, Odin, Balder, Valkyres." The gloom and cold drive man into himself; do not open him. In the East one can live in quiet solitude, with no effort, close to nature. The representatives of all faiths wear ostentatiously their badges, pray in public, and no one sneers at all religions. Oriental faiths have no organization; there is no head of Hinduism, Buddhism, or hardly of Mohammedanism. There are no missions, but religion grows rankly from a rich soil, so the boy wrote three demands: a reasonable theory of the universe, a workable and working code of conduct, and a promise of something desirable hereafter. So he read books and tried to make a system.

On a hill, in a thunder-storm in the East, he realized how Thor was born. Man fears thunder; it seems the voice of a greater man. Deny eyes, legs, and body of the Deity, and nothing is left. God as an abstract spirit is unthinkable, but Buddhism offers us no God, only law. Necessity, blind force, law, or a free personal will—that is the alternative. Freedom limits omnipotence; the two can never mix. "The German Emperor's God, clanking round the heavenly mansions wearing a German *Pickelhaube* and swearing German oaths," is not satisfactory. Man's God is what he admires most in himself; he can be propitiated, hence atonement; you can not break a law, but you can study it. Inquiry, not submission, is the attitude. Perhaps both destiny and freedom are true, but truth is for the sake of light.

Thor had no moral code; the Greeks were unmoral. Jehovah at first asked only fear, reverence, and worship. This gives no guide to life. Most codes are directed against a foe and against pain. Truth, mercy, courtesy— these were slowly added to reverence; then sanitary rules, hence castes. Two codes, those of Christ and Buddha, tower above all others. They are the same in praising not wealth, greatness, or power, but purity, renunciation of the world, as if one fitted one's self for one by being unfitted for the other world.

Is heaven a bribe? Its ideals are those of children, of girl angels, white wings, floating dresses, no sheep, but lambs. "Surely there is nothing in all the world so babyish." One can hardly imagine a man with a deep voice, with the storm of life beating his soul, amid those baby faces. If happiness in any act or attitude is perfect, it will last forever. Where is due the weariness or satiety? But if happiness be perfect, this is impossible; so life would be monotony akin to annihilation. But life is change, and change is misery. There is effort here; but there will be none in the great peace that passes understanding; no defeat, therefore no victory; no friends, because no enemies; no joyous meetings, because no farewells. It is the shadows and the dark mysteries that sound the depths of our hearts. No man that ever lived, if told that he could be young again or go to any heaven, would choose the latter. Men die for many things, but all fear the beyond. Thus no religion gives us an intelligible First Cause, a code or a heaven that we want.

The most religious man is the peasant listening to the angelus, putting out a little *ghi* for his God; the woman crying in the pagoda. Thus we can only turn to the hearts of men for the truth of religion.

Biographies and autobiographies furnish many photographic glimpses of the struggles and experiences of early adolescent years.

Anthony Trollope's autobiography[33] is pitiful. He was poor and disliked by most of his masters and treated with ignominy by his fellow pupils. He describes himself as always in disgrace. At fifteen he walked three miles each way twice a day to and from school. As a sizar he seemed a wretched farmer's boy, reeking from the dunghill, sitting next the sons of big peers. All were against him, and he was allowed to join no games, and learned, he tells us, absolutely nothing but a little Greek and Latin. Once only, goaded to desperation, he rallied and whipped a bully. The boy was never able to overcome the isolation of his school position, and while he coveted popularity with an eagerness which was almost mean, and longed exceedingly to excel in cricket or with the racquet, was allowed to know nothing of them. He remembers at nineteen never to have had a lesson in writing, arithmetic, French, or German. He knew his masters by their ferules and they him. He believes that he has "been flogged oftener than any human being alive. It was just possible to obtain five scourgings in one day at Winchester, and I have often boasted that I have obtained them all." Prizes were distributed prodigally, but he never got one. For twelve years of tuition, he says, "I do not remember that I ever knew a lesson."

At this age he describes himself as "an idle, desolate, hanger on ... without an idea of a career or a profession or a trade," but he was tolerably happy because he could fancy himself in love with pretty girls and had been removed from the real misery of school, but had not a single aspiration regarding his future. Three of his household were dying of consumption, and his mother was day nurse, night nurse, and divided her time between pill-boxes and the ink-bottle, for when she was seventy-six she had written one hundred and forty volumes, the first of which was not written till she was fifty.

Gradually the boy became alive to the blighted ambition of his father's life and the strain his mother was enduring, nursing the dying household and writing novels to provide a decent roof for them to die under. Anthony got a position at the post-office without an examination. He knew no French nor science; was a bad speller and worse writer and could not have sustained an examination on any subject. Still he could not bear idleness, and was always going about with some castle in the air finely built in his mind, carrying on for weeks and years the same continuous story; binding himself down to certain laws, proprieties, and unities; always his own hero, excluding everything violently improbable. To this practise, which he calls dangerous and which began six or seven years before he went to the post-office, he ascribes his power to maintain an interest in a fictitious story and to live in a entirely outside imaginative life. During these seven years he acquired a character of irregularity and grew reckless.

Mark Pattison[34] shows us how his real life began in the middle teens, when his energy was "directed to one end, to improve myself"; "to form my own mind; to sound things thoroughly; to be free from the bondage of unreason and the traditional prejudices which, when I first began to think, constituted the whole of my mental fabric." He entered upon life with a "hide-bound and contracted intellect," and depicts "something of the steps by which I emerged from that frozen condition." He believes that to "remember the dreams and confusions of childhood and never to lose the recollection of the curiosity and simplicity of that age, is one of the great gifts of the poetic character," although this, he tells us, was extraordinarily true of George Sand, but not of himself. From the age of twelve on, a Fellowship at Oriel was the ideal of his life, and although he became a commoner there at seventeen, his chief marvel is that he was so immature and unimpressionable.

William Hale White[35] learned little at school, save Latin and good penmanship, but his very life was divided into halves—Sundays and week days—and he reflects at some length upon the immense dangers of the early teens; the physiological and yet subtler psychic penalties of error; callousness to fine pleasures; hardening of the conscience; and deplores the misery which a little instruction might have saved him. At fourteen he underwent conversion, understood in his sect to be a transforming miracle, releasing higher and imprisoning lower powers. He compares it to the saving of a mind from vice by falling in love with a woman who is adored, or the reclamation of a young woman from idleness and vanity by motherhood. But as a boy he was convinced of many things which were mere phrases, and attended prayer-meetings for the clanship of being marked off from the world and of walking home with certain girls. He learned to say in prayer that there was nothing good in him, that he was rotten and filthy and his soul a mass of putrefying sores; but no one took him at his word and expelled him from society, but thought the better of him. Soon he began to study theology, but found no help in suppressing tempestuous lust, in understanding the Bible, or getting his doubts answered, and all the lectures seemed irrelevant chattering. An infidel was a monster whom he had rarely ever seen. At nineteen he began to preach, but his heart was untouched till he read Wordsworth's lyrical ballads, and this recreated a living God for him, melted his heart to tears, and made him long for companionship;

its effect was instantly seen in his preaching, and soon made him slightly suspected as heretical.[36]

John Addington Symonds, in his autobiography, describes his "insect-like" devotion to creed in the green infancy of ritualism. In his early teens at boarding-school he and his mates, with half sincerity, followed a classmate to compline, donned surplices, tossed censers, arranged altars in their studies, bought bits of painted glass for their windows and illuminated crucifixes with gold dust and vermilion. When he was confirmed, this was somewhat of an epoch. Preparation was like a plowshare, although it turned up nothing valuable, and stimulated esthetic and emotional ardor. In a dim way he felt God near, but he did not learn to fling the arms of the soul in faith around the cross of Christ. Later the revelation he found in Plato removed him farther from boyhood. He fell in love with gray Gothic churches, painted glass, organ lofts, etc.

Walter Pater has described phases of ferment, perhaps largely his own, in the character of Florian Deleal; his rapture of the red hawthorn blossoms, "absolutely the reddest of all things"; his times of "seemingly exclusive predominance of interest in beautiful physical things, a kind of tyranny of the senses"; and his later absorbing efforts to estimate the proportion of the sensuous and ideal, assigning most importance to sensible vehicles and occasions; associating all thoughts with touch and sight as a link between himself and things, till he became more and more "unable to care for or think of soul but as in an actual body"; comforted in the contemplation of death by the thought of flesh turning to violets and almost oppressed by the pressure of the sensible world, his longings for beauty intensifying his fear of death. He loved to gaze on dead faces in the Paris Morgue although the haunt of them made the sunshine sickly for days, and his long fancy that they had not really gone nor were quite motionless, but led a secret, half fugitive life, freer by night, and perhaps dodging about in their old haunts with no great good-will toward the living, made him by turns pity and hate the ghosts who came back in the wind, beating at the doors. His religious nature gradually yielded to a mystical belief in Bible personages in some indefinite place as the reflexes and patterns of our nobler self, whose companionship made the world more satisfying. There was "a constant substitution of the typical for the actual," and angels might be met anywhere. "A deep mysticity brooded over real things and partings," marriages and many acts and accidents of life. "The very colors of things became themselves weighty with meanings," or "full of penitence and peace." "For a time he walked through the world in a sustained, not unpleasurable awe generated by the habitual recognition, beside every circumstance and event of life, of its celestial correspondent."

In D. C. Boulger's Life of General Charles Gordon[37] he records how, like Nelson Clive, his hero was prone to boys' escapades and outbreaks that often made him the terror of his superiors. He was no bookworm, but famous as the possessor of high spirits, very often involved in affairs that necessitated discipline, and seemed greatly out of harmony with the popular idea of the ascetic of Mount Carmel. As a schoolboy he made wonderful squirts "that would wet you through in a minute." One Sunday twenty-seven panes of glass in a large storehouse were broken with screws shot through them by his cross-bow "for ventilation." Ringing bells and pushing young boys in, butting an unpopular officer severely in the stomach with his head and taking the punishment, hitting a bully with a clothes-brush and being put back six months in the Royal Military Academy at Woolwich; these are the early outcrops of one side of his dual character. Although more soldier than saint, he had a very cheery, genial side. He was always ready to take even the severest punishment for all his scrapes due to excessive high spirits. When one of his superiors declared that he would never make an officer, he felt his honor touched, and his vigorous and expressive reply was to tear the epaulets from his shoulders and throw them at his superior's feet. He had already developed some of the rather moody love of seclusion that was marked later, but religion did not strike him deeply enough to bring him into the church until he was twenty-one, when he took his first sacrament. On one occasion he declined promotion within his reach because he would have had to pass a friend to get it. He acted generally on his impulses, which were perhaps better than his judgments, took great pleasure in corresponding on religious topics with his elder sister, and early formed the habit of excessive smoking which gravely affected his health later. His was the rare combination of inner repose and confidence, interrupted by spells of gaiety.

Williamson, in his "Life of Holman Hunt,"[38] tells us that at thirteen he was removed from school as inapt in study. He began to spend his time in drawing in his copybooks. He was made clerk to an auctioneer, who fortunately encouraged his passion, and at sixteen was with a calico printer. Here he amused himself by drawing flies on the window, which his employer tried to brush off. There was the greatest home opposition to his studying art. After being rejected twice, he was admitted at seventeen to the Academy school as a probationer, and the next year, in 1845, as a student. Here he met Millais and Rossetti and was able to relieve the strain on his mind, which the worry of his father concerning his course caused him, and very soon his career began.

At thirteen Fitzjames Stephen[39] roused himself to thrash a big boy who had long bullied him, and became a fighter. In his sixteenth year, he grew nearly five inches, but was so shy and timid at Eton that he says, "I was like a sensible grown-up woman among a crowd of rough boys"; but in the reaction to the long abuse his mind was steeled against oppression, tyranny, and every kind of unfairness. He read Paine's "Age of Reason," and went "through the Bible as a man might go through a wood, cutting down trees. The priests can stick them in again, but they will not make them grow."

Dickens has given us some interesting adolescents. Miss Dingwall in "Sketches by Boz," "very sentimental and romantic"; the tempery young Nickleby, who, at nineteen, thrashed Squeers; Barnaby Rudge, idiotic and very muscular; Joe Willet, persistently treated as a boy till he ran away to join the army and married Dolly Varden, perhaps the most exuberant, good-humored, and beautiful girl in all the Dickens gallery; Martin Chuzzlewit, who also ran away, as did David Copperfield, perhaps the most true to adolescence because largely reminiscent of the author's own life; Steerforth, a stranger from home, and his victim, Little Emily; and to some extent Sam Weller, Dick Swiveller, the Marchioness, young Podsnap, the Artful Dodger, and Charley Bates; while Oliver Twist, Little Nell, and Little Dorrit, Joe and Turveydrop in Bleak House, and Paul Dombey, young as they were, show the beginning of the pubescent change. Most of his characters, however, are so overdrawn and caricatured as to be hardly true to life.[40]

In the "Romance of John Inglesant,"[41] by J. H. Shorthouse, we have a remarkable picture of an unusually gifted youth, who played an important rôle in the days of Cromwell and King Charles, and who was long poised in soul between the Church of Rome and the English party. He was very susceptible to the fascination of superstition, romance, and day-dreaming, and at eleven absorbed his master's Rosicrucian theories of spiritual existence where spirits held converse with each other and with mankind. A mystic Platonism, which taught that Pindar's story of the Argo was only a recipe for the philosopher's stone, fascinated him at fourteen. The philosophy of obedience and of the subjection of reason to authority was early taught him, and he sought to live from within, hearing only the divine law, as the worshipers of Cybele heard only the flutes. His twin brother Eustace was an active worldling, and soon he followed him to court as page to the Queen, but delighted more and more in wandering apart and building air castles. For a time he was entirely swayed, and his life directed, by a Jesuit Father, who taught him the crucifix and the rosary. At sixteen the doctrine of divine illumination fascinated him. He struggled to find the path of true devotion; abandoned himself to extremely ritualistic forms of worship; dabbled a little in alchemy and astrology to help develop the divine nature within him and to attain the beatific vision. Soon he was introduced to the "Protestant nunnery," as it was called, where the venerable Mr. Ferran, a friend of George Herbert's, was greatly taken by Inglesant's accomplishments and grace of manner. Various forms of extremely High Church yet Protestant worship were celebrated here each day with great devotion, until he became disgusted with Puritanism and craved to participate in the office of mass. At this point, however, he met Mr. Hobbes, whose rude but forcible condemnation of papacy restrained him from casting his lot with it. At seventeen, he saw one night a real apparition of the just executed Strafford. The last act of his youth, which we can note here, was soon after he was twenty, when he fell in love with the charming and saintly Mary Collet. The rough Puritan Thorne had made her proposals at which she revolted, but she and Inglesant confessed love to each other; she saw, however, that they had a way of life marked out for themselves by an inner impulse and light. This calling they must follow and abandon love, and now John plunged into the war on the side of the King.

W. J. Stillman[42] has written with unusual interest and candor the story of his own early life.

As a boy he was frenzied at the first sight of the sea; caught the whip and lashed the horses in an unconscious delirium, and always remembered this as one of the most vivid experiences of his life. He had a period of nature worship. His first trout was a delirium, and he danced about wildly and furiously. He relates his very vivid impressions of the religious orthodoxy in which he was reared, especially revival sermons; his occasional falsehoods to escape severe punishment; his baptism at ten or eleven in a river in midwinter; the somberness of his intellectual life, which was long very apathetic; his phenomenal stupidity for years; his sudden insurrections in which he thrashed bullies at school; his fear that he should be sent home in disgrace for bad scholarship; and how at last, after seven years of dulness, at the age of fourteen, "the mental fog broke away suddenly, and before the term ended I could construe the Latin in less time than it took to recite it, and the demonstrations of Euclid were as plain and clear as a fairy story. My memory came back so distinctly that I could recite long poems after a single reading, and no member of the class passed a more brilliant examination at the end of the term than I; and, at the end of the second term, I could recite the whole of Legendre's geometry, plane and spherical, from beginning to end without a question, and the class examination was recorded as the most remarkable which the academy had witnessed for many years. I have never been able to conceive an explanation of this curious phenomenon, which I record only as of possible interest to some one interested in psychology."

A. Bronson Alcott[43] was the son of a Connecticut farmer. He began a diary at twelve; aspired vainly to enter Yale, and after much restlessness at the age of nineteen left home with two trunks for Virginia to peddle on foot, hoping to teach school. Here he had a varying and often very hard experience for years.

Hornes Bushnell's[44] parents represented the Episcopal and liberal Congregational Church. His early life was spent on a farm and in attending a country academy. He became profoundly interested in religion in the early teens and developed extreme interest in nature. At seventeen, while tending a carding machine, he wrote a paper on Calvinism. At nineteen he united with the church, and entered Yale when he was twenty-one, in 1823. Later he tried to teach school, but left it, declaring he would rather lay stone wall; worked on a journal, but withdrew, finding it a terrible life; studied law for a year, became a tutor at Yale, experienced a reconversion and entered the ministry.

A well-known American, who wishes his name withheld, writes me of his youth as follows:

'First came the love of emotion and lurid romance reading. My mind was full of adventure, dreams of underground passages, and imprisoned beauties whom I rescued. I wrote a story in red ink, which I never read, but a girl friend did, and called it magnificent. The girl fever, too, made me idealize first one five years older than I, later another three years older, and still later one of my own age. I would have eaten dirt for each of them for a year or two; was extremely gallant and the hero of many romances for two, but all the time so bashful that I scarcely dared speak to one of them, and no schoolmate ever suspected it all. Music also became a craze at fourteen. Before, I had hated lessons, now I was thrilled and would be a musician, despite my parents' protests. I practised the piano furiously; wrote music and copied stacks of it; made a list of several hundred pieces and tunes, including everything musical I knew; would imagine a crowded hall, where I played and swayed with fine airs. The vast assembly applauded and would not let me go, but all the time it was a simple piece and I was a very ordinary player. At fifty years, this is still a relic. I now in hours of fatigue pound the piano and dreamily imagine dazed and enchanted audiences. Then came oratory, and I glowed and thrilled in declaiming Webster's "Reply to Hayne," "Thanatopsis," Byron's "Darkness," Patrick Henry, and best of all "The Maniac," which I spouted in a fervid way wearing a flaming red necktie. I remember a fervid scene with myself on a high solitary hill with a bald summit two miles from home, where I once went because I had been blamed. I tried to sum myself up, inventory my good and bad points. It was Sunday, and I was keyed up to a frenzy of resolve, prayer, idealization of life; all grew all in a jumble. My resolve to go to college was clinched then and there, and that hill will always remain my Pisgah and Moriah,

Horeb and Sinai all in one. I paced back and forth in the wind and shouted, 'I will make people know and revere me; I will do something'; and called everything to witness my vow that I never again would visit this spot till all was fulfilled." "Alas!" he says, "I have never been there since. Once, to a summer party who went, I made excuse for not keeping this rendezvous. It was too sacramental. Certainly it was a very deep and never-to-be-forgotten experience there all alone, when something of great moment to me certainly took place in my soul."

In the biography of Frederick Douglas[45] we are told that when he was about thirteen he began to feel deeply the moral yoke of slavery and to seek means of escaping it. He became interested in religion, was converted, and dreamed of and prayed for liberty. With great ingenuity he extracted knowledge of the alphabet and reading from white boys of his acquaintance. At sixteen, under a brutal master he revolted and was beaten until he was faint from loss of blood, and at seventeen he fought and whipped the brutal overseer Covey, who would have invoked the law, which made death the punishment for such an offense, but for shame of having been worsted by a negro boy and from the reflection that there was no profit from a dead slave. Only at twenty did he escape into the new world of freedom.

Jacob Riis[46] "fell head over heels in love with sweet Elizabeth" when he was fifteen and she thirteen. His "courtship proceeded at a tumultuous pace, which first made the town laugh, then put it out of patience and made some staid matrons express the desire to box my ears soundly." She played among the lumber where he worked, and he watched her so intently that he scarred his shinbone with an adze he should have been minding. He cut off his forefinger with an ax when she was dancing on a beam near by, and once fell off a roof when craning his neck to see her go round a corner. At another time he ordered her father off the dance-floor, because he tried to take his daughter home a few minutes before the appointed hour of midnight. Young as he was, he was large and tried to run away to join the army, but finally went to Copenhagen to serve his apprenticeship with a builder, and here had an interview with Hans Christian Andersen.

Ellery Sedgwick tells as that at thirteen the mind of Thomas Paine ran on stories of the sea which his teacher had told him, and that he attempted to enlist on the privateer *Terrible*. He was restless at home for years, and shipped on a trading vessel at nineteen.

Indeed, modern literature in our tongue abounds in this element, from "Childe Harold" to the second and third long chapters in Mrs. Ward's "David Grieve," ending with his engagement to Lucy Purcell; Thackeray's Arthur Pendennis and his characteristic love of the far older and scheming Fanny Fotheringay; David in James Lane Allen's "Reign of Law," who read

Darwin, was expelled from the Bible College and the church, and finally was engaged to Gabriella; and scores more might be enumerated. There is even Sonny,[47] who, rude as he was and poorly as he did in all his studies, at the same age when he began to keep company, "tallered" his hair, tied a bow of ribbon to the buggy whip, and grew interested in manners, passing things, putting on his coat and taking off his hat at table, began to study his menagerie of pet snakes, toads, lizards, wrote John Burroughs, helped him and got help in return, took to observing, and finally wrote a book about the forest and its occupants, all of which is very *bien trouvé* if not historic truth.

Two singular reflections always rearise in reading Goethe's autobiographical writings: first, that both the age and the place, with its ceremonies, festivals, great pomp and stirring events in close quarters in the little province where he lived, were especially adapted to educate children and absorb them in externals; and, second, that this wonderful boy had an extreme propensity for moralizing and drawing lessons of practical service from all about him. This is no less manifest in Wilhelm Meister's Apprenticeship and Travels, which supplements the autobiography. Both together present a very unique type of adolescence, the elaborate story of which defies epitome. From the puppet craze well on into his precocious university life it was his passion to explore the widest ranges of experience and then to reflect, moralize, or poetize upon them. Perhaps no one ever studied the nascent stages of his own life and elaborated their every incident with such careful observation and analysis. His peculiar diathesis enabled him to conserve their freshness on to full maturity, when he gave them literary form. Most lack power to fully utilize their own experience even for practical self-knowledge and guidance, but with Goethe nothing was wasted from which self-culture could be extracted.

Goethe's first impression of female loveliness was of a girl named Gretchen, who served wine one evening, and whose face and form followed him for a long time. Their meetings always gave him a thrill of pleasure, and though his love was like many first loves, very spiritual and awakened by goodness and beauty, it gave a new brightness to the whole world, and to be near her seemed to him an indispensable condition of his being. Her *fiancé* was generally with her, and Goethe experienced a shock in finding that she had become a milliner's assistant for although, like all natural boys of aristocratic families, he loved common people, this interest was not favored by his parents. The night following the coronation day several were compelled to spend in chairs, and he and his Gretchen, with others, slept, she with her head upon his shoulder, until all the others had awakened in the morning. At last they parted at her door, and for the first and last time they kissed but never met again, although he often wept in thinking of her.

He was terribly affronted to fully realize that, although only two years older than himself, she should have regarded him as a child. He tried to strip her of all loving qualities and think her odious, but her image hovered over him. The sanity of instinct innate in youth prompted him to lay aside as childish the foolish habit of weeping and railing, and his mortification that she regarded him somewhat as a nurse might, gradually helped to work his cure.

He was very fond of his own name, and, like young and uneducated people, wrote or carved it anywhere; later placed near it that of a new love, Annette, and afterward on finding the tree he shed tears, melted toward her, and made an idyl. He was also seized with a passion of teasing her and dominating over her devotedness with wanton and tyrannical caprice, venting upon her the ill humor of his disappointments, and grew absurdly jealous and lost her after she had borne with him with incredible patience and after terrible scenes with her by which he gained nothing. Frenzied by his loss, he began to abuse his physical nature and was only saved from illness by the healing power of his poetic talent; the "Lover's Caprice" was written with the impetus of a boiling passion. In the midst of many serious events, a reckless humor, which was due to the excess of life, developed which made him feel himself superior to the moment, and even to court danger. He played tricks, although rarely with premeditation. Later he mused much upon the transient nature of love and the mutability of character; the extent to which the senses could be indulged within the bounds of morality; he sought to rid himself of all that troubled him by writing song or epigram about it, which made him seem frivolous and prompted one friend to seek to subdue him by means of church forms, which he had severed on coming to Leipzig. By degrees he felt an epoch approaching when all respect for authority was to vanish, and he became suspicious and even despairing with regard to the best individuals he had known before and grew chummy with a young tutor whose jokes and fooleries were incessant. His disposition fluctuated between gaiety and melancholy, and Rousseau attracted him. Meanwhile his health declined until a long illness, which began with a hemorrhage, caused him to oscillate for days between life and death; and convalescence, generally so delightful, was marred by a serious tumor. His father's disposition was stern, and he could become passionate and bitter, and his mother's domesticity made her turn to religion, so that on coming home he formed the acquaintance of a religious circle. Again Goethe was told by a hostile child that he was not the true son of his father. This inoculated him with a disease that long lurked in his system and prompted various indirect investigations to get at the truth, during which he compared all distinguished guests with his own physiognomy to detect his own likeness.

Up to the Leipzig period he had great joy in wandering unknown, unconscious of self; but he soon began to torment himself with an almost hypertrophied fancy that he was attracting much attention, that others' eyes were turned on his person to fix it in their memories, that he was scanned and found fault with; and hence he developed a love of the country, of the woods and solitary places, where he could be hedged in and separated from all the world. Here he began to throw off his former habit of looking at things from the art standpoint and to take pleasure in natural objects for their own sake. His mother had almost grownup to consciousness in her two oldest children, and his first disappointment in love turned his thought all the more affectionately toward her and his sister, a year younger. He was long consumed with amazement over the newly awakening sense impulse that took intellectual forms and the mental needs that clothed themselves in sense images. He fell to building air castles of opposition lecture courses and gave himself up to many dreams of ideal university conditions. He first attended lectures diligently, but suffered much harm from being too advanced; learned a great deal that he could not regulate, and was thereby made uncomfortable; grew interested in the fit of his clothes, of which hitherto he had been careless. He was in despair at the uncertainty of his own taste and judgment, and almost feared he must make a complete change of mind, renouncing what he had hitherto learned, and so one day in great contempt for his past burned up his poetry, sketches, etc.

He had learned to value and love the Bible, and owed his moral culture to it. Its events and symbols were deeply stamped upon him, so without being a pietist he was greatly moved at the scoffing spirit toward it which he met at the university. From youth he had stood on good terms with God, and at times he had felt that he had some things to forgive God for not having given better assistance to his infinite good-will. Under all this influence he turned to cabalism and became interested in crystals and the microcosm and macrocosm, and fell into the habit of despair over what he had been and believed just before. He conceived a kind of hermetical or neoplatonic godhead creating in more and more eccentric circles, until the last, which rose in contradiction, was Lucifer to whom creation was committed. He first of all imagined in detail an angelic host, and finally a whole theology was wrought out *in petto*. He used a gilt ornamented music-stand as a kind of altar with fumigating pastils for incense, where each morning God was approached by offerings until one day a conflagration put a sudden end to these celebrations.

Hans Anderson,[48] the son of a poor shoemaker, taught in a charity school at the dawn of puberty; vividly animated Bible stories from pictures painted on the wall; was dreamy and absent-minded; told continued stories to his mates; at confirmation vowed he would be famous and finally, at fourteen, left home for Copenhagen, where he was violently stage-struck and worked his way from friendship with the bill-poster to the stage as page, shepherd, etc.; called on a famous dancer, who scorned him, and then, feeling that he had no one but God to depend on, prayed earnestly and often. For nearly a year, until his voice broke, he was a fine singer. He wet with his tears the eyes of a portrait of a heartless man that he might feel for him. He played with a puppet theater and took a childish delight in decking the characters with gay remnants that he begged from shops; wrote several plays which no one would accept; stole into an empty theater one New Year's day to pray aloud on the middle of the stage; shouted with joy; hugged and kissed a beech-tree till people thought him insane; abhorred the thought of apprenticeship to Latin as he did to that of a trade, which was a constant danger; and was one of the most dreamy and sentimental, and by spells religious and prayerful, of youth.

George Ebers[49] remembered as a boy of eleven the revolution of '48 in Berlin, soon after which he was placed in Froebel's school at Keilhau. This great teacher with his noble associates, Middendorf, Barop, and Langekhal, lived with the boys; told the stirring stories of their own lives as soldiers in the war of liberation; led their pupils on long excursions in vacation, often lasting for months, and gave much liberty to the boys, who were allowed to haze not only their new mates, but new teachers. This transfer from the city to the country roused a veritable passion in the boy, who remained here till he was fifteen. Trees and cliffs were climbed, collections made, the Saale by moonlight and the lofty Steiger at sunset were explored. There were swimming and skating and games, and the maxim of the school, "*Friede, Freude, Freiheit,*" [Peace, joy, freedom] was lived up to. The boys hung on their teachers for stories. The teachers took their boys into their confidence for all their own literary aims, loves, and ideals. One had seen the corpse of Körner and another knew Prohaska. "The Roman postulate that knowledge should be imparted to boys according to a thoroughly tested method approved by the mature human intellect and which seems most useful to it for later life" was the old system of sacrificing the interests of the child for those of the man. Here childhood was to live itself out completely and naturally into an ever renewed paradise. The temperaments, dispositions, and characters of each of the sixty boys were carefully studied and recorded. Some of these are still little masterpieces of psychological penetration, and this was made the basis of development. The extreme Teutonism cultivated by wrestling, shooting, and fencing, giving each a spot of land to sow, reap, and shovel, and all in an atmosphere of adult life, made an environment that fitted the transition period as well as any that the history of education affords. Every tramp and battle were described in a book by each boy. When at fifteen Ebers was transferred to the Kottbus Gymnasium, he felt like a colt led from green pastures to the stable, and the period of effervescence made him almost possessed by a demon, so many sorts of follies did he commit. He wrote "a poem of the world," fell in love with an actress older than himself, became known as foolhardy for his wild escapades, and only slowly sobered down.

In Gottfried Kelley's "Der grüne Heinrich,"[50] the author, whom R.M. Meyer calls "the most eminent literary German of the nineteenth century," reviews the memories of his early life. This autobiography is a plain and very realistic story of a normal child, and not adulterated with fiction like Goethe's or with psychoses like Rousseau or Bashkirtseff. He seems a boy like all other boys, and his childhood and youth were in no wise extraordinary. The first part of this work, which describes his youth up to the age of eighteen, is the most important, and everything is given with remarkable fidelity and minuteness. It is a tale of little things. All the friendships and loves and impulses are there, and he is fundamentally selfish and utilitarian; God and nature were one, and only when his beloved Army died did he wish to believe in immortality. He, too, as a child, found two kinds of love in his heart—the idea and the sensual, very independent—the one for a young and innocent girl and the other for a superb young woman years older than he, pure, although the personification of sense. He gives a rich harvest of minute and sagacious observations about his strange simultaneous loves; the peculiar tastes of food; his day-dream period; and his rather prolonged habit of lying, the latter because he had no other vent for invention. He describes with great regret his leaving school at so early an age; his volcanic passion of anger; his self-distrust; his periods of abandon; his passion to make a success of art though he did not of life; his spells of self-despair and cynicism; his periods of desolation in his single life; his habit of story-telling; his wrestling with the problem of theology and God; the conflict between his philosophy and his love of the girls, etc.

From a private school in Leipzig, where he had shown all a boy's tact in finding what his masters thought the value of each subject they taught; where he had joined in the vandalism of using a battering-ram to break a way to the hated science apparatus and to destroy it; feeling that the classical writers were overpraised; and where at the age of sixteen he had appeared several times in public as a reciter of his own poems, Max Müller returned to Leipzig and entered upon the freedom of university life there at the age of seventeen. For years his chief enjoyment was music.[51] He played the piano well, heard everything he could in concert or opera, was an oratorio tenor, and grew more and more absorbed in music, so that he planned to devote himself altogether to it and also to enter a musical school at Dessau, but nothing came of it. At the university he saw little of society, was once incarcerated for wearing a club ribbon, and confesses that with his boon companions he was guilty of practises which would now bring culprits into collision with authorities. He fought three duels, participated in many pranks and freakish escapades, but nevertheless attended fifty-three different courses of lectures in three years. When Hegelism was the state philosophy, he tried hard to understand it, but dismissed it with the sentiments expressed by a French officer to his tailor, who refused to take the trousers he had ordered to be made very tight because they did not fit so closely that he could not get into them. Darwin attracted him, yet the wildness of his followers repelled. He says, "I confess I felt quite bewildered for a time and began to despair altogether of my reasoning powers." He wonders how young minds in German universities survive the storms and fogs through which they pass. With bated breath he heard his elders talk of philosophy and tried to lay hold of a word here and there, but it all floated before his mind like mist. Later he had an Hegelian period, but found in Herbart a corrective, and at last decided upon Sanskrit and other ancient languages, because he felt that he must know something that no other knew, and also that the Germans had then heard only the after-chime and not the real striking of the bells of Indian philosophy. From twenty his struggles and his queries grew more definite, and at last, at the age of twenty-two, he was fully launched upon his career in Paris, and later went to Oxford.

At thirteen Wagner[52] translated about half the "Odyssey" voluntarily; at fourteen began the tragedy which was to combine the grandeur of two of Shakespeare's dramas; at sixteen he tried "his new-fledged musical wings by soaring at once to the highest peaks of orchestral achievement without wasting any time on the humble foot-hills." He sought to make a new departure, and, compared to the grandeur of his own composition, "Beethoven's Ninth Symphony appeared like a simple Pleyel Sonata." To facilitate the reading of his astounding score, he wrote it in three kinds of ink—red for strings, green for the wood-wind, and black for the brass instruments. He writes that this overture was the climax of his absurdities, and although the audience before which an accommodating orchestra played it were disgusted and the musicians were convulsed with laughter, it made a deep impression upon the author's mind. Even after matriculating at the university he abandoned himself so long to the dissipations common to student life before the reaction came that his relatives feared that he was a good-for-nothing.

In his "Hannele," Hauptmann, the dramatist, describes in a kind of dream poem what he supposed to pass through the mind of a dying girl of thirteen or fourteen, who does not wish to live and is so absorbed by the "Brownies of her brain" that she hardly knows whether she is alive on earth or dead in heaven, and who sees the Lord Jesus in the form of the schoolmaster whom she adores. In her closing vision there is a symbolic representation of her own resurrection. To the passionate discussions in Germany, England, and France, as to whether this character is true to adolescence, we can only answer with an emphatic affirmative; that her heaven abounds in local color and in fairy tale items, that it is very material, and that she is troubled by fears of sin against the Holy Ghost, is answer enough in an ill-used, starving child with a fevered brain, whose dead mother taught her these things.

Saint-Pierre's "Paul and Virginia" is an attempt to describe budding adolescence in a boy and girl born on a remote island and reared in a state of natural simplicity The descriptions are sentimental after the fashion of the age in France, and the pathos, which to us smacks of affectation and artificiality, nevertheless has a vein of truth in it. The story really begins when the two children were twelve; and the description of the dawn of love and melancholy in Virginia's heart, for some time concealed from Paul, of her disquiet and piety, of the final frank avowal of eternal love by each, set of by the pathetic separation, and of the undying love, and finally the tragic death and burial of each—all this owes its charm, for its many generations of readers, to its merits as an essentially true picture of the human heart at this critical age. This work and Rousseau[53] have contributed to give French literature its peculiar cast in its description of this age.

'The first explosions of combustible constitution" in Rousseau's, precocious nature were troublesome, and he felt premature sensations of erotic voluptuousness, but without any sin. He longed "to fall at the feet of an imperious mistress, obey her mandates or implore pardon." He only wanted a lady, to become a knight errant. At ten he was passionately devoted to a Mlle. Vulson, whom he publicly and tyrannically claimed as his own and would allow no other to approach. He had very different sensuous feelings toward Mlle. Goton, with whom his relations were very passionate, though pure. Absolutely under the power of both these mistresses, the effects they produced upon him were in no wise related to each other. The former was a brother's affection with the jealousy of a lover added, but the latter a furious, tigerish, Turkish rage. When told of the former's marriage, in his indignation and heroic fury he swore never more to see a perfidious girl. A slightly neurotic vein of prolonged ephebeitis pervades much of his life.

Pierre Loti's "Story of a Child"[54] was written when the author was forty-two, and contains hardly a fact, but it is one of the best of inner autobiographies, and is nowhere richer than in the last chapters, which bring the author down to the age of fourteen and a half. He vividly describes the new joy at waking, which he began to feel at twelve or thirteen; the clear vision into the bottomless pit of death; the new, marvelous susceptibility to nature as comradeship with boys of his own age was lacking; the sudden desires from pure bravado and perversity to do something unseemly, e. g., making a fly omelet and carrying it in a procession with song; the melting of pewter plates and pouring them into water and salting a wild tract of land with them; organizing a band of miners, whom he led as if with keen scent to the right spot and rediscovered his nuggets, everything being done mysteriously and as a tribal secret. Loti had a new feeling for the haunting music of Chopin, which he had been taught to play but had not been interested in; his mind was inflamed, by a home visit of an elder brother, with the idea of going to the South Sea Islands, and this became a long obsession which finally led him to enlist in the navy, dropping, with a beating heart, the momentous letter into the post-office after long misgivings and delays. He had a superficial and a hidden self, the latter somewhat whimsical and perhaps ridiculous, shared only with a few intimate friends for whom he would have let himself be cut into bits. He believes his transition period lasted longer than with the majority of men, and during it he was carried from one extreme to another; had rather eccentric and absurd manners, and touched moat of the perilous rocks on the voyage of life. He had an early love for an older girl whose name he wrote in cipher on his books, although he felt it a little artificial, but believed it might have developed into a great and true hereditary friendship, continuing that which their ancestors had felt for many generations. The birth of love in his heart was in a dream after having read the forbidden poet, Alfred de Musset. He was fourteen, and in his dream it was a soft, odorous twilight. He walked amid flowers seeking a nameless some one whom he ardently desired, and felt that something strange and wonderful, intoxicating as it advanced, was going to happen. The twilight grew deeper, and behind a rose-bush he saw a young girl with a languorous and mysterious smile, although her forehead and eyes were hidden. As it darkened rather suddenly, her eyes came out, and they were very personal and seemed to belong to some one already much beloved, who had been found with "transports of infinite joy and tenderness." He woke with a start and sought to retain the phantom, which faded. He could not conceive that was a mere illusion, and as he realized that she had vanished he felt overwhelmed with hopelessness. It was the first stirring "of true love with all its great melancholy and deep mystery, with its overwhelming but sad enchantment—love which like a perfume endows with a fragrance all it touches."

It is, I believe, high time that ephebic literature should be recognized as a class by itself, and have a place of its own in the history of letters and in criticism. Much of it should be individually prescribed for the reading of the young, for whom it has a singular zest and is a true stimulus and corrective. This stage of life now has what might almost be called a school of its own. Here the young appeal to and listen to each other as they do not to adults, and in a way the latter have failed to appreciate. Again, no biography, and especially no autobiography, should henceforth be complete if it does not describe this period of transformation so all-determining for future life to which it alone can often give the key. Rightly to draw the lessons of this age not only saves us from waste ineffable of this rich but crude area of experience, but makes maturity saner and more complete. Lastly, many if not most young people should be encouraged to enough of the confessional private journalism to teach them self-knowledge, for the art of self-expression usually begins now if ever, when it has a wealth of subjective material and needs forms of expression peculiar to itself.

For additional references on the subject of this chapter, see:

Alcafarado, Marianna, Love Letters of a Portuguese Nun. Translated by R. H., New York, 1887. Richardson, Abby Sage, Abelard and Héloise, and Letters of Héloise, Houghton, Mifflin and Co., Boston. Smith, Theodote L., Types of Adolescent Affection. Pedagogical Seminary, June, 1904, vol. II, pp. 178-203.

[Footnote 1: Pedagogical Seminary, June 1901, vol. 8, pp. 163-205]

[Footnote 2: Being a Boy.]

[Footnote 3: Story of a Bad Boy.]

[Footnote 4: A Boy's Town.]

[Footnote 5: Court of Boyville.]

[Footnote 6: The Spoilt Child, by Peary Chandmitter. Translated by G. D. Oswell. Thacker, Spink and Co., Calcutta, 1893.]

[Footnote 7: The Golden Age]

[Footnote 8: Frau Spyri.]

[Footnote 9: The One I Knew the Best of All.]

[Footnote 10: The Study of the Boyhood of Great Men. Pedagogical Seminary, October, 1894, vol. 3, pp. 134-156.]

[Footnote 11: The Vanishing Character of Adolescent Experiences. Northwestern Monthly, June, 1898, vol. 8, p. 644.]

[Footnote 12: The Count of Boyville, by William Allen White. New York, 1899, p. 358.]

[Footnote 13: The Study of Adolescence. Pedagogical Seminary, June, 1891, vol. 1, pp. 174-195.]

[Footnote 14: Lancaster: The Psychology and Pedagogy of Adolescence. Pedagogical Seminary, July, 1897, vol. 5, p. 106.]

[Footnote 15: Standards of Efficiency in School and in Life. Pedagogical Seminary, March, 1903, vol. 10, pp. 3-22.]

[Footnote 16: See also Vittorio da Feltre and other Humanist Educators, by W. H. Woodward. Cambridge University Press, 1897.]

[Footnote 17: See The Private Life of Galileo; from his Correspondence and that of his Eldest Daughter. Anon, Macmillan, London, 1870.]

[Footnote 18: See Sir David Brewster's Life of Newton. Harper, New York, 1874.]

[Footnote 19: Louis Agassiz, His Life and Work, by C. F. Holder. G. P. Putnam's Sons, New York, 1893.]

[Footnote 20: Life and Letters of Thomas H. Huxley, by his son Leonard Huxley. D. Appleton and Co., New York, 1901.]

[Footnote 21: See also Sully: A Girl's Religion. Longman's Magazine, May, 1890, pp. 89-99.]

[Footnote 22: Sheldon (Institutional Activities of American Children; American Journal of Psychology, July, 1898, vol. 9, p. 434) describes a faintly analogous case of a girl of eleven, who organised the worship of Pallas Athena on two flat rocks, in a deep ravine by a stream where a young sycamore grew from an old stump, as did Pallas from the head of her father Zeus. There was a court consisting of king, queen and subjects, and priests who officiated at sacrifices. The king and queen wore goldenrod upon their heads and waded in streams attended by their subjects; gathered flowers for Athena; caught crayfish which were duly smashed upon her altar. "Sometimes there was a special celebration, when, in addition to the slaughtered crayfish and beautiful flower decorations, and pickles stolen from the dinner-table, there would be an elaborate ceremony," which because of its uncanny acts was intensely disliked by the people at hand.]

[Footnote 23: The One I Know The Best of All. A Memory of the Mind of a Child. By Frances Hodgson Burnett. Scribner's Sons, New York, 1893]

[Footnote 24: The Beth Book, by Sarah Grand. D. Appleton and Co., New York, 1897.]

[Footnote 25: Autobiography of a Child. Hannah Lynch, W. Blackwood and Sons, London, 1899, p. 255.]

[Footnote 26: The Story of My Life. By Helen Keller. Doubleday, Page and Co., New York, 1903, p. 39.]

[Footnote 27: Journal of a Young Artist. Cassell and Co., New York, 1889, p. 434.]

[Footnote 28: The Story of Mary MacLane. By herself. Herbert S. Stone and Co., Chicago, 1902, p. 322.]

[Footnote 29: Fate. Translated from the Italian by A.M. Von Blomberg. Copeland and Day, Boston, 1898.]

[Footnote 30: Confessions of an Opium Eater. Part I. Introductory Narrative. (Cambridge Classics) 1896.]

[Footnote 31: Longmans, Green and Co. London, 1891, 2nd ed.]

[Footnote 32: The Hearts of Men. Macmillan, London, 1891, p. 324.]

[Footnote 33: An Autobiography. Edited by H.M. Trollope. 2 vols. London, 1883.]

[Footnote 34: See his Memoirs. London, 1885.]

[Footnote 35: See Autobiography of Mark Rutherford (pseudonym for W.H. White), edited by Reuben Shapcott. 2 vols. London, 1881.]

[Footnote 36: The rest of the two volumes is devoted to his further life as a dissenting minister, who later became something of a literary man; relating how he was slowly driven to leave his little church, how he outgrew and broke with the girl to whom he was engaged, whom he marvelously met and married when both were well on in years, and how strangely he was influenced by the free-thinker Mardon and his remarkable daughter. All in all it is a rare study of emancipation.]

[Footnote 37: London, 1896, vol. 1.]

[Footnote 38: Macmillan, 1902.]

[Footnote 39: Life of Sir J.F. Stephen. By his brother, Leslie Stephen, London, 1895.]

[Footnote 40: See the very impressive account of Dicken's characterization of childhood and youth, and of his great but hitherto inadequately recognized interest and influence as an educator. Dickens as an Educator. James L. Hughes. D. Appleton and Co., New York, 1901, p. 319.]

[Footnote 41: John Inglesant: A Romance. 6th ed. Macmillan, 1886.]

[Footnote 42: The Autobiography of a Journalist. 2 vols. Houghton, Mifflin and Co., Boston, 1901.]

[Footnote 43: A. Bronson Alcott, His Life and Philosophy. By F. B. Sanborn and W. T. Harris. Roberts Bros., Boston, 1893.]

[Footnote 44: Horace Bushnell, Preacher and Theologian. By Theodore F. Munger. Houghton, Mifflin and Co., Boston, 1899.]

[Footnote 45: By C.W. Chesnutt. (Beacon Biographies.) Small, Maynard and Co., Boston, 1899.]

[Footnote 46: The Making of an American. Macmillan, 1901.]

[Footnote 47: Sonny. By Ruth McEnery Stuart. The Century Co., New York, 1896.]

[Footnote 48: The Story of My Life. Works, vol. 8 new edition. Houghton, Mifflin and Co., Boston, 1894.]

[Footnote 49: The Story of My Life. Translated by M. J. Safford. D. Appleton and Co., New York 1893.]

[Footnote 50: Gesammelte Werke. Vierter Band. Wilhelm Hertz, Berlin, 1897.]

[Footnote 51: My Autobiography, p. 106. Chas. Scribner's Sons, New York, 1901.]

[Footnote 52: Wagner and His Works. By Henry T. Finck. Chas. Scribner's Sons, New York, 1893.]

[Footnote 53: Les Confessions. Oeuvres Complètes, vols. 8 and 9. Hachette et Cie., Paris, 1903.]

[Footnote 54: Translated from the French by C.F. Smith. C.C. Birchard and Co., Boston, 1901.]

* * * * *

CHAPTER IX - THE GROWTH OF SOCIAL IDEALS

Change from childish to adult friends — Influence of favorite teachers — What children wish or plan to do or be — Property and the money sense — Social judgments — The only child — First social organizations — Student life — Associations for youth, controlled by adults.

In a few aspects we are already able to trace the normal psychic outgrowing of the home of childhood as its interests irradiate into an ever enlarging environment. Almost the only duty of small children is habitual and prompt obedience. Our very presence enforces one general law — that of keeping our good-will and avoiding our displeasure. They respect all we smile at or even notice, and grow to it like the plant toward the light. Their early lies are often saying what they think will please. At bottom, the most restless child admires and loves those who save him from too great fluctuations by coercion, provided the means be rightly chosen and the ascendency extend over heart and mind. But the time comes when parents are often shocked at the lack of respect suddenly shown by the child. They have ceased to be the highest ideals. The period of habituating morality and making it habitual is ceasing; and the passion to realize freedom, to act on personal experience, and to keep a private conscience is in order. To act occasionally with independence from the highest possible ideal motives develops the impulse and the joy of pure obligation, and thus brings some new and original force into the world and makes habitual guidance by the highest and best, or by inner as opposed to outer constraint, the practical rule of life. To bring the richest streams of thought to bear in interpreting the ethical instincts, so that the youth shall cease to live in a moral interregnum, is the real goal of self-knowledge. This is true education of the will and prepares the way for love of overcoming obstacles of difficulty, perhaps even of conflict. This impulse is often the secret of obstinacy.[1] And yet, "at no time in life will a human being respond So heartily if treated by older and wiser people as if he were an equal or even a superior. The attempt to treat a child at adolescence as you would treat an inferior is instantly fatal to good discipline."[2] Parents still think of their offspring as mere children, and tighten the rein when they should loosen it. Many young people feel that they have the best of homes and yet that they will go crazy if they must remain in them. If the training of earlier years has been good, guidance by command may now safely give way to that by ideals, which are sure to be heroic. The one unpardonable thing for the adolescent is dullness, stupidity, lack of life, interest, and enthusiasm in school or teachers, and, perhaps above all, too great stringency. Least of all, at this stage, can the curriculum school be an ossuary. The child must now be taken into the family councils and find the parents interested in all that interests him. Where this is not done, we have the conditions for the interesting cases of so many youth, who now begin to suspect that father, mother, or both, are not their true parents. Not only is there interest in rapidly widening associations with coevals, but a new lust to push on and up to maturity. One marked trait now is to seek friends and companions older than themselves, or next to this, to seek those younger. This is marked contrast with previous years, when they seek associates of their own age. Possibly the merciless teasing instinct, which culminates at about the same time, may have some influence, but certain it is that now interest is transpolarized up and down the age scale. One reason is the new hunger for information, not only concerning reproduction, but a vast variety of other matters, so that there is often an attitude of silent begging for knowledge. In answer to Lancaster's[3] questions on this subject, some sought older associates because they could learn more from them, found them better or more steadfast friends, craved sympathy and found most of it from older and perhaps married people. Some were more interested in their parents' conversation with other adults than with themselves, and were particularly entertained by the chance of hearing things they had no business to. There is often a feeling that adults do not realize this new need of friendship with them and show want of sympathy almost brutal.

Stableton,[4] who has made interesting notes on individual boys entering the adolescent period, emphasizes the importance of sympathy, appreciation, and respect in dealing with this age. They must now be talked to as equals, and in this way their habits of industry and even their dangerous love affairs run be controlled. He says, "There is no more important question before the teaching fraternity today than how to deal justly and successfully with boys at this time of life. This is the age when they drop out of school" in far too large numbers, and he thinks that the small percentage of male graduates from our high schools is due to "the inability of the average grammar grade or high-school teacher to deal rightly with boys in this critical period of their school life." Most teachers "know all their bad points, but fail to discover their good ones." The fine disciplinarian, the mechanical movement of whose school is so admirable and who does not realize the new need of liberty or how loose-jointed, mentally and physically, all are at this age, should be supplanted by one who can look into the heart and by a glance make the boy feel that he or she is his friend. "The weakest work in our schools is the handling of boys entering the adolescent period of life, and there is no greater blessing that can come to a boy at this age, when he does not understand himself, than a good strong teacher that understands him, has faith in him, and will day by day lead him till he can walk alone."

Small[5] found the teacher a focus of imitation whence many influences, both physical and mental, irradiated to the pupils. Every accent, gesture, automatism, like and dislike is caught consciously and unconsciously. Every intellectual interest in the teacher permeates the class—liars, if trusted, became honest; those treated as ladies and gentlemen act so; those told by favorite teachers of the good things they are capable of feel a strong impulsion to do them; some older children are almost transformed by being made companions to teachers, by having their good traits recognized, and by frank apologies by the teacher when in error.

An interesting and unsuspected illustration of the growth of independence with adolescence was found in 2,411 papers from the second to eighth grades on the characteristics of the best teacher as seen by children. [6] In the second and third grades, all, and in the fourth, ninety-five per cent specified help in studies. This falls off rapidly in the sixth, seventh, and eighth grades to thirty-nine per cent, while at the same time the quality of patience in the upper grades rises from a mention by two to twenty-two per cent.

Sanford Bell[7] collated the answers of 543 males and 488 females as to who of all their past teachers did them most good, and wherein; whom they loved and disliked most, and why. His most striking result is presented in which shows that fourteen in girls and sixteen in boys is the age in which most good was felt to have been done, and that curves culminating at twelve for both sexes but not falling rapidly until fifteen or sixteen represent the period when the strongest and most indelible dislikes were felt. What seems to be most appreciated in teachers is the giving of purpose, arousing of ideals, kindling of ambition to be something or do something and so giving an object in life, encouragement to overcome circumstances, and, in general, inspiring self-confidence and giving direction. Next came personal sympathy and interest, kindness, confidence, a little praise, being understood; and next, special help in lessons, or timely and kindly advice, while stability and poise of character, purity, the absence of hypocrisy, independence, personal beauty, athleticism and vigor are prominent. It is singular that those of each sex have been most helped by their own sex and that this prominence is far greatest in men. Four-fifths of the men and nearly one-half of the women, however, got most help from men. Male teachers, especially near adolescence, seem most helpful for both sexes.

The qualities that inspire most dislike are malevolence, sarcasm, unjust punishment, suspicion, severity, sternness, absence of laughing and smiling, indifference, threats and broken vows, excessive scolding and "roasting," and fondness for inflicting blows. The teacher who does not smile is far more liable to excite animosity. Most boys dislike men most, and girls' dislikes are about divided. The stories of school cruelties and indignities are painful. Often inveterate grudges are established by little causes, and it is singular how permanent and indelible strong dislike, are for the majority of children. In many cases, aversions engendered before ten have lasted with little diminution till maturity, and there is a sad record of children who have lost a term, a year, or dropped school altogether because of ill treatment or partiality.

Nearly two thousand children were asked what they would do in a specific case of conflict between teacher and parents. It was found that, while for young children parental authority was preferred, a marked decline began about eleven and was most rapid after fourteen in girls and fifteen in boys, and that there was a nearly corresponding increase in the number of pubescents who preferred the teacher's authority. The reasons for their choice were also analyzed, and it was found that whereas for the young, unconditioned authority was generally satisfactory, with pubesecents, abstract authority came into marked predominance, "until when the children have reached the age of sixteen almost seventy-five per cent of their reasons belong to this class, and the children show themselves able to extend the idea of authority without violence to their sense of justice."

On a basis of 1,400 papers answering the question whom, of anyone ever heard or read of, they would like to resemble, Barnes[8] found that girls' ideals were far more often found in the immediate circle of their acquaintance than boys, and that those within that circle were more often in their own family, but that the tendency to go outside their personal knowledge and choose historical and public characters was greatly augmented at puberty, when also the heroes of philanthropy showed marked gain in prominence. Boys rarely chose women as their ideals; but in America, half the girls at eight and two-thirds at eighteen chose male characters. The range of important women ideals among the girls was surprisingly small. Barnes fears that if from the choice of relative as ideals, the expansion to remote or world heroes is too fast, it may "lead to disintegration of character and reckless living." "If, on the other hand, it is expanded too slowly we shall have that arrested development which makes good ground in which to grow stupidity, brutality, and drunkenness—the first fruits of a sluggish and self-contained mind." "No one can consider the regularity with which local ideals die out and are replaced by world ideals without feeling that he is in the presence of law-abiding forces," and this emphasizes the fact that the teacher or parent does not work in a world governed by caprice.

The compositions written by thousands of children in New York on what they wanted to do when they were grown up were collated by Dr. Thurber.[9] The replies were serious, and showed that poor children looked forward willingly to severe labor and the increased earnestness of adolescent years, and the better answers to the question *why* were noteworthy. All anticipated giving up the elastic joyousness of childhood and felt the need of patience. Up to ten, there was an increase in the number of those who had two or more desires. This number declined rapidly at eleven, rose as rapidly at twelve, and slowly fell later. Preferences for a teacher's life exceeded in girls up to nine, fell rapidly at eleven, increased slightly the next year, and declined thereafter. The ideal of becoming a dressmaker and milliner increased till ten, fell at eleven, rose rapidly to a maximum at thirteen, when it eclipsed teaching, and then fell permanently again. The professions of clerk and stenographer showed a marked rise from eleven and a half. The number of boys who chose the father's occupation attained its maximum at nine and its minimum at twelve, with a slight rise to fourteen, when the survey ended. The ideal of tradesman culminated at eight, with a second rise at thirteen. The reason "to earn money" reached its high maximum of fifty per cent at twelve, and fell very rapidly. The reason "because I like it" culminated at ten and fell steadily thereafter. The motive that influenced the choice of a profession and which was altruistic toward parents or for their benefit culminated at twelve and a half, and then declined. The desire for character increased somewhat throughout, but rapidly after twelve, and the impulse to do good to the world, which had risen slowly from nine, mounted sharply after thirteen. Thus, "at eleven all the ideas and tendencies are increasing toward a maximum. At twelve we find the altruistic desires for the welfare of parents, the reason 'to earn money'; at thirteen the desire on the part of the girls to be dressmakers, also to be clerks and stenographers. At fourteen culminates the desire for a business career in bank or office among the boys, the consciousness of life's uncertainties which appeared first at twelve, the desire for character, and the hope of doing the world good."

'What would you like to be in an imaginary new city?" was a question answered by 1,234 written papers.[10] One hundred and fourteen different occupations were given; that of teacher led with the girls at every age except thirteen and fourteen, when dressmaker and milliner took precedence. The motive of making money led among the boys at every age except fourteen and sixteen, when occupations chosen because they were liked led. The greatest number of those who chose the parent's occupation was found at thirteen, but from that age it steadily declined and independent choice came into prominence. The maximum of girls who chose parental vocations was at fourteen. Motives of philanthropy reached nearly their highest point in girls and boys at thirteen.

Jegi[11] obtained letters addressed to real or imaginary friends from 3,000 German children in Milwaukee, asking what they desired to do when they grew up, and why, and tabulated returns from 200 boys and 200 girls for each age from eight its fourteen inclusive. He also found a steadily decreasing influence of relatives to thirteen; in early adolescence, the personal motive of choosing an occupation because it was liked increased, while from twelve in boys and thirteen in girls the consideration of finding easy vocations grew rapidly strong.

L. W. Cline[12] studied by the census method returns from 2,594 children, who were asked what they wished to be and do. He found that in naming both ideals and occupations girls were more conservative than boys, but more likely to give a reason for their choice. In this respect country children resembled boys more than city children. Country boys were prone to inattention, were more independent and able to care for themselves, suggesting that the home life of the country child is more effective in shaping ideals and character than that of the city child. Industrial occupations are preferred by the younger children, the professional and technical pursuits increasing with age. Judgments of rights and justice with the young are more prone to issue from emotional rather than from intellectual processes. Country children seem more altruistic than those in the city, and while girls are more sympathetic than boys, they are also more easily prejudiced. Many of these returns bear unmistakable marks that in some homes and schools moralization has been excessive and has produced a sentimental type of morality and often a feverish desire to express ethical views instead of trusting to suggestion. Children are very prone to have one code of ideals for themselves and another for others. Boys, too, are more original than girls, and country children more than city children.

Friedrich[13] asked German school children what person they chose as their pattern. The result showed differences of age, sex, and creed. First of all came characters in history, which seemed to show that this study for children of the sixth and seventh grades was essentially ethical or a training of mood and disposition (*Gesinnungsunterricht*), and this writer suggests reform in this respect. He seems to think that the chief purpose of history for this age should be ethical. Next came the influence of the Bible, although it was plain that this was rather in spite of the catechism and the method of memoriter work. Here, too, the immediate environment at this age furnished few ideals (four and one-fifth per cent), for children seem to have keener eyes for the faults than for the virtues of those near them. Religion, therefore, should chiefly be directed to the emotions and not to the understanding. This census also suggested more care that the reading of children should contain good examples in their environment, and also that the matter of instruction should be more fully adapted to the conditions of sex.

Friedrich found as his chief age result that children of the seventh or older class in the German schools laid distinctly greater stress upon characters distinguished by bravery and courage than did the children of the sixth grade, while the latter more frequently selected characters illustrating piety and holiness. The author divided his characters into thirty-five classes, illustrating qualities, and found that national activity led, with piety a close second; that then came in order those illustrating firmness of faith, bravery, modesty, and chastity; then pity and sympathy, industry, goodness, patience, etc.

Taylor, Young, Hamilton, Chambers, and others, have also collected interesting data on what children and young people hope to be, do, whom they would like to be, or resemble, etc. Only a few at adolescence feel themselves so good or happy that they are content to be themselves. Most show more or less discontent at their lot. From six to eleven or twelve, the number who find their ideals among their acquaintances falls off rapidly, and historical characters rise to a maximum at or before the earliest teens. From eleven or twelve on into the middle teens contemporary ideals increase steadily. London children are more backward in this expansion of ideals than Americans, while girls choose more acquaintance ideals at all ages than do boys. The expansion, these authors also trace largely to the study of history. The George Washington ideal, which leads all the rest by far and is greatly overworked, in contrast with the many heroes of equal rank found in England, pales soon, as imperfections are seen and those now making history loom up. This is the normal age to free from bondage to the immediate present, and this freedom is one measure of education. Bible heroes are chosen as ideals by only a very small percentage, mostly girls, far more characters being from fiction and mythology; where Jesus is chosen, His human is preferred to His divine side. Again, it would seem that teachers would be ideals, especially as many girls intend to teach, but they are generally unpopular as choices. In an ideal system they would be the first step in expansion from home ideals. Military heroes and inventors play leading rôles in the choices of pubescent boys.

Girls at all school ages and increasingly up the grades prefer foreign ideals, to be the wife of a man of title, as aristocracies offer special opportunities for woman to shine, and life near the source of fashion is very attractive, at least up to sixteen. The saddest fact in these studies is that nearly half our American pubescent girls, or nearly three times as many as in England, choose male ideals, or would be men. Girls, too, have from six to fifteen times as many ideals as boys. In this significant fact we realize how modern woman has cut loose from all old moorings and is drifting with no destination and no anchor aboard. While her sex has multiplied in all lower and high school grades, its ideals are still too masculine. Textbooks teach little about women. When a woman's Bible, history, course of study, etc., is proposed, her sex fears it may reduce her to the old servitude. While boys rarely, and then only when very young, choose female ideals, girls' preference for the life of the other sex sometimes reaches sixty and seventy per cent. The divorce between the life preferred and that demanded by the interests of the race is often absolute. Saddest and most unnatural of all is the fact that this state of things increases most rapidly during just those years when ideals of womanhood should be developed and become most dominant, till it seems as if the female character was threatened with disintegration. While statistics are not yet sufficient to be reliable on the subject, there is some indication that woman later slowly reverts toward ideals not only from her own sex but also from the circle of her own acquaintances.

The reasons for the choice of ideals are various and not yet well determined. Civic virtues certainly rise; material and utilitarian considerations do not seem to much, if at all, at adolescence, and in some data decline. Position, fame, honor, and general greatness increase rapidly, but moral qualities rise highest and also fastest just before and near puberty and continue to increase later yet. By these choices both sexes, but girls far most, show increasing admiration of ethical and social qualities. Artistic and intellectual traits also rise quite steadily from ten or eleven onward, but with no such rapidity, and reach no such height as military ability and achievement for boys. Striking in these studies is the rapid increase, especially from eight to fourteen, of the sense of historic time for historic persons. These long since dead are no longer spoken of as now living. Most of these choices are direct expressions of real differences of taste and character.

Property, Kline and France[14] have defined as "anything that the individual may acquire which sustains and prolongs life, favors survival, and gives an advantage over opposing forces." Many animals and even insects store up food both for themselves and for their young. Very early in life children evince signs of ownership. Letourneau[15] says that the notion of private property, which seems to us so natural, dawned late and slowly, and that common ownership was the rule among primitive people. Value is sometimes measured by use and sometimes by the work required to produce it. Before puberty, there is great eagerness to possess things that are of immediate service; but after its dawn, the desire of possession takes another form, and money for its own sake, which is at first rather an abstraction, comes to be respected or regarded as an object of extreme desire, because it is seen to be the embodiment of all values.

The money sense, as it is now often called, is very complex and has not yet been satisfactorily analyzed by psychology. Ribot and others trace its origin to provision which they think animals that hoard food feel. Monroe[16] has tabulated returns from 977 boys and 1,090 girls from six to sixteen in answer to the question as to what they would do with a small monthly allowance. The following table shows the marked increase at the dawn of adolescence of the number who would save it:

Age. Boys. Girls. | Age. Boys. Girls.
7....43 per cent 36 per cent | 12....82 per cent 64 per cent
8....45 " 34 " | 13....88 " 78 "
9....48 " 35 " | 14....85 " 80 "
10....58 " 50 " | 15....83 " 78 "
11....71 " 58 " | 16....85 " 82 "

This tendency to thrift is strongest in boys, and both sexes often show the tendency to moralize, that is so strong in the early teens. Much of our school work in arithmetic is dominated by the money sense; and school savings-banks, at first for the poor, are now extending to children of all classes. This sense tends to prevent pauperism, prodigality, is an immense stimulus to the imagination and develops purpose to pursue a distant object for a long time. To see all things and values in terms of money has, of course, its pedagogic and ethical limitations; but there is a stage when it is a great educational advance, and it, too, is full of phylogenetic suggestions.

Social judgement, cronies, solitude — The two following observations afford a glimpse of the development of moral judgments. From 1,000 boys and 1,000 girls of each age from six to sixteen who answered the question as to what should be done to a girl with a new box of paints who beautified the parlor chairs with them with a wish to please her mother, the following conclusion was drawn.[17] Most of the younger children would whip the girl, but from fourteen on the number declines very rapidly. Few of the young children suggest explaining why it was wrong; while at twelve, 181, and at sixteen, 751 would explain. The motive of the younger children in punishment is revenge; with the older ones that of preventing a repetition of the act comes in; and higher and later comes the purpose of reform. With age comes also a marked distinction between the act and its motive and a sense of the girl's ignorance. Only the older children would suggest extracting a promise not to offend again. Thus with puberty comes a change of viewpoint from judging actions by results to judging by motives, and only the older ones see that wrong can be done if there are no bad consequences. There is also with increased years a great development of the quality of mercy.

One hundred children of each sex and age between six and sixteen asked what they would do with a burglar, the question stating that the penalty was five years in prison.[18] Of the younger children nearly nine-tenths ignored the law and fixed upon some other penalty, but from twelve years there is a steady advance in those who would inflict the legal penalty, while at sixteen, seventy-four per cent would have the criminal punished according to law. Thus "with the dawn of adolescence at the age of twelve or shortly after comes the recognition of a larger life, a life to be lived in common with others, and with this recognition the desire to sustain the social code made for the common welfare," and punishment is no longer regarded as an individual and arbitrary matter.

From another question answered by 1,914 children[19] it was found that with the development of the psychic faculties in youth, there was an increasing appreciation of punishment as preventive; an increasing sense of the value of individuality and of the tendency to demand protection of personal rights; a change from a sense of justice based on feeling and on faith in authority to that based on reason and understanding. Children's attitude toward punishment for weak time sense, tested by 2,536 children from six to sixteen,[20] showed also a marked pubescent increase in the sense of the need of the remedial function of punishment as distinct from the view of it as vindictive, or getting even, common in earlier years. There is also a marked increase in discriminating the kinds and degrees of offenses; in taking account of mitigating circumstances, the inconvenience caused others, the involuntary nature of the offense and the purpose of the culprit. All this continues to increase up to sixteen, where these studies leave the child.

An interesting effect of the social instinct appears in August Mayer's[21] elaborate study made up on fourteen boys in the fifth and sixth grade of a Würzburg school to determine whether they could work better together or alone. The tests were in dictation, mental and written arithmetic, memory, and Ebbinghaus's combination exercises and all were given with every practicable precaution to make the other conditions uniform. The conclusions demonstrate the advantages of collective over individual instruction. Under the former condition, emulation is stronger and work more rapid and better in quality. From this it is inferred that pupils should not be grouped according to ability, for the dull are most stimulated by the presence of the bright, the bad by the good, etc. Thus work at home is prone to deteriorate, and experimental pedagogy shows that the social impulse is on the whole a stronger spur for boys of eleven or twelve than the absence of distraction which solitude brings.

From the answers of 1,068 boys and 1,268 girls from seven to sixteen on the kind of chum they liked best,[22] it appears that with the teens children are more anxious for chums that can keep secrets and dress neatly, and there is an increased number who are liked for qualities that supplement rather than duplicate those of the chooser. "There is an apparent struggle between the real actual self and the ideal self; a pretty strong desire to have a chum that embodies the traits youth most desire but which they are conscious of lacking." The strong like the weak; those full of fun the serious; the timid the bold; the small the large, etc. Only children[23] illustrate differing effects of isolation, while "mashes" and "crushes" and ultra-crony-ism with "selfishness for two" show the results of abnormal restriction of the irradiation of the social instinct which should now occur.[24]

M. H. Small,[25] after pointing out that communal animals are more intelligent than those with solitary habits, and that even to name all the irradiations of the social instinct would be write a history of the human race, studied nearly five hundred cases of eminent men who developed proclivities to solitude. It is interesting to observe in how many of these cases this was developed in adolescence when, with the horror of mediocrity, comes introspection, apathy, irresolution, and subjectivism. The grounds of repulsion from society at this age may be disappointed hunger for praise, wounded vanity, the reaction from over-assertion, or the nursing of some high ideals, as it is slowly realized that in society the individual cannot be absolute. The motives to self-isolation may be because youth feels its lack of physical or moral force to compete with men, or they may be due to the failure of others to concede to the exactions of inordinate egotism and are directly proportional to the impulse to magnify self, or to the remoteness of common social interests from immediate personal desire or need, and inversely as the number and range of interests seen to be common and the clearness with which social relations are realized. While maturity of character needs some solitude, too much dwarfs it, and more or less of the same paralysis of association follows which is described in the nostalgia of arctic journeys, deserts, being lost in the jungle, solitary confinement, and in the interesting stories of feral men.[26] In some of these cases the mind is saved from entire stultification by pets, imaginary companions, tasks, etc. Normally "the tendency to solitude at adolescence indicates not fulness but want"; and a judicious balance between rest and work, pursuit of favorite lines, genuine sympathy, and wise companionship will generally normalize the social relation.

First forms of spontaneous social organizations. — Gulick has studied the propensity of boys from thirteen on to consort in gangs, do "dawsies" and stumps, get into scrapes together, and fight and suffer for one another. The manners and customs of the gang are to build shanties or "hunkies," hunt with sling shots, build fires before huts in the woods, cook their squirrels and other game, play Indian, build tree-platforms, where they smoke or troop about some leader, who may have an old revolver. They find or excavate caves, or perhaps roof them over; the barn is a blockhouse or a battleship. In the early teens boys begin to use frozen snowballs or put pebbles in them, or perhaps have stone-fights between gangs than which no contiguous African tribes could be more hostile. They become toughs and tantalize policemen and peddlers; "lick" every enemy or even stranger found alone on their grounds; often smash windows; begin to use sticks and brass knuckles in their fights; pelt each other with green apples; carry shillalahs, or perhaps air-rifles. The more plucky arrange fights beforehand; rifle unoccupied houses; set ambushes for gangs with which they are at feud; perhaps have secrets and initiations where new boys are triced up by the legs and butted against trees and rocks. When painted for their Indian fights, they may grow so excited as to perhaps rush into the water or into the school-room yelling; mimic the violence of strikes; kindle dangerous bonfires; pelt policemen, and shout vile nicknames.

The spontaneous tendency to develop social and political organizations among boys in pubescent years was well seen in a school near Baltimore in the midst of an eight-hundred-acre farm richly diversified with swamp and forest and abounding with birds, squirrels, rabbits, etc. Soon after the opening of this school[27] the boys gathered nuts in parties. When a tree was reached which others had shaken, an unwritten law soon required those who wished to shake it further first to pile up all nuts under the tree, while those who failed to do so were universally regarded as dishonest and every boy's hand was against them. To pile them involved much labor, so that the second party usually sought fresh trees, and partial shaking practically gave possession of all the fruits on a tree. They took birds' eggs freely, and whenever a bird was found in building, or a squirrel's hole was discovered, the finder tacked his name on the tree and thereby confirmed his ownership, as he did if he placed a box in which a nest was built. The ticket must not blow off, and the right at first lasted only one season. In the rabbit-land every trap that was set preëmpted ground for a fixed number of yards about it. Some grasping boys soon made many traps and set them all over a valuable district, so that the common land fell into a few hands. Traps were left out all winter and simply set the next spring. All these rights finally came into the ownership of two or three boys, who slowly acquired the right and bequeathed their claims to others for a consideration, when they left school. The monopolists often had a large surplus of rabbits which they bartered for "butters," the unit being the ounce of daily allowance. These could be represented by tickets transferred, so that debts were paid with "butters" that had never been seen. An agrarian party arose and demanded a redistribution of land from the monopolists, as Sir Henry Maine shows often happened in the old village community. Legislation and judicial procedure were developed and quarrels settled by arbitration, ordeal, and wager, and punishment by bumping often followed the decision of the boy folk-mote. Scales of prices for commodities in "butters" or in pie-currency were evolved, so that we here have an almost entirely spontaneous but amazingly rapid recapitulation of the social development of the race by these boys.

From a study of 1,166 children's organizations described as a language lesson in school composition, Mr. Sheldon[28] arrives at some interesting results. American children tend strongly to institutional activities, only about thirty per cent of all not having belonged to some such organization. Imitation plays a very important rôle, and girls take far more kindly than boys to societies organized by adults for their benefit. They are also more governed by adult and altruistic motives in forming their organizations, while boys are nearer to primitive man. Before ten comes the period of free spontaneous imitation of every form of adult institution. The child reproduces sympathetically miniature copies of the life around him. On a farm, his play is raking, threshing, building barns, or on the seashore he makes ships and harbors. In general, he plays family, store, church, and chooses officers simply because adults do. The feeling of caste, almost absent in the young, culminates about ten and declines thereafter. From ten to fourteen, however, associations assume a new character; boys especially cease to imitate adult organizations and tend to form social units characteristic of lower stages of human evolution — pirates, robbers, soldiers, lodges, and other savage reversionary combinations, where the strongest and boldest is the leader. They build huts, wear feathers and tomahawks as badges, carry knives and toy-pistols, make raids and sell the loot. Cowards alone, together they fear nothing. Their imagination is perhaps inflamed by flash literature and "penny-dreadfuls." Such associations often break out in decadent country communities where, with fewer and feebler offspring, lax notions of family discipline prevail and hoodlumism is the direct result of the passing of the rod. These barbaric societies have their place and give vigor; but if unreduced later, as in many unsettled portions of this country, a semisavage state of society results. At twelve the predatory function is normally subordinated, and if it is not it becomes dangerous, because the members are no longer satisfied with mere play, but are stronger and abler to do harm, and the spice of danger and its fascination may issue in crime. Athleticism is now the form into which these wilder instincts can be best transmuted, and where they find harmless and even wholesome vent. Another change early in adolescence is the increased number of social, literary, and even philanthropic organizations and institutions for mutual help—perhaps against vice, for having a good time, or for holding picnics and parties. Altruism now begins to make itself felt as a motive.

Student life and organizations. Student life is perhaps the best of all fields, unworked though it is, for studying the natural history of adolescence. Its modern record is over eight hundred years old and it is marked with the signatures of every age, yet has essential features that do not vary. Cloister and garrison rules have never been enforced even in the hospice, bursa, inn, "house," "hall," or dormitory, and *in loco parentis* [In place of a parent] practises are impossible, especially with large numbers. The very word "school" means leisure, and in a world of toil and moil suggests paradise. Some have urged that *élite* youth, exempt from the struggle to live and left to the freedom of their own inclinations, might serve as a biological and ethnic compass to point out the goal of human destiny. But the spontaneous expressions of this best age and condition of life, with no other occupation than their own development, have shown reversions as often as progress. The rupture of home ties stimulates every wider vicarious expression of the social instinct. Each taste and trait can find congenial companionship in others and thus be stimulated to more intensity and self-consciousness. Very much that has been hitherto repressed in the adolescent soul is now reënforced by association and may become excessive and even aggressive. While many of the race-correlates of childhood are lost, those of this stage are more accessible in savage and sub-savage life. Freedom is the native air and vital breath of student life. The sense of personal liberty is absolutely indispensable for moral maturity; and just as truth can not be found without the possibility of error, so the *posse non peccare* [Ability not to sin] precedes the *non posse peccare*, [Inability to sin] and professors must make abroad application of the rule *abusus non tollit usum* [Abuse does not do away with use]. The student must have much freedom to be lazy, make his own minor morals, vent his disrespect for what he can see no use in, be among strangers to act himself out and form a personality of his own, be baptized with the revolutionary and skeptical spirit, and go to extremes at the age when excesses teach wisdom with amazing rapidity, if he is to become a true knight of the spirit and his own master. Ziegler[29] frankly told German students that about one-tenth of them would be morally lost in this process, but insisted that on the whole more good was done than by restraint; for, he said, "youth is now in the stage of Schiller's bell when it was molten metal."

Of all safeguards I believe a rightly cultivated sense of honor is the most effective at this age. Sadly as the written code of student honor in all lands needs revision, and partial, freaky, and utterly perverted, tainted and cowardly as it often is, it really means what Kant expressed in the sublime precept, "Thou canst because thou oughtest." Fichte said that *Faulheit, Feigheit,* and *Falschheit* [Laziness, cowardice, falsehood] were the three dishonorable things for students. If they would study the history and enter into the spirit of their own fraternities, they would often have keener and broader ideas of honor to which they are happily so sensitive. If professors made it always a point of honor to confess and never to conceal the limitation of their knowledge, would scorn all pretense of it, place credit for originality frankly where it belongs, teach no creeds they do not profoundly believe, or topics in which they are not interested, and withhold nothing from those who want the truth, they could from this vantage with more effect bring students to feel that the laziness that, while outwardly conforming, does no real inner work; that getting a diploma, as a professor lately said, an average student could do, on one hour's study a day; living beyond one's means, and thus imposing a hardship on parents greater than the talent of the son justifies; accepting stipends not needed, especially to the deprivation of those more needy; using dishonest ways of securing rank in studies or positions on teams, or social standing, are, one and all, not only ungentlemanly but cowardly and mean, and the axe would be laid at the root of the tree. Honor should impel students to go nowhere where they conceal their college, their fraternity, or even their name; to keep themselves immaculate from all contact with that class of women which, Ziegler states, brought twenty-five per cent of the students of the University of Berlin in a single year to physicians; to remember that other's sisters are as cherished as their own; to avoid those sins against confiding innocence which cry for vengeance, as did Valentine against Faust, and which strengthen the hate of social classes and make mothers and sisters seem tedious because low ideas of womanhood have been implanted, and which give a taste for mucky authors that reek with suggestiveness; and to avoid the waste of nerve substance and nerve weakness in ways which Ibsen and Tolstoi have described. These things are the darkest blot on the honor of youth.

Associations for youth, devised or guided by adults. Here we enter a very different realm. Forbush[30] undertakes an analysis of many such clubs which he divides according to their purpose into nine chief classes: physical training, handicraft, literary, social, civic and patriotic, science-study, hero-love, ethical, religious. These he classifies as to age of the boys, his purview generally ending at seventeen; discusses and tabulates the most favorable number, the instincts chiefly utilized, the kinds of education gained in each and its percentage of interest, and the qualities developed. He commends Riis's mode of pulling the safety-valve of a rather dangerous boy-gang by becoming an adult honorary member, and interpreting the impulsions of this age in the direction of adventure instead of in that of mischief. He reminds us that nearly one-third of the inhabitants of America are adolescents, that 3,000,000 are boys between twelve and sixteen, "that the do-called heathen people are, whatever their age, all in the adolescent stage of life."

A few American societies of this class we may briefly characterize as follows:

(a) Typical of a large class of local juvenile clubs is the "Captains of Ten," originally for boys of from eight to fourteen, and with a later graduate squad of those over fifteen. The "Ten" are the fingers; and whittling, scrap-book making, mat-weaving, etc., are taught. The motto is, "The hand of the diligent shall bear rule"; its watchword is "Loyalty"; and the prime objects are "to promote a spirit of loyalty to Christ among the boys of the club," and to learn about and work for Christ's kingdom. The members wear a silver badge; have an annual photograph; elect their leaders; vote their money to missions (on which topic they hold meetings); act Bible stories in costume; hear stories and see scientific experiments; enact a Chinese school; write articles for the children's department of religious journals; develop comradeship, and "have a good time."

(b) The Agassiz Association, founded in 1875 "to encourage personal work in natural science," now numbers some 25,000 members, with chapters distributed all over the country, and was said by the late Professor Hyatt to include "the largest number of persons ever bound together for the purpose of mutual help in the study of nature." It furnishes practical courses of study in the sciences; has local chapters in thousands of towns and cities in this and other countries; publishes a monthly organ, The Swiss Cross, to facilitate correspondence and exchange of specimens; has a small endowment, a badge, is incorporated, and is animated by a spirit akin to that of University Extension; and, although not exclusively for young people, is chiefly sustained by them.

(c) The Catholic Total Abstinence Union is a strong, well-organized, and widely extended society, mostly composed of young men. The pledge required of all members explains its object: "I promise with the Divine assistance and in honor of the Sacred Thirst and the Agony of our Saviour, to abstain from all intoxicating drinks and to prevent as much as possible by advice and example the sin of intemperance in others and to discountenance the drinking customs of society." A general convention of the Union has been held annually since 1877.

(d) The Princely Knights of Character Castle is an organization founded in 1895 for boys from twelve to eighteen to "inculcate, disseminate, and practise the principles of heroism—endurance—love, purity, and patriotism." The central incorporated castle grants charters to local castles, directs the ritual and secret work. Its officers are supreme prince, patriarch, scribes, treasurer, director, with captain of the guard, watchman, porter, keeper of the dungeon, musician, herald, and favorite son. The degrees of the secret work are shepherd lad, captive, viceroy, brother, son, prince, knight, and royal knight. There are jewels, regalia, paraphernalia, and initiations. The pledge for the first degree is, "I hereby promise and pledge that I will abstain from the use of intoxicating liquor in any form as a beverage; that I will not use profane or improper language; that I will discourage the use of tobacco in any form; that I will strive to live pure in body and mind; that I will obey all rules and regulations of the order and not reveal any of the secrets in any way." There are benefits, reliefs, passwords, a list of offenses and penalties.

(e) Some 35,000 Bands of Mercy are now organized under the direction of the American Humane Education Society. The object of the organization is to cultivate kindness to animals and sympathy with the poor and oppressed. The prevention of cruelty in driving, cattle transportation, humane methods of killing, care for the sick and abandoned or overworked animals, are the themes of most of its voluminous literature. It has badges, hymnbooks, cards, and certificates of membership, and a motto, "Kindness, Justice, and Mercy to All." Its pledge is, "I will try to be kind to all harmless living creatures, and try to protect them from cruel usage," and is intended to include human as well as dumb creatures. The founder and secretary, with great and commendable energy, has instituted prize contests for speaking on humane subjects in schools, and has printed and circulated prize stories; since the incorporation of the society in 1868, he has been indefatigable in collecting funds, speaking before schools and colleges, and prints fifty to sixty thousand copies of the monthly organ. In addition to its mission of sentiment, and to make it more effective, this organization clearly needs to make more provision for the intellectual element by well-selected or constructed courses, or at least references on the life, history, habits, and instincts of animals, and it also needs more recognition that modern charity is a science as well as a virtue.

(f) The Coming Men of America, although organized only in 1894, now claims to be the greatest chartered secret society for boys and young men in the country. It began two years earlier in a lodge started by a nineteen-year-old boy in Chicago in imitation of such ideas of Masons, Odd-Fellows, etc., as its founder could get from his older brother, and its meetings were first held in a basement. On this basis older heads aided in its development, so that it is a good example of the boy-imitative helped out by parents. The organization is now represented in every State and Territory, and boys travel on its badge. There is an official organ, The Star, a badge, sign, and a secret sign language called "bestography." Its secret ritual work is highly praised. Its membership is limited to white boys under twenty-one.

(g) The first Harry Wadsworth Club was established in 1871 as a result of E.E. Hale's Ten Times One, published the year before. Its motto is, "Look up, and not down; look forward, and not back; look out, and not in; lend a hand," or "Faith, Hope, and Charity." Its organ is the Ten Times One Record; its badge is a silver Maltese cross. Each club may organize as it will, and choose its own name, provided it accepts the above motto. Its watchword is, "In His Name." It distributes charities, conducts a Noonday Rest, outings in the country, and devotes itself to doing good.[31]

[Footnote 1: Tarde: L'Opposition Universelle. Alcan, Paris, 1897, p. 461.]

[Footnote 2: The Adolescent at Home and in School. By E. G. Lancaster. Proceedings of the National Educational Association, 1899, p. 1039.]

[Footnote 3: The Psychology and Pedagogy of Adolescence. Pedagogical Seminary, July, 1897, vol. 5, p. 87.]

[Footnote 4: Study of Boys Entering the Adolescent Period of Life. North Western Monthly, November, 1897, vol. 8, pp. 248-250, and a series thereafter.]

[Footnote 5: The Suggestibility of Children. Pedagogical Seminary, December, 1896, vol. 4, p. 211]

[Footnote 6: Characteristics of the Best Teacher as Recognized by Children. By H.E. Kratz. Pedagogical Seminary, June, 1896, vol. 3, pp. 413-418. See also The High School Teacher from the Pupil's Point of View, by W.F. Book. Pedagogical Seminary, September, 1905, vol. 12, pp. 239-288.]

[Footnote 7: A Study of the Teacher's Influence. Pedagogical Seminary, December, 1900, vol. 7, pp. 492-525.]

[Footnote 8: Children's Ideals. Pedagogical Seminary, April, 1900, vol. 7, pp. 3-12]

[Footnote 9: Transactions of the Illinois Society for Child Study, vol. 2, No. 2, 1896, pp. 41-46.]

[Footnote 10: Children's Ambitions. By H.M. Willard. Barnes's Studies in Education, vol. 2, pp. 243-258. (Privately printed by Earl Barnes, 4401 Sansom Street, Philadelphia.)]

[Footnote 11: Transactions of the Illinois Society for Child Study, October, 1898, vol. 3, No. 3, pp. 131-144.]

[Footnote 12: A Study in Juvenile Ethics. Pedagogical Seminary, June, 1903, vol. 10, pp. 239-266]

[Footnote 13: Die Ideale der Kinder. Zeitschrift für pädagogische Psychologie, Pathologie und Hygiene, Jahrgang 3, Heft 1, pp. 38-64.]

[Footnote 14: The Psychology of Ownership, Pedagogical Seminary, December, 1899, vol. 6, pp. 421-470.]

[Footnote 15: Property: Its Origin and Development. Chas. Scribner's Sons, 1892.]

[Footnote 16: Money-Sense of Children. Will S. Monroe. Pedagogical Seminary, March, 1899, vol. 6, pp. 152-156]

[Footnote 17: A Study of Children's Rights, as Seen by Themselves. By M.E. Schallenberger. Pedagogical Seminary, October, 1894, vol. 3, pp. 87-96.]

[Footnote 18: Children's Attitude toward Law. By E. M Darrah. Barnes's Studies in Education, vol. 1, pp. 213-216. (Stanford University, 1897.) G. E. Stechert and Co., New York.]

[Footnote 19: Class Punishment. By Caroline Frear. Barnes's Studies in Education, vol. 1, pp. 332-337.]

[Footnote 20: Children's Attitude toward Punishment for Weak Time Sense. By D.S. Snedden. Barnes's Studies in Education, vol. 1, pp. 344-351]

[Footnote 21: Ueber Einzel- und Gesamtleistung des Schulkindes. Archiv für die gesamte Psychologie, 1 Band, 2 and 3 Heft, 1903, pp. 276-416]

[Footnote 22: Development of the Social Consciousness of Children. By Will S. Monroe. North-Western Monthly, September, 1898, vol. 9, pp. 31-36.]

[Footnote 23: Bohannon: The Only Child in a Family. Pedagogical Seminary, April, 1898, vol. 5, pp. 475-496.]

[Footnote 24: J. Delitsch: Über Schülerfreundschaften in einer Volksschulklasse, Die Kinderfehler. Fünfter Jahrgang, Mai, 1900, pp. 150-163.]

[Footnote 25: On Some Psychical Relations of Society and Solitude. Pedagogical Seminary, April 1900, vol. 7, pp. 13-69]

[Footnote 26: A. Rauber: Homo Sapiens Ferus. J. Brehse, Leipzig, 1888. See also my Social Aspects of Education; Pedagogical Seminary,

March, 1902, vol. 9, pp. 81-91. Also Kropotkin: Mutual Aid a Factor of Evolution. W. Heinemann, London, 1902.]

[Footnote 27: Rudimentary Society among Boys, by John H. Johnson, McDonogh, Md. McDonogh School, 1983, reprinted from Johns Hopkins University Studies Series 2 (Historical and Political Studies, vol. 2, No. 11).]

[Footnote 28: The Institutional Activities of American Children. American Journal of Psychology, July, 1898, vol. 9, pp. 425-448.]

[Footnote 29: Der deutsche Student am Ende des 19. Jahrhunderts. 6th Ed. Göschen, Leipzig, 1896.]

[Footnote 30: The Social Pedagogy of Boyhood. Pedagogical Seminary, October, 1900, vol. 7, pp. 307-346. See also his The Boy Problem, with an introduction by G. Stanley Hall, The Pilgrim Press, Boston, 1901, p. 194. Also Winifred Buck (Boys' Self-governing Clubs, Macmillan, New York, 1903), who thinks ten million dollars could be used in training club advisers who should have the use of schools and grounds after hours and evenings, conduct excursions, organize games, etc., but avoid all direct teaching and book work generally. This writer thinks such an institution would soon result in a marked increase of public morality and an augmented demand for technical instruction, and that for the advisers themselves the work would be the best training for high positions in politics and reform. Clubs of boys from eight to sixteen or eighteen must not admit age disparities of more than two years.]

[Footnote 31: See Young People's Societies, by L.W. Bacon. D. Appleton and Co., New York, 1900, p. 265. Also, F.G. Cressey: The Church and Young Men. Fleming H. Revell Co., New York, 1903, p. 233.]

* * * * *

CHAPTER X - INTELLECTUAL EDUCATION AND SCHOOL WORK

The general change and plasticity at puberty—English teaching—Causes of its failure: (1) too much time to other languages, (2) subordination of literary content to form, (3) too early stress on eye and hand instead of ear and mouth, (4) excessive use of concrete words—Children's interest in words—Their favorites—Slang—Story telling—Age of reading crazes—What to read—The historic sense—Growth of memory span.

Just as about the only duty of young children is implicit obedience, so the chief mental training from about eight to twelve is arbitrary memorization, drill, habituation, with only limited appeal to the understanding. After the critical transition age of six or seven, when the brain has achieved its adult size and weight, and teething has reduced the chewing surface to its least extent, begins a unique stage of life marked by reduced growth and increased activity and power to resist both disease and fatigue, which suggests what was, in some just post-simian age of our race, its period of maturity. Here belong discipline in writing, reading, spelling, verbal memory, manual training, practise of instrumental technic, proper names, drawing, drill in arithmetic, foreign languages by oral methods, the correct pronunciation of which is far harder if acquired later, etc. The hand is never so near the brain. Most of the content of the mind has entered it through the senses, and the eye-and ear-gates should be open at their widest. Authority should now take precedence of reason. Children comprehend much and very rapidly if we can only refrain from explaining, but this slows down intuition, tends to make casuists and prigs and to enfeeble the ultimate vigor of reason. It is the age of little method and much matter. The good teacher is now a *pedotrieb*, or boy-driver. Boys of this age at now not very affectionate. They take pleasure in obliging and imitating those they like and perhaps in disobliging those they dislike. They have much selfishness and little sentiment. As this period draws to a close and the teens begin, the average normal child will not be bookish but should read and write well, know a few dozen well-chosen books, play several dozen games, be well started in one or more ancient and modern languages—if these must be studied at all, should know something of several industries and how to make many things he is interested in, belong to a few teams and societies, know much about nature in his environment, be able to sing and draw, should have memorized much more than he now does, and be acquainted, at least in story form, with the outlines of many of the best works in literature and the epochs and persons in history. [1] Morally he should have been through many if not most forms of what parents and teachers commonly call "badness," and Professor Yoder even calls "meanness". He should have fought, whipped and been whipped, used language offensive to the prude and to the prim precisian, been in some scrapes, had something to do with bad, if more with good, associates, and been exposed to and already recovering from as many forms of ethical mumps and measles as, by having in mild form now he can be rendered immune to later when they become far more dangerous, because his moral and religious as well as his rational nature is normally rudimentary. He is not depraved, but only in a savage or half-animal stage, although to a large-brained, large-hearted and truly parental soul that does not call what causes it inconvenience by opprobrious names, an altogether lovable and even fascinating stage. The more we know of boyhood the more narrow and often selfish do adult ideals of it appear. Something is amiss with the lad of ten who is very good, studious, industrious, thoughtful, altruistic, quiet, polite, respectful, obedient, gentlemanly, orderly, always in good toilet, docile to reason, who turns away from stories that reek with gore, prefers adult companionship to that of his mates, refuses all low associates, speaks standard English, or is as pious and deeply in love with religious services as the typical maiden teacher or the *à la mode* parent wishes. Such a boy is either under-vitalized and anemic and precocious by nature, a repressed, overtrained, conventionalized manikin, a hypocrite, as some can become under pressure thus early in life, or else a genius of some kind with a little of all these.

But with the teens all this begins to be changed and many of these precepts must be gradually reversed. There is an outburst of growth that needs a large part of the total kinetic energy of the body. There is a new interest in adults, a passion to be treated like one's elders, to make plans for the future, a new sensitiveness to adult praise or blame. The large muscles have their innings and there is a new clumsiness of body and mind. The blood-vessels expand and blushing is increased, new sensations and feelings arise, the imagination blossoms, love of nature is born, music is felt in a new, more inward way, fatigue comes easier and sooner; and if heredity and environment enable the individual to cross this bridge successfully there is sometimes almost a break of continuity, and a new being emerges. The drill methods of the preceding period must be slowly relaxed and new appeals made to freedom and interest. We can no longer coerce a break, but must lead and inspire if we would avoid arrest. Individuality must have a longer tether. Never is the power to appreciate so far ahead of the power to express, and never does understanding so outstrip ability to explain. Overaccuracy is atrophy. Both mental and moral acquisition sink at once too deep to be reproduced by examination without injury both to intellect and will. There is nothing in the environment to which the adolescent nature does not keenly respond. With pedagogic tact we can teach about everything we know that is really worth knowing; but if we amplify and morselize instead of giving great wholes, if we let the hammer that strikes the bell rest too long against it and deaden the sound, and if we wait before each methodic step till the pupil has reproduced all the last, we starve and retard the soul, which is now all insight and receptivity. Plasticity is at its maximum, utterance at its minimum. The inward traffic obstructs the outer currents. Boys especially are often dumb-bound, monophrastic, inarticulate, and semi-aphasic save in their own vigorous and inelegant way. Nature prompts to a modest reticence for which the deflowerers of all ephebic naiveté should have some respect. Deep interests arise which are almost as sacred as is the hour of visitation of the Holy Ghost to the religious teacher. The mind at times grows in leaps and bounds in a way that seems to defy the great enemy, fatigue; and yet when the teacher grows a little tiresome the pupil is tired in a moment. Thus we have the converse danger of forcing knowledge upon unwilling and unripe minds that have no love for it, which is in many ways psychologically akin to a nameless crime that in some parts of the country meets summary vengeance.

(A) The heart of education as well as its phyletic root is the vernacular literature and language. These are the chief instruments of the social as well as of the ethnic and patriotic instinct. The prime place of the former we saw in the last chapter, and we now pass to the latter, the uniqueness of which should first be considered.

The Century, the largest complete dictionary of English, claims to have 250,000 words, as against 55,000 in the old Webster's Unabridged. Worcester's Unabridged of 1860 has 105,000; Murray's, now in L, it is said, will contain 240,000 principal and 140,000 compound words, or 380,000 words in all. The dictionary of the French Academy has 33,000; that of the Royal Spanish Academy, 50,000; the Dutch dictionary of Van Dale, 86,000; the Italian and Portuguese, each about 50,000 literary, or 150,000 encyclopedic words. Of course, words can really be counted hardly more than ideas or impressions, and compounds, dialects, obsolete terms, localisms, and especially technical terms, swell the number indefinitely. A competent philologist[2] says, if given large liberty, he "will undertake to supply 1,000,000 English words for 1,000,000 American dollars." Chamberlain[3] estimates that our language contains more than two score as many words as all those left us from the Latin. Many savage languages contain only a very few thousand, and some but a few hundred, words. Our tongue is essentially Saxon in its vocabulary and its spirit and, from the time when it was despised and vulgar, has followed an expansion policy, swallowing with little modification terms not only from classical antiquity, but from all modern languages—Indian, African, Chinese, Mongolian—according to its needs, its adopted children far outnumbering those of its own blood. It absorbs at its will the slang of the street gamin, the cant of thieves and beggars; is actually creative in the baby talk of mothers and nurses; drops, forgets, and actually invents new words with no pedigree like those of Lear, Carrol, and many others.[4]

In this vast field the mind of the child early begins to take flight. Here his soul finds its native breath and vital air. He may live as a peasant, using, as Max Müller says many do, but a few hundred words during his lifetime; or he may need 8,000, like Milton, 15,000, like Shakespeare, 20,000 or 30,000, like Huxley, who commanded both literary and technical terms; while in understanding, which far outstrips, use, a philologist may master perhaps 100,000 or 200,000 words. The content of a tongue may contain only folk-lore and terms for immediate practical life, or this content may be indefinitely elaborated in a rich literature and science. The former is generally well on in its development before speech itself becomes an abject of study. Greek literature was fully grown when the Sophists, and finally Aristotle, developed the rudiments of grammar, the parts of speech being at first closely related with his ten metaphysical categories. Our modern tongue had the fortune, unknown to those of antiquity, when it was crude and despised, to be patronized and regulated by Latin grammarians, and has had a long experience, both for good and evil, with their conserving and uniformitizing instincts. It has, too, a long history of resistance to this control. Once spelling was a matter of fashion or even individual taste; and as the constraint grew, two pedagogues in the thirteenth century fought a duel for the right spelling of the word, and that maintained by the survivor prevailed. Phonic and economic influences are now again making some headway against orthographic orthodoxy here; so with definitions. In the days of Johnson's dictionary, individuality still had wide range in determining meanings. In pronunciation, too: we may now pronounce the word *tomato* in six ways, all sanctioned by dictionaries. Of our tongue in particular it is true, as Tylor says in general, condensing a longer passage, "take language all in all, it is the product of a rough-and-ready ingenuity and of the great rule of thumb. It is an old barbaric engine, which in its highest development is altered, patched, and tinkered into capability. It is originally and naturally a product of low culture, developed by ages of conscious and unconscious improvement to answer more or less perfectly the requirements of modern civilization."

It is plain, therefore, that no grammar, and least of all that derived from the prim, meager Latin contingent of it, is adequate to legislate for the free spirit of our magnificent tongue. Again, if this is ever done and English ever has a grammar that is to it what Latin grammar is to that language, it will only be when the psychology of speech represented, e.g., in Wundt's Psychologie der Sprache,[5] which is now compiling and organizing the best elements from all grammars, is complete. The reason why English speakers find such difficulty in learning other languages is because ours has so far outgrown them by throwing off not only inflections but many old rules of syntax, that we have had to go backward to an earlier and more obsolescent stage of human development. In 1414, at the Council of Constance, when Emperor Sigismund was rebuked for a wrong gender, he replied, "I am King of the Romans and above grammar." Thomas Jefferson later wrote, "Where strictures of grammar does not weaken expression it should be attended to; but where by a small grammatical negligence the energy of an idea is condensed or a word stands for a sentence, I hold grammatical rigor in contempt." Browning, Whitman, and Kipling deliberately violate grammar and secure thereby unique effects neither asking nor needing excuse.

By general consent both high school and college youth in this country are in an advanced stage of degeneration in the command of this the world's greatest organ of the intellect; and that, despite the fact that the study of English often continues from primary into college grades, that no topic counts for more, and that marked deficiency here often debars from all other courses. Every careful study of the subject for nearly twenty years shows deterioration, and Professor Shurman, of Nebraska, thinks it now worse than at any time for forty years. We are in the case of many Christians described by Dante, who strove by prayers to get nearer to God when in fact with every petition they were departing farther from him. Such a comprehensive fact must have many causes.

I. One of these is the excessive time given to other languages just at the psychological period of greatest linguistic plasticity and capacity for growth. School invention and tradition is so inveterate that it is hard for us to understand that there is little educational value—and perhaps it is deëducational—to learn to tell the time of day or name a spade in several different tongues or to learn to say the Lord's Prayer in many different languages, any one of which the Lord only can understand. The polyglot people that one meets on great international highways of travel are linguists only in the sense that the moke on the variety stage who plays a dozen instruments equally badly is a musician. It is a psychological impossibility to pass through the apprenticeship stage of learning foreign languages at the age when the vernacular is setting without crippling it. The extremes are the youth in ancient Greece studying his own language only and the modern high school boy and girl dabbling in three or perhaps four languages. Latin, which in the eight years preceding 1898 increased one hundred and seventy-four per cent. in American high schools, while the proportion entering college in the country and even in Massachusetts steadily declined, is the chief offender. In the day of its pedagogical glory Latin was the universal tongue of the learned. Sturm's idea was to train boys so that if suddenly transported to ancient Rome or Greece they would be at home there. Language, it was said, was the chief instrument of culture; Latin, the chief language and therefore a better drill in the vernacular than the vernacular itself. Its rules were wholesome swathing bands for the modern languages when in their infancy. Boys must speak only Latin on the playground. They thought, felt, and developed an intellectual life in and with that tongue.[6] But how changed all this is now. Statistical studies show that five hours a week for a year gives command of but a few hundred words, that two years does not double this number, and that command of the language and its resources in the original is almost never attained, but that it is abandoned not only by the increasing percentage that do not go to college but also by the increasing percentage who drop it forever at the college door. Its enormous numerical increase due to high school requirements, the increasing percentage of girl pupils more ready to follow the teacher's advice, in connection with the deteriorating quality of the girls — inevitable with their increasing numbers, the sense that Latin means entering upon a higher education, the special reverence for it by Catholic children, the overcrowded market for Latin teachers whom a recent writer says can be procured by the score at less rates than in almost any other subject, the modern methods of teaching it which work well with less knowledge of it by the teacher than in the case of other school topics, have been attended perhaps inevitably by steady pedagogic decline despite the vaunted new methods; until now the baby Latin in the average high school class is a kind of sanctified relic, a ghost of a ghost, suggesting Swift's Struldbrugs, doomed to physical immortality but shriveling and with increasing horror of all things new. In 1892 the German emperor declared it a shame for a boy to excel in Latin composition, and in the high schools of Sweden and Norway it has been practically abandoned. In the present stage of its educational decadence the power of the dead hand is strongly illustrated by the new installation of the old Roman pronunciation with which our tongue has only remote analogies, which makes havoc with proper names which is unknown and unrecognized in the schools of the European continent, and which makes a pedantic affectation out of more vocalism. I do not know nor care whether the old Romans pronounced thus or not, but if historic fidelity in this sense has pedagogic justification, why still teach a text like the *Viri Romae*, which is not a classic but a modern pedagogue's composition?

I believe profoundly in the Latin both as a university specialty and for all students who even approach mastery, but for the vast numbers who stop in the early stages of proficiency it is disastrous to the vernacular. Compare the evils of translation English, which not even the most competent and laborious teaching can wholly prevent and which careless mechanical instruction directly fosters, with the vigorous fresh productions of a boy or girl writing or speaking of something of vital present interest. The psychology of translation shows that it gives the novice a consciousness of etymologies which rather impedes than helps the free movement of the mind. Jowett said in substance that it is almost impossible to render either of the great dead languages into English without compromise, and this tends to injure the idiomatic mastery of one's own tongue, which can be got only by much hard experience in uttering our own thoughts before trying to shape the dead thoughts of others into our language. We confound the little knowledge of word-histories which Latin gives with the far higher and subtler sentence-sense which makes the soul of one language so different from that of another, and training in which ought not to end until one has become more or less of a stylist and knows how to hew out modes of expressing his own individuality in great language. There is a sense in which Macaulay was not an Englishman at all, but a Ciceronian Latinist who foisted an alien style upon our tongue; and even Addison is a foreigner compared to the virile Kipling. The nature and needs of the adolescent mind demand bread and meat, while Latin rudiments are husks. In his autobiography, Booker Washington says that for ten years after their emancipation, the two chief ambitions of the young negro of the South were to hold office and to study Latin, and he adds that the chief endeavor of his life has been against these tendencies. For the American boy and girl, high school too often means Latin. This gives at first a pleasing sense of exaltation to a higher stage of life, but after from one to three years the great majority who enter the high school drop out limp and discouraged for many reasons, largely, however, because they are not fed. Defective nutrition of the mind also causes a restlessness, which enhances all the influences which make boys and girls leave school.

II. The second cause of this degeneration is the subordination of literature and content to language study. Grammar arises in the old age of language. As once applied to our relatively grammarless tongue it always was more or less of a school-made artifact and an alien yoke, and has become increasingly so as English has grown great and free. Its ghost, in the many textbooks devoted to it, lacks just the quality of logic which made and besouled it. Philology, too, with all its magnificence, is not a product of the nascent stages of speech. In the college, which is its stronghold, it has so inspired professors of English that their ideal is to be critical rather than creative till they prefer the minute reading of a few masterpieces to a wide general knowledge, and a typical university announces that "in every case the examiners will treat mere knowledge of books as less important than the ability to write good English" that will parse and that is spelled, punctuated, capitalized, and paragraphed aright. Good professors of English literature are hard to find, and upon them philologists, who are plentiful, look with a certain condescension. Many academic chairs of English are filled by men whose acquaintance of our literature is very narrow, who wish to be linguistic and not literary, and this is true even in ancient tongues.

At a brilliant examination, a candidate for the doctor's degree who had answered many questions concerning the forms of Lucretius, when asked whether he was a dramatist, historian, poet, or philosopher, did not know, and his professor deemed the question improper. I visited the eleventh recitation in Othello in a high school class of nineteen pupils, not one of whom knew how the story ended, so intent had they been kept on its verbiage. Hence, too, has come the twelve feet of text-books on English on my shelves with many standard works, edited for schools, with more notes than text. Fashion that works from above down the grades and college entrance requirements are in large measure responsible for this, perhaps now the worst case of the prostitution of content to form.

Long exposure to this method of linguistic manicuring tends to make students who try to write ultra-fastidiously, seeking an over-refined elaboration of petty trifles, as if the less the content the greater the triumph of form alone could be. These petty but pretty nothings are like German confectionery, that appeals to the eye but has little for taste and is worse than nothing for the digestion. It is like straining work on an empty stomach. For youth this embroidery of details is the precocious senescence that Nordau has so copiously illustrated as literary decadence. Language is vastly larger than all its content, and the way to teach it is to focus the mind upon story, history, oratory, drama, Bible, for their esthetic, mental, and above all, moral content, as shown in the last chapter. The more unconscious processes that reflect imitatively the linguistic environment and that strike out intuitively oral and written vents for interests so intense that they must be told and shared, are what teach us how to command the resources of our mother tongue. These prescriptions and corrections and consciousness of the manifold ways of error are never so peculiarly liable to hinder rather than to help as in early adolescence, when the soul has a new content and a new sense for it, and so abhors and is so incapable of precision and propriety of diction. To hold up the flights of exuberant youth by forever being on the hunt for errors is, to borrow the language of the gridiron, low tackle, and I would rather be convicted of many errors by such methods than use them. Of course this has its place, but it must always be subordinated to a larger view, as in one of the newly discovered *logia* ascribed to Jesus, who, when he found a man gathering sticks on Sunday, said to him, "If you understand what you are doing, it is well, but if not, thou shalt be damned." The great teacher who, when asked how he obtained such rare results in expression, answered, "By carefully neglecting it and seeking utter absorption in subject-matter," was also a good practical psychologist. This is the inveterate tendency that in other ages has made pedagogic scribes, Talmudists, epigoni, and sophists, who have magnified the letter and lost the spirit. But there are yet other seats of difficulty.

III. It is hard and, in the history of the race, a late change, to receive language through the eye which reads instead of through the ear which hears. Not only is perception measurably quite distinctly slower, but book language is related to oral speech somewhat as an herbarium is to a garden, or a museum of stuffed specimens to a menagerie. The invention of letters is a novelty in the history of the race that spoke for countless ages before it wrote. The winged word of mouth is saturated with color, perhaps hot with feeling, musical with inflection, is the utterance of a living present personality, the consummation of man's gregarious instincts. The book is dead and more or less impersonal, best apprehended in solitude, its matter more intellectualized; it deals in remoter second-hand knowledge so that Plato reproached Aristotle as being a reader, one remove from the first spontaneous source of original impressions and ideas, and the doughty medieval knights scorned reading as a mere clerk's trick, not wishing to muddle their wits with other people's ideas when their own were good enough for them. But although some of the great men in history could not read, and though some of the illiterate were often morally and intellectually above some of the literate, the argument here is that the printed page must not be too suddenly or too early thrust between the child and life. The plea is for moral and objective work, more stories, narratives, and even vivid readings, as is now done statedly in more than a dozen of the public libraries of the country, not so often by teachers as by librarians, all to the end that the ear, the chief receptacle of language, be maintained in its dominance, that the fine sense of sound, rhythm, cadence, pronunciation, and speech-music generally be not atrophied, that the eye which normally ranges freely from far to near be not injured by the confined treadmill and zigzag of the printed page.

Closely connected with this, and perhaps psychologically worse, is the substitution of the pen and the scribbling fingers for the mouth and tongue. Speech is directly to and from the soul. Writing, the deliberation of which fits age better than youth, slows down its impetuosity many fold, and is in every way farther removed from vocal utterance than is the eye from the ear. Never have there been so many pounds of paper, so many pencils, and such excessive scribbling as in the calamopapyrus [Pen-paper] pedagogy of to-day and in this country. Not only has the daily theme spread as infection, but the daily lesson is now extracted through the point of a pencil instead of from the mouth. The tongue rests and the curve of writer's cramp takes a sharp turn upward, as if we were making scribes, reporters, and proof-readers. In some schools, teachers seem to be conducting correspondence classes with their own pupils. It all makes excellent busy work, keeps the pupils quiet and orderly, and allows the school output to be quantified, and some of it gives time for more care in the choice of words. But is it a gain to substitute a letter for a visit, to try to give written precedence over spoken forms? Here again we violate the great law that the child repeats the history of the race, and that, from the larger historic standpoint, writing as a mode of utterance is only the latest fashion.

Of course the pupils must write, and write well, just as they must read, and read much; but that English suffers from insisting upon this double long circuit too early and cultivates it to excess, devitalizes school language and makes it a little unreal, like other affectations of adult ways, so that on escaping from its thraldom the child and youth slump back to the language of the street as never before. This is a false application of the principle of learning to do by doing. The young do not learn to write by writing, but by reading and hearing. To become a good writer one must read, feel, think, experience, until he has something to say that others want to hear. The golden age of French literature, as Gaston Deschamps and Brunetière have lately told us, was that of the salon, when conversation dominated letters, set fashions, and made the charm of French style. Its lowest ebb was when bookishness led and people began to talk as they wrote.

IV. The fourth cause of degeneration of school English is the growing preponderance of concrete words for designating things of sense and physical acts, over the higher element of language that names and deals with concepts, ideas, and non-material things. The object-lesson came in as a reaction against the danger of merely verbal and definition knowledge and word memory. Now it has gone so far that not only things but even languages, vernacular and foreign, are taught by appeals to the eye. More lately, elementary science has introduced another area of pictures and things while industrial education has still further greatly enlarged the material sensori-motor element of training. Geography is taught with artifacts, globes, maps, sand boxes, drawing. Miss Margaret Smith[7] counted two hundred and eighty objects that must be distributed and gathered for forty pupils in a single art lesson. Instruction, moreover, is more and more busied upon parts and details rather than wholes, upon analysis rather than synthesis. Thus in modern pedagogy there is an increased tyranny of things, a growing neglect or exclusion of all that is unseen.

The first result of this is that the modern school child is more and more mentally helpless without objects of sense. Conversation is increasingly concrete, if not of material things and persons present in time and even place. Instead of dealing with thoughts and ideas, speech and writing is close to sense and the words used are names for images and acts. But there is another higher part of language that is not so abjectly tied down to perception, but that lives, moves, and has its being in the field of concepts rather than percepts, which, to use Earle's distinction, is symbolic and not presentative, that describes thinking that is not mere contiguity in space or sequence in time but that is best in the far higher and more mental associations of likeness, that is more remote from activity, that, to use logical terminology, is connotative and not merely denotative, that has extension as well as intension, that requires abstraction and generalization. Without this latter element higher mental development is lacking because this means more than word-painting the material world.

Our school youth today suffer from just this defect. If their psychic operations can be called thought it is of that elementary and half animal kind that consists imagery. Their talk with each other is of things of present and immediate interest. They lack even the elements of imagination, which makes new combinations and is creative, because they are dominated by mental pictures of the sensory. Large views that take them afield away from the persons and things and acts they know do not appeal to them. Attempts to think rigorously are too hard. The teacher feels that all the content of mind must come in through the senses, and that if these are well fed, inferences and generalizations will come of themselves later. Many pupils have never in their lives talked five minutes before others on any subject whatever that can properly be called intellectual. It irks them to occupy themselves with purely mental processes, so enslaved are they by what is near and personal, and thus they are impoverished in the best elements of language. It is as if what are sometimes called the associative fibers, both ends of which are in the brain, were dwarfed in comparison with the afferent and efferent fibers that mediate sense and motion.

That the soul of language as an instrument of thought consists in this non-presentative element, so often lacking, is conclusively shown in the facts of speech diseases. In the slowly progressive aphasias, of late so carefully studied, the words first lost are those of things and acts most familiar to the patient, while the words that persist longest in the wreckage of the speech-centers are generally words that do not designate the things of sense. A tailor loses the power to name his chalk, measure, shears, although he can long talk fluently of what little he may chance to know of God, beauty, truth, virtue, happiness, prosperity, etc. The farmer is unable to name the cattle in his yard or his own occupations, although he can reason as well as ever about politics; can not discuss coin or bills, but can talk of financial policies and securities, or about health and wealth generally. The reason obvious. It is because concrete thinking has two forms, the word and the image, and the latter so tends to take the place of the former that it can be lost to both sense and articulation without great impairment, whereas conceptual thinking lacks imagery and depends upon words alone, and hence these must persist because they have no alternate form which vicariates for them.

In its lower stages, speech is necessarily closely bound up with the concrete world; but its real glory appears in its later stages and its higher forms, because there the soul takes flight in the intellectual world, learns to live amidst its more spiritual realities, to put names to thoughts, which is far higher than to put names to things. It is in this world that the best things in the best books live; and the modern school-bred distaste for them, the low-ranged mental action that hovers near the coastline of matter and can not launch out with zest into the open sea of thoughts, holding communion with the great dead of the past or the great living of the distant present, seems almost like a slow progressive abandonment of the high attribute of speech and the lapse toward infantile or animal picture-thinking. If the school is slowly becoming speechless in this sense, if it is lapsing in all departments toward busy work and losing silence, repose, the power of logical thought, and even that of meditation, which is the muse of originality, this is perhaps the gravest of all these types of decay. If the child has no resources in solitude, can not think without the visual provocation, is losing subjective life, enthusiasm for public, social, ethical questions, is crippled for intellectual pursuits, cares only in a languid way for literary prose and poetry, responds only to sensuous stimuli and events at short range, and is indifferent to all wide relations and moral responsibility, cares only for commercial self-interest, the tactics of field sport, laboratory occupations and things which call be illustrated from a pedagogic museum, then the school is dwarfing, in dawning maturity, the higher powers that belong to this stage of development and is responsible for mental arrest.

In this deplorable condition, if we turn to the child study of speech for help, we find that, although it has been chiefly occupied with infant vocabularies, there are already a very few and confessedly crude and feeble beginnings, but even these shed more light on the lost pathway than all other sources combined. The child once set in their midst again corrects the wise men. We will first briefly recapitulate these and then state and apply their lessons.

Miss Williams[8] found that out of 253 young ladies only 133 did not have favorite sounds, *[long "a"]* and *a* leading among the vowels, and *l*, *r* and *m* among the constants. Eighty-five had favorite words often lugged in, 329 being good. Two hundred and twenty-one, as children, had favorite proper names in geography, and also for boys, but especially for girls. The order of a few of the latter is as follows: Helen, 36; Bessie, 25; Violet and Lilly, 20; Elsie and Beatrice, 18; Dorothy and Alice, 17; Ethel, 15; Myrtle, 14; Mabel, Marguerite, Pearl, and Rose, 13; May, 12; Margaret, Daisy, and Grace, 11; Ruth and Florence, 9; Gladys, 8; Maud, Nellie, and Gertrude, 7; Blanche and Mary, 6; Eveline and Pansy, 5; Belle, Beulah, Constance, Eleanor, Elizabeth, Eve, Laura, Lulu, Pauline, Virginia, and Vivian, 4 each, etc.

Of ten words found interesting to adolescents, murmur was the favorite, most enjoying its sound. Lullaby, supreme, annannamannannaharoumlemay, immemorial, lillibulero, burbled, and incarnadine were liked by most, while zigzag and shigsback were not liked. This writer says that adolescence is marked by some increased love of words for motor activity and in interest in words as things in themselves, but shows a still greater rise of interest in new words and pronunciations; "above all, there is a tremendous rise in interest in words as instruments of thought." The flood of new experiences, feelings, and views finds the old vocabulary inadequate, hence "the dumb, bound feeling of which most adolescents at one time or another complain and also I suspect from this study in the case of girls, we have an explanation of the rise of interest in slang." "The second idea suggested by our study is the tremendous importance of hearing in the affective side of language."

Conradi[9] found that of 273 returns concerning children's pleasure in knowing or using new words, ninety-two per cent were affirmative, eight per cent negative, and fifty per cent gave words especially "liked." Some were partial to big words, some for those with z in them. Some found most pleasure in saying them to themselves and some in using them with others. In all there were nearly three hundred such words, very few of which were artificial. As to words pretty or queer in form or sound, his list was nearly as large, but the greater part of the words were different. Sixty per cent of all had had periods of spontaneously trying to select their vocabulary by making lists, studying the dictionary, etc. The age of those who did so would seem to average not far from early puberty, but the data are too meager for conclusion. A few started to go through the dictionary, some wished to astonish their companions or used large new words to themselves or their dolls. Seventy percent had had a passion for affecting foreign words when English would do as well. Conradi says "the age varies from twelve to eighteen, most being fourteen to sixteen." Some indulge this tendency in letters, and would like to do so in conversation, but fear ridicule. Fifty-six per cent reported cases of superfine elegance or affected primness or precision in the use of words. Some had spells of effort in this direction, some belabor compositions to get a style that suits them, some memorise fine passages to this end, or modulate their voices to aid them, affect elegance with a chosen mate by agreement soliloquize before a glass with poses. According to his curve this tendency culminates at fourteen.

Adjectivism, adverbism, and nounism, or marked disposition to multiply one or more of the above classes of words, and in the above order, also occur near the early teens. Adjectives are often used as adverbial prefixes to other adjectives, and here favorite words are marked. Nearly half of Conradi's reports show it, but the list of words so used is small.

Miss Williams presents on interesting curve of slang confessed as being both attractive and used by 226 out of 251. From this it appears that early adolescence is the curve of greatest pleasure in its use, fourteen being the culminating year. There is very little until eleven, when the curve for girls rises very rapidly, to fall nearly us rapidly from fifteen to seventeen. Ninety-three out of 104 who used it did so despite criticism.

Conradi, who collected and prints a long list of current slang words and phrases, found that of 295 young boys and girls not one failed to confess their use, and eighty-five per cent of all gave the age at which they thought it most common. On this basis he constructs the above curve, comparing with this the curve of a craze for reading and for precision in speech.

The reasons given are, in order of frequency, that slang was more emphatic, more exact, more concise, convenient, sounded pretty, relieved formality, was natural, manly, appropriate, etc. Only a very few thought it was vulgar, limited the vocabulary, led to or was a substitute for swearing, destroyed exactness, etc. This writer attempts a provisional classification of slang expressions under the suggestive heads of rebukes to pride, boasting and loquacity, hypocrisy, quaint and emphatic negatives, exaggerations, exclamations, mild oaths, attending to one's own business and not meddling or interfering, names for money, absurdity, neurotic effects of surprise or shock, honesty and lying, getting confused, fine appearance and dress, words for intoxication which Partridge has collected,[10]for anger collated by Chamberlain,[11] crudeness or innocent naïveté, love and sentimentality, etc. Slang is also rich in describing conflicts of all kinds, praising courage, censuring inquisitiveness, and as a school of moral discipline, but he finds, however, a very large number unclassified; and while he maintains throughout a distinction between that used by boys and by girls, sex differences are not very marked. The great majority of terms are mentioned but once, and a few under nearly all of the above heads have great numerical precedence. A somewhat striking fact is the manifold variations of a pet typical form. Twenty-three shock expletives, e.g., are, "Wouldn't that — — you?" the blank being filled by jar, choke, cook, rattle, scorch, get, start, etc., or instead of *you* adjectives are devised. Feeling is so intense and massive, and psychic processes are so rapid, forcible, and undeveloped that the pithiness of some of those expressions makes them brilliant and creative works of genius, and after securing an apprenticeship are sure of adoption. Their very lawlessness helps to keep speech from rigidity and desiccation, and they hit off nearly every essential phrase of adolescent life and experience.

Conventional modes of speech do not satisfy the adolescent, so that he is often either reticent or slangy. Walt Whitman[12] says that slang is "an attempt of common humanity to escape from bald literalism and to express itself illimitably, which in the highest walks produces poets and poems"; and again, "Daring as it is to say so, in the growth of language it is certain that the retrospect of slang from the start would be the recalling from their nebulous condition of all that is poetical in the stores of human utterance." Lowell[13] says, "There is death in the dictionary, and where language is too strictly limited by convention, the ground for expression to grow in is limited also, and we get a potted literature, Chinese dwarfs instead of healthy trees." Lounsbury asserts that "slang is an effort on the part of the users of language to say something more vividly, strongly, concisely than the language existing permits it to be said. It is the source from which the decaying energies of speech are constantly refreshed." Conradi adds in substance that weak or vicious slang is too feeble to survive, and what is vital enough to live fills a need. The final authority is the people, and it is better to teach youth to discriminate between good and bad slang rather than to forbid it entirely. Emerson calls it language in the making, its crude, vital, material. It is often an effective school of moral description, a palliative for profanity, and expresses the natural craving for superlatives. Faults are hit off and condemned with the curtness sententiousness of proverbs devised by youth to sanctify itself and correct its own faults. The pedagogue objects that it violates good form and established usage, but why should the habits of hundreds of years ago control when they can not satisfy the needs of youth, which requires a *lingua franca* of its own, often called "slanguage"? Most high school and college youth of both sexes have two distinct styles, that of the classroom which is as unnatural as the etiquette of a royal drawing-room reception or a formal call, and the other, that of their own breezy, free, natural life. Often these two have no relation to or effect upon each other, and often the latter is at times put by with good resolves to speak as purely and therefore as self-consciously as they knew, with petty fines for every slang expression. But very few, and these generally husky boys, boldly try to assert their own rude but vigorous vernacular in the field of school requirements.

These simple studies in this vast field demonstrate little or nothing, but they suggest very much. Slang commonly expresses a moral judgment and falls into ethical categories. It usually concerns ideas, sentiment, and will, has a psychic content, and is never, like the language of the school, a mere picture of objects of sense or a description of acts. To restate it in correct English would be a course in ethics, courtesy, taste, logical predication and opposition, honesty, self-possession, modesty, and just the ideal and non-presentative mental content that youth most needs, and which the sensuous presentation methods of teaching have neglected. Those who see in speech nothing but form condemn it because it is vulgar. Youth has been left to meet these high needs alone, and the prevalence of these crude forms is an indictment of the delinquency of pedagogues in not teaching their pupils to develop and use their intellect properly. Their pith and meatiness are a standing illustration of the need of condensation for intellectual objects that later growth analyzes. These expressions also illustrate the law that the higher and larger the spiritual content, the grosser must be the illustration in which it is first couched. Further studies now in progress will, I believe, make this still clearer.

Again, we see in the above, outcrops of the strong pubescent instinct to enlarge the vocabulary in two ways. One is to affect foreign equivalents. This at first suggests an appetency for another language like the dog-Latin gibberish of children. It is one of the motives that prompts many to study Latin or French, but it has little depth, for it turns out, on closer study, to be only the affectation of superiority and the love of mystifying others. The other is a very different impulse to widen the vernacular. To pause to learn several foreign equivalents of things of sense may be anti-educational if it limits the expansion of thought in our own tongue. The two are, in fact, often inversely related to each other. In giving a foreign synonym when the mind seeks a new native word, the pedagogue does not deal fairly. In this irradiation into the mother tongue, sometimes experience with the sentiment or feeling, act, fact, or object precedes, and then a name for it is demanded, or conversely the sound, size, oddness or jingle of the word is first attractive and the meaning comes later. The latter needs the recognition and utilization which the former already has. Lists of favorite words should be wrought out for spelling and writing and their meanings illustrated, for these have often the charm of novelty as on the frontier of knowledge and enlarge the mental horizon like new discoveries. We must not starve this voracious new appetite "for words as instruments of thought."

Interest in story-telling rises till twelve or thirteen, and thereafter falls off perhaps rather suddenly, partly because youth is now more interested in receiving than in giving. As in the drawing curve we saw a characteristic age when the child loses pleasure in creating as its power of appreciating pictures rapidly arises, so now, as the reading curve rises, auditory receptivity makes way for the visual method shown in the rise of the reading curve with augmented zest for book-method of acquisition. Darkness or twilight enhances the story interest in children, for it eliminates the distraction of sense and encourages the imagination to unfold its pinions, but the youthful fancy is less bat-like and can take its boldest flights in broad daylight. A camp-fire, or an open hearth with tales of animals, ghosts, heroism, and adventure can teach virtue, and vocabulary, style, and substance in their native unity.

The pubescent reading passion is partly the cause and partly an effect of the new zest in and docility to the adult world and also of the fact that the receptive are now and here so immeasurably in advance of the creative powers. Now the individual transcends his own experience and learns to profit by that of others. There is now evolved a penumbral region in the soul more or less beyond the reach of all school methods, a world of glimpses and hints, and the work here is that of the prospector and not of the careful miner. It is the age of skipping and sampling, of pressing the keys lightly. What is acquired is not examinable but only suggestive. Perhaps nothing read now fails to leave its mark. It can not be orally reproduced at call, but on emergency it is at hand for use. As Augustine said of God, so the child might say of most of his mental content in these psychic areas, "If you ask me, I do not know; but if you do not ask me, I know very well"—a case analogous to the typical girl who exclaimed to her teacher, "I can do and understand this perfectly if you only won't explain it." That is why examinations in English, if not impossible, as Goldwin Smith and Oxford hold, are very liable to be harmful, and recitations and critical notes an impertinence, and always in danger of causing arrest of this exquisite romantic function in which literature comes in the closest relation to life, keeping the heart warm, reënforcing all its good motives, preforming choices, and universalizing its sympathies.

R. W. Bullock[14] classified and tabulated 2,000 returns from schoolchildren from the third to the twelfth grade, both inclusive, concerning their reading. From this it appeared that the average boy of the third grade "read 4.9 books in six months; that the average falls to 3.6 in the fourth and fifth grades and rises to a maximum of 6.5 at the seventh grade, then drops quite regularly to 3 in the twelfth grade at the end of the high school course." The independent tabulation of returns from other cities showed little variation. "Grade for grade, the girls read more than the boys, and as a rule they reach their maximum a year sooner, and from a general maximum of 5.9 books there is a drop to 3.3 at the end of the course." The age of reading may be postponed or accelerated perhaps nearly a year by the absence or presence of library facilities. Tabulating the short stories read per week, it was found that these averaged 2.1 in the third grade, rose to 7.7 per week in the seventh grade, and in the twelfth had fallen to 2.3, showing the same general tendency.

The percentage tables for boys' preference for eight classes of stories are here only suggestive. "War stories seem popular with third grade boys, and that liking seems well marked through the sixth, seventh, and eighth grades. Stories of adventure are popular all through the heroic period, reaching their maximum in the eighth and ninth grades. The liking for biography and travel or exploration grows gradually to a climax in the ninth grade, and remains well up through the course. The tender sentiment has little charm for the average grade boy, and only in the high school course does he acknowledge any considerable use of love stories. In the sixth grade he is fond of detective stories, but they lose their charm for him as he grows older." For girls, "stories of adventure are popular in the sixth grade, and stories of travel are always enjoyed. The girl likes biography, but in the high school, true to her sex, she prefers stories of great women rather than great men, but because she can not get them reads those of men. Pity it is that the biographies of so few of the world's many great women are written. The taste for love stories increases steadily to the end of the high school course. Beyond that we have no record." Thus "the maximum amount of reading is done in every instance between the sixth and eighth grades, the average being in the seventh grade at an average age of fourteen and one-tenth years." Seventy-five per cent of all discuss their reading with some one, and the writer urges that "when ninety-five per cent of the boys prefer adventure or seventy-five per cent of the girls prefer love stories, that is what they are going to read," and the duty of the teacher or librarian is to see that they have both in the highest, purest form.

Henderson[15] found that of 2,989 children from nine to fifteen, least books were read at the age of nine and most at the age of fifteen, and that there was "a gradual rise in amount throughout, the only break being in the case of girls at the age of fourteen and the boys at the age of twelve." For fiction the high-water mark was reached for both sexes at eleven, and the subsequent fall is far less rapid for girls than for boys. "At the age of thirteen the record for travel and adventure stands highest in the case of the boys, phenomenally so. There is a gradual rise in history with age, and a corresponding decline in fiction."

Kirkpatrick[16] classified returns from 5,000 children from the fourth to the ninth grade in answer to questions that concerned their reading. He found a sudden increase in the sixth grade, when children are about twelve, when there is often a veritable, reading craze. Dolls are abandoned and "plays, games, and companionship of others are less attractive, and the reading hunger in many children becomes insatiable and is often quite indiscriminate." It seems to "most frequently begin at about twelve years of age and continue at least three or four years," after which increased home duties, social responsibilities, and school requirements reduce it and make it more discriminating in quality. "The fact that boys read about twice, as much history and travel as girls and only about two-thirds as much poetry and stories shows beyond question that the emotional and intellectual wants of boys and girls are essentially different before sexual maturity."

Miss Vostrovsky[17] found that among 1,269 children there was a great increase of taste for reading as shown by the number of books taken from the library, which began with a sharp rise at eleven and increased steadily to nineteen, when her survey ended; that boys read most till seventeen, and then girls took the precedence. The taste for juvenile stories was declining and that for fiction and general literature was rapidly increased. At about the sixteenth year a change took place in both sexes, "showing then the beginning of a greater interest in works of a more general character." Girls read more fiction than boys at every age, but the interest in it begins to be very decided at adolescence. With girls it appears to come a little earlier and with greater suddenness, while the juvenile story maintains a strong hold upon boys even after the fifteenth year. The curve of decline in juvenile stories is much more pronounced in both sexes than the rise of fiction. Through the teens there is a great increase in the definiteness of answers to the questions why books were chosen. Instead of being read because they were "good" or "nice," they were read because recommended, and later because of some special interest. Girls relied on recommendations more than boys. The latter were more guided by reason the former by sentiment. Nearly three times as many boys in the early teens chose books because they were exciting or venturesome. Even the stories which girls called exciting were tame compared with those chosen by boys. Girls chose books more than four times as often because of children in them, and more often because they ware funny. Boys care very little for style, but must have incidents and heroes. The author says "the special interest that girls have in fiction begins about the age of adolescence. After the sixteenth year the extreme delight in stories fades," or school demands become more imperative and uniform. Girls prefer domestic stories and those with characters like themselves and scenes like those with which they are familiar. "No boy confesses to a purely girl's story, while girls frankly do to an interesting story about boys. Women writers seem to appeal more to girls, men writers to boys. Hence, the authors named by each sex are almost entirely different. In fiction more standard works, were drawn by boys than by girls." "When left to develop according to chance, the tendency is often toward a selection of books which unfit one for every-day living, either by presenting, on the one hand, too many scenes of delicious excitement or, on the other, by narrowing the vision to the wider possibilities of life."

Out of 523 full answers, Lancaster found that 453 "had what might be called a craze for reading at some time in the adolescent period," and thinks parents little realize the intensity of the desire to read or how this nascent period is the golden age to cultivate taste and inoculate against reading what is bad. The curve rises rapidly from eleven to fourteen, culminates at fifteen, after which it falls rapidly. Some become omnivorous readers of everything in their way; others are profoundly, and perhaps for life, impressed with some single book; others have now crazes for history, now for novels, now for dramas or for poetry; some devour encyclopedias; some imagine themselves destined to be great novelists and compose long romances; some can give the dates with accuracy of the different periods of the development of their tastes from the fairy tales of early childhood to the travels and adventures of boyhood and then to romance, poetry, history, etc; and some give the order of their development of taste for the great poets.

The careful statistics of Dr. Reyer show that the greatest greed of reading is from the age of fifteen to twenty-two, and is on the average greatest of all at twenty. He finds that ten per cent of the young people of this age do forty per cent of all the reading. Before twenty the curve ascends very rapidly, to fall afterward yet more rapidly as the need of bread-winning becomes imperative. After thirty-five the great public reads but little. Every youth should have his or her own library, which, however small, should be select. To seal some knowledge of their content with the delightful sense of ownership helps to preserve the apparatus of culture, keeps green early memories, or makes one of the best tangible mementoes of parental care and love. For the young especially, the only ark of safety in the dark and rapidly rising flood of printer's ink is to turn resolutely away from the ideal of quantity to that of quality. While literature rescues youth from individual limitations and enables it to act and think more as spectators of all time, and sharers of all existence, the passion for reading may be excessive, and books which from the silent alcoves of our nearly 5,500 American libraries rule the world more now than ever before, may cause the young to neglect the oracles within, weaken them by too wide reading, make conversation bookish, and overwhelm spontaneity and originality with a superfetation of alien ideas.

The reading passion may rage with great intensity when the soul takes its first long flight in the world of books, and ninety per cent of all Conradi's cases showed it. Of these, thirty-two per cent read to have the feelings stirred and the desire of knowledge was a far less frequent motive. Some read to pass idle time, others to appear learned or to acquire a style or a vocabulary. Romance led. Some specialized, and with some the appetite was omnivorous. Some preferred books about or addressed to children, some fairy tales, and some sought only those for adults. The night is often invaded and some become "perfectly wild" over exciting adventures or the dangers and hardships of true lovers, laughing and crying as the story turns from grave to gay, and a few read several books a week. Some were forbidden and read by stealth alone, or with books hidden in their desks or under school books. Some few live thus for years in an atmosphere highly charged with romance, and burn out their fires wickedly early with a sudden and extreme expansiveness that makes life about them uninteresting and unreal, and that reacts to commonplace later. Conradi prints some two or three hundred favorite books and authors of early and of later adolescence. The natural reading of early youth is not classic nor blighted by compulsion or uniformity for all. This age seeks to express originality and personality in individual choices and tastes.

Suggestive and briefly descriptive lists of best books and authors by authorities in different fields on which some time is spent in making selection, talks about books, pooling knowledge of them, with no course of reading even advised and much less prescribed, is the best guidance for developing the habit of rapid cursory reading. Others before professor De Long, of Colorado, have held that the power of reading a page in moment, as a mathematician sums up a column of figures and as the artist Doré was able to read a book by turning the leaves, can be attained by training and practise. School pressure should not suppress this instinct of omnivorous reading, which at this age sometimes prompts the resolve to read encyclopedias, and even libraries, or to sample everything to be found in books at home. Along with, but never suppressing, it there should be some stated reading, but this should lay down only kinds of reading like the four emphasized in the last chapter or offer a goodly number of large alternative groups of books and authors, like the five of the Leland Stanford University, and permit wide liberty of choice to both teacher and pupil. Few triumphs of the uniformitarians, who sacrifice individual needs to mechanical convenience in dealing with youth in masses, have been so sad as marking off and standardizing a definite quantum of requirements here. Instead of irrigating a wide field, the well-springs of literary interest are forced to cut a deep canyon and leave wide desert plains of ignorance on either side. Besides imitation, which reads what others do, is the desire to read something no one else does, and this is a palladium of individuality. Bad as is the principle, the selections are worse, including the saccharinity ineffable of Tennyson's Princess (a strange expression of the progressive feminization of the high school and yet satirizing the scholastic aspiration of girls) which the virile boy abhors, books about books which are two removes from life, and ponderous Latinity authors which for the Saxon boy suggest David fighting in Saul's armor, and which warp and pervert the nascent sentence-sense on a foreign model. Worst of all, the prime moral purpose of youthful reading is ignored in choices based on form and style; and a growing profusion of notes that distract from content to language, the study of which belongs in the college if not in the university, develops the tendencies of criticism before the higher powers of sympathetic appreciation have done their work.[18]

(B) Other new mental powers and aptitudes are as yet too little studied. Very slight are the observations so far made, of children's historic, which is so clearly akin to literary, interest and capacity. With regard to this and several other subjects in the curriculum we are in the state of Watts when he gazed at the tea-kettle and began to dream of the steam-engine; we are just recognizing a new power and method destined to reconstruct and increase the efficiency of education, but only after a long and toilsome period of limited successes.

Mrs. Barnes[19], told a story without date, place, name, or moral and compared the questions which 1,250 children would like to have answered about it. She found that the interest of girls in persons, or the number who asked the question "who," culminated at twelve, when it coincided with that of boys, but that the latter continued to rise to fifteen. The interest to know "place where" events occurred culminated at eleven with girls, and at fifteen, and at a far higher point, with boys. The questions "how" and "why," calling for the method and reason, both culminated at twelve for girls and fifteen for boys, but were more infrequent and showed less age differences than the preceding question. Interest in the results of the action was most pronounced of all, culminating at twelve in girls and fifteen in boys. Details and time excited far less interest, the former jointly culminating for both sexes at eleven. Interest in the truth of the narrative was extremely slight, although it became manifest at fifteen, and was growing at sixteen. The number of inferences drawn steadily increased with age, although the increase was very slight after thirteen. Both legitimate and critical inferences increased after eleven, while imaginative inferences at that age had nearly reached their maximum. Interest in names was very strong throughout, as in primitive people. Boys were more curious concerning "who," "where," and "how"; girls as to "why." In general, the historic curiosity of boys was greater than that of girls, and culminated later. The inferences drawn from an imagined finding of a log-house, boat, and arrows on a lonely island indicate that the power of inference, both legitimate and imaginative, develops strongly at twelve and thirteen, after which doubt and the critical faculties are apparent; which coincides with Mr. M.A. Tucker's conclusion, that doubt develops at thirteen and that personal inference diminishes about that age.

The children were given two accounts of the fall of Fort Sumter, one in the terms of a school history and the other a despatch of equal length from Major Anderson, and asked which was best, should be kept, and why. Choice of the narrative steadily declined after eleven and that of the despatch increased, the former reaching its lowest, the latter its highest, point at fifteen, indicating a preference for the first-hand record. The number of those whose choice was affected by style showed no great change, from twelve to fifteen, but rose very rapidly for the nest two years. Those who chose the despatch because it was true, signed, etc., increased rapidly in girls and boys throughout the teens, and the preference for the telegram as a more direct source increased very rapidly from thirteen to seventeen.

Other studies of this kind led Mrs. Barnes to conclude that children remembered items by groups; that whole groups were often omitted; that those containing most action were best remembered; that what is remembered is remembered with great accuracy; that generalities are often made more specific; that the number of details a child carries away from a connected narrative is not much above fifty, so that their numbers should be limited; and from it all was inferred the necessity of accuracy, of massing details about central characters or incidents, letting action dominate, omitting all that is aside from the main line of the story, of bringing out cause and effect and dramatizing where possible.

Miss Patterson[20] collated the answers of 2,237 children to the question "What does 1895 mean?" The blanks "Don't know" decreased very rapidly from six to eight, and thereafter maintained a slight but constant percentage. Those who expanded the phase a little without intelligence were most numerous from eight to ten, while the proportion who gave a correct explanation rose quite steadily for both sexes and culminated at fourteen for girls and fifteen for boys. The latter only indicates the pupils of real historic knowledge. The writer concludes that "the sense of historical time is altogether lacking with children of seven, and may be described as slight up to the age of twelve." History, it is thought, should be introduced early with no difference between boys and girls, but "up to the age of twelve or thirteen it should be presented in a series of striking biographies and events, appearing if possible in contemporary ballads and chronicles, and illustrated by maps, chronological charts, and as richly as possible by pictures of contemporary objects, buildings, and people." At the age of fourteen or fifteen, another sort of work should appear. Original sources should still be used, but they should illustrate not "the picture of human society moving before us in a long panorama, but should give us the opportunity to study the organization, thought, feeling, of a time as seen in its concrete embodiments, its documents, monuments, men, and books." The statesmen, thinkers, poets, should now exceed explorers and fighters; reflection and interpretation, discrimination of the true from the false, comparison, etc., are now first in order; while later yet, perhaps in college, should come severer methods and special monographic study.

Studies of mentality, so well advanced for infants and so well begun for lower grades, are still very meager for adolescent stages so far as they bear on growth in the power to deal with arithmetic, drawing and pictures, puzzles, superstitions, collections, attention, reason, etc. Enough has been done to show that with authority to collect data on plans and by methods that can now be operated and with aid which should now be appropriated by school boards and teachers' associations, incalculable pedagogic economy could be secured and the scientific and professional character of teaching every topic in upper grammar and high school and even in the early college grades be greatly enhanced. To enter upon this laborious task in every branch of study is perhaps our chief present need and duty to our youth in school, although individual studies like that of Binet[21] belong elsewhere.

(C) The studies of memory up the grades show characteristic adolescent changes, and some of these results are directly usable in school.

Bolton[22] tested the power of 1,500 children to remember and write dictated digits, and found, of course, increasing accuracy with the older pupils. He also found that the memory span increased with age rather than with the growth of intelligence as determined by grade. The pupils depended largely upon visualisation, and this and concentrated attention suggested that growth of memory did not necessarily accompany intellectual advancement. Girls generally surpassed boys, and as with clicks too rapid to be counted, it was found that when the pupils reached the limits of their span, the number of digits was overestimated. The power of concentrated and prolonged attention was tested. The probability of error for the larger number of digits, 7 and 8, decreased in a marked way with the development of pubescence, at least up to fourteen years, with the suggestion of a slight rise again at fifteen.

In comprehensive tests of the ability of Chicago children to remember figures seen, heard, or repeated by them, it was found that, from seven to nine, auditory were slightly better remembered than visual impressions. From that age the latter steadily increased over the former. After thirteen, auditory memory increased but little, and was already about ten per cent behind visual, which continued to increase at least till seventeen. Audiovisual memory was better than either alone, and the span of even this was improved when articulatory memory was added. When the tests were made upon pupils of the same age in different grades it was found in Chicago that memory power, whether tested by sight, hearing, or articulation, was best in those pupils whose school standing was highest, and least where standing was lowest.

When a series of digits was immediately repeated orally and a record made, it was found[23] that while from the age of eight to twelve the memory span increased only eight points, from fourteen to eighteen it increased thirteen points. The number of correct reproductions of numbers of seven places increased during the teens, although this class of children remain about one digit behind normal children of corresponding age. In general, though not without exceptions, it was found that intelligence grew with memory span, although the former is far more inferior to that of the normal child than the latter, and also that weakness of this kind of memory is not an especially prominent factor of weak-mindedness.

Shaw[24] tested memory in 700 school children by dividing a story of 324 words into 152 phrases, having it read and immediately reproduced by them, and selecting alternate grades from the third grammar to the end of the high school, with a few college students. The maximum power of this kind of memory was attained by boys in the high school period. Girls remembered forty-three per cent in the seventh grade, and in the high school forty-seven per cent. The increase by two-year periods was most rapid between the third and fifth grades. Four terms were remembered on the average by at least ninety per cent of the pupils, 41 by fifty per cent, and 130 by ten per cent. The story written out in the terms remembered by each percentage from ten to ninety affords a most interesting picture of the growth of memory, and even its errors of omission, insertion, substitution and displacement. "The growth of memory is more rapid in the case of girls than boys, and the figures suggest a coincidence with the general law, that the rapid development incident to puberty occurs earlier in girls than in boys."

In a careful study of children's memory, Kemsies[25] concludes that the quality of memory improves with age more rapidly than the quantity.

W.G. Monroe tested 275 boys and 293 girls, well distributed, from seven to seventeen years of age, and found a marked rise for both visual and auditory memory at fifteen for both sexes. For both sexes, also, auditory memory was best at sixteen and visual at fifteen.

When accuracy in remembering the length of tone was used as a test, it was found there was loss from six to seven and gain from seven to eight for both sexes. From eight to nine girls lost rapidly for one and gained rapidly for the following year, while boys were nearly stationary till ten, after which both sexes gained to their maximum at fourteen years of age and declined for the two subsequent years, both gaining power from sixteen to seventeen, but neither attaining the accuracy they had at fourteen.[26]

Netschajeff[27] subjected 637 school children, well distributed between the ages of nine and eighteen, to the following tests. Twelve very distinct objects were shown them, each for two seconds, which must them be immediately written down. Twelve very distinct noises were made out of sight; numbers of two figures each were read; three-syllable words, which were names of familiar objects, objects that suggested noises, words designating touch, temperature, and muscle sensations, words describing states of feeling, and names of abstract ideas also were given them. The above eight series of twelve each were all reproduced in writing, and showed that each kind of memory here tested increased with age, with some slight tendency to decline at or just before puberty, then to rise and to slightly decline after the sixteenth or seventeenth year. Memory for objects showed the greatest amount of increase during the year studied, and works for feeling next, although at all ages the latter was considerably below the former. Boys showed stronger memory for real impressions, and girls excelled for numbers and words. The difference of these two kinds of memory was less with girls than with boys. The greatest difference between the sexes lay between eleven and fourteen years. This seems, at eighteen or nineteen, to be slightly increased. "This is especially great at the age of puberty." Children from nine to eleven have but slight power of reproducing emotions, but this increases in the next few years very rapidly, as does that of the abstract words. Girls from nine to eleven deal better with words than with objects; boys slightly excel with objects. Illusions in reproducing words which mistake sense, sound, and rhythm, which is not infrequent with younger children, decline with age especially at puberty.

Up to this period girls are most subject to these illusions, and afterward boys. The preceding tables, in which the ordinates represent the number of correct reproductions and the abscissas the age, are interesting.

Lobsien made tests similar to those of Netschajeff,[28] with modifications for greater accuracy, upon 238 boys and 224 girls from nine to fourteen and a half years of age. The preceding tables show the development of the various kinds of memory for boys and girls:

BOYS.

Age. Objects Noises Number Visual Acoustic Touch Feeling Sounds
Concepts Concepts Concepts Concepts

13-14-1/2 92.56 71.89 80.67 73.00 74.78 75.33 75.44 40.56 12-13 76.45 57.38 72.33 69.67 64.89 73.67 58.67 37.87 11-12 89.78 57.19 70.22 59.67 63.00 73.33 55.33 19.99 10-11 87.12 55.33 49.33 55.11 48.44 57.11 38.33 12.44 9-10 64.00 53.33 49.09 46.58 43.78 43.67 27.22 7.22

Normal 82.2 59.02 64.8 60.6 59.4 64.2 31.2 24.0 value.

GIRLS.

13-14-1/2 99.56 82.67 87.22 96.67 71.44 82.00 70.22 41.33 12-13 92.89 75.56 74.89 77.22 63.11 74.67 67.33 34.89 11-12 94.00 56.00 73.56 72.78 72.11 70.89 73.33 28.22 10-11 75.78 46.22 62.44 56.22 54.78 58.78 43.22 10.44 9-10 89.33 46.22 50.44 54.22 38.22 51.11 32.89 6.89

Normal 91.4 62.2 71.8 71.0 60.2 67.2 59.4 23.8 value.

The table for boys shows in the fourteenth year a marked increase of memory for objects, noises, and feelings, especially as compared with the marked relative decline the preceding year, when there was a decided increase in visual concepts and senseless sounds. The twelfth year shows the greatest increase in number memory, acoustic impressions, touch, and feeling. The tenth and eleventh years show marked increase of memory for objects and their names. Thus the increase in the strength of memory is by no means the same year by year, but progress focuses on some forms and others are neglected. Hence each type of memory shows an almost regular increase and decrease in relative strength.

The table for girls shown marked increase of all memory forms about the twelfth year. This relative increase is exceeded only in the fourteenth year for visual concepts. The thirteenth year shows the greatest increase for sounds and a remarkable regression for objects in passing from the lowest to the next grade above.

In the accuracy of reproducing the order of impressions, girls much exceeded boys at all ages. For seen object, their accuracy was twice that of boys, the boys excelling in order only in number. In general, ability to reproduce a series of impressions increases and decreases with the power to reproduce in any order, but by no means in direct proportion to it. The effect of the last member in a series by a purely mechanical reproduction is best in boys. The range and energy of reproduction is far higher than ordered sequence. In general girls slightly exceed boys in recalling numbers, touch concepts, and sounds, and largely exceed in recalling feeling concepts, real things and visual concept.

Colegrove[29] tabulated returns from the early memories of 1,658 correspondents with 6,069 memories, from which he reached the conclusions, represented in the following curves, for the earliest three memories of white males and females.

In the cuts on the following page, the heavy line represents the first memory, the broken the second, and the dotted the third. Age at the time of reporting is represented in distance to the right, and the age of the person at the time of the occurrence remembered is represented by the distance upward. "There is a rise in all the curves at adolescence. This shows that, from the age of twelve to fifteen, boys do not recall so early memories as they do both before and after this period." This Colegrove ascribes to the fact that the present seems so large and rich. At any rate, "the earliest memories of boys at the age of fourteen average almost four years." His curves for girls show that the age of all the first three memories which they are able to recall is higher at fourteen than at any period before or after; that at seven and eight the average age of the first things recalled is nearly a year earlier than it is at fourteen. This means that at puberty there is a marked and characteristic obliteration of infantile memories which lapse to oblivion with augmented absorption in the present.

It was found that males have the greatest number of memories for protracted or repeated occurrences, for people, and clothing, topographical and logical matters; that females have better memories for novel occurrences or single impressions. Already at ten and eleven motor memories begin to decrease for females and increase for males. At fourteen and fifteen, motor memories nearly culminate for males, but still further decline for females. The former show a marked decrease in memory for relatives and playmates and an increase for other persons. Sickness and accidents to self are remembered less by males and better by females, as are memories of fears. At eighteen and nineteen there is a marked and continued increase in the visual memories of each sex and the auditory memory of females. Memory for the activity of others increases for both, but far more strongly for males.

Colegrove concludes from his data that "the period of adolescence is one of great psychical awaking. A wide range of memories is found at this time. From the fourteenth year with girls and the fifteenth with boys the auditory memories are strongly developed. At the dawn of adolescence the motor memory of voice nearly culminates, and they have fewer memories of sickness and accidents to self. During this time the memory of other persons and the activity of others is emphasized in case of both boys and girls. In general, at this period the special sensory memories are numerous, and it is the golden age for motor memories. Now, too, the memories of high ideals, self-sacrifice, and self-forgetfulness are cherished. Wider interests than self and immediate friends become the objects of reflection and recollection."

After twenty there is marked change in the memory content. The male acquires more and the female less visual and auditory memories. The memories of the female are more logical, and topographical features increase. Memories of sickness and accidents to self decrease with the males and increase with the females, while in the case of both there is relative decline in the memories of sickness and accident to others. From all this it would appear that different memories culminate at different periods, and bear immediate relation to the whole mental life of the period. While perhaps some of the finer analyses of Colegrove may invite further confirmation, his main results given above are not only suggestive, but rendered very plausible by his evidence.

Statistics based upon replies to the question as to whether pleasant or unpleasant experiences were best remembered, show that the former increase at eleven, rise rapidly at fourteen, and culminate at eighteen for males, and that the curve of painful memories follows the same course, although for both there is a drop at fifteen. For females, the pleasant memories increase rapidly from eleven to thirteen, decline a little at fourteen, rise again at sixteen, and culminate at seventeen, and the painful memories follow nearly the same course, only with a slight drop at fifteen. Thus, up to twenty-two for males, there is a marked preponderance of pleasant over painful memories, although the two rise and fall together. After thirty, unpleasant memories are but little recalled. For the Indians and negroes in this census, unpleasant memories play a far more and often preponderating rôle suggesting persecution and sad experiences. Different elements of the total content of memory come to prominence at different ages. He also found that the best remembered years of life are sixteen to seventeen for males and fifteen for females, and that in general the adolescent period has more to do than any other in forming and furnishing the memory plexus, while the seventh and eighth year are most poorly remembered.

It is also known that many false memories insert themselves into the texture of remembered experiences. One dreams a friend is dead and thinks she is till she is met one day in the street; or dreams of a fire and inquires about it in the morning; dreams of a present and searches the house for it next day; delays breakfast for a friend, who arrived the night before in a dream, to come down to breakfast; a child hunts for a bushel of pennies dreamed of, etc. These phantoms falsify our memory most often, according to Dr. Colegrove, between sixteen and nineteen.

Mnemonic devices prompt children to change rings to keep appointments, tie knots in the handkerchief, put shoes on the dressing-table, hide garments, associate faces with hoods, names with acts, things, or qualities they suggest; visualize, connect figures, letters with colors, etc. From a scrutiny of the original material, which I was kindly allowed to make, this appears to rise rapidly at puberty.

[Footnote 1: See my Ideal School as Based on Child Study. Proceedings of the National Educational Association, 1901, pp. 470-490.]

[Footnote 2: Charles P.G. Scott: The Number of Words in the English and Other Languages. Princeton University Bulletin, May, 1902, vol. 13, pp. 106-111.]

[Footnote 3: The Teaching of English. Pedagogical Seminary, June, 1902, vol. 9, pp. 161-168.]

[Footnote 4: See my Some Aspects of the Early Sense of Self. American Journal of Psychology, April, 1898, vol. 9, pp. 351-395.]

[Footnote 5: Sprachgeschichte und Sprachpsychologie, mit Rucksicht auf B. Delbrück's "Grundfragen der Sprachforschung." Leipzig, W. Engelmann, 1901]

[Footnote 6: Latin in the High School. By Edward Conradi. Pedagogical Seminary, March, 1905, vol. 12, pp. 1-26.]

[Footnote 7: The Psychological and Pedagogical Aspect of Language. Pedagogical Seminary, December, 1903, vol. 10, pp. 438-458.]

[Footnote 8: Children's Interest in Words. Pedagogical Seminary, September, 1902, vol. 9, pp. 274-295.]

[Footnote 9: Children's Interests in Words, Slang, Stories, etc. Pedagogical Seminary, October, 1903, vol. 10, pp. 359-404.]

[Footnote 10: American Journal of Psychology, April, 1900, vol. 11, p. 345 *et seq.*]

[Footnote 11: American Journal of Psychology, January, 1895, vol. 6, pp. 585-592. See also vol. 10, p. 517 *et seq.*]

[Footnote 12: North American Review, November, 1885, vol. 141, pp. 431-435.]

[Footnote 13: Introduction to the Biglow Papers, series ii.]

[Footnote 14: Some Observations on Children's Reading. Proceedings of the National Educational Association, 1897, pp. 1015-1021.]

[Footnote 15: Report on Child Reading. New York Report of State Superintendent, 1897, vol. 2, p. 979.]

[Footnote 16: Children's reading. North-Western Monthly, December, 1898, vol. 9, pp. 188-191, and January, 1899, vol. 9, pp. 229-233.]

[Footnote 17: A study of Children's Reading Tastes. Pedagogical Seminary, December, 1899, vol. 6, pp. 523-535.]

[Footnote 18: Perhaps the best and most notable school reader is Das Deutsche Lesebuch, begun nearly fifty years ago by Hopf and Paulsiek, and lately supplemented by a corps of writers headed by Döbeln, all in ten volumes of over 3,500 pages and containing nearly six times as much matter as the largest American series. Many men for years went over the history of German literature, from the Eddas and Nibelungenlied down, including a few living writers, carefully selecting saga, legends, *Märchen*, fables, proverbs, hymns, a few prayers, Bible tales, conundrums, jests, and humorous tales, with many digests, epitomes and condensation of great standards, quotations, epic, lyric, dramatic poetry, adventure, exploration, biography, with sketches of the life of each writer quoted, with a large final volume on the history of German literature. All this, it is explained, is "*stataric*" or required to be read between *Octava*[A] and *Obersecunda*. It is no aimless anthology or chrestomathy like Chambers's Encyclopedia, but it is perhaps the best product of prolonged concerted study to select from a vast field the best to feed each nascent stage of later childhood and early youth, and to secure the maximum of pleasure and profit. The ethical end is dominant throughout this pedagogic canon.]

[Footnote A: The Prussian gymnasium, whose course is classical and fits for the University, has nine classes in three divisions of three classes each. The lower classes are Octava, Septa, Sexta, Quinta, and Quarta; the middle classes, Untertertia, Obertertia, and Untersecunda; the higher classes, Obersecunda, Unterprima, and Oberprima. Pupils must be at least nine years of age and have done three years preparatory work before entrance.]

[Footnote 19: The Historic Sense among Children. In her Studies in Historical Method. D. C. Heath and Co., Boston, 1896, p. 57.]

[Footnote 20: Special Study on Children's Sense of Historical Time. Mrs. Barnes's Studies in Historical Method, D.C. Heath and Co., Boston, 1896, p. 94.]

[Footnote 21: L'Etude expérimentale de l'intelligence. Schleicher Frères, Paris, 1903.]

[Footnote 22: The Growth of Memory in School Children. American Journal of Psychology, April, 1892, vol. 9, pp. 362-380.]

[Footnote 23: Contribution to the Psychology and Pedagogy of Feeble-minded Children. By G.E. Johnson. Pedagogical Seminary, October, 1895, vol. 3, p. 270.]

[Footnote 24: A Test of Memory in School Children. Pedagogical Seminary, October, 1898, vol. 4, pp. 61-78.]

[Footnote 25: Zeitschrift für pädagogische Psychologie, Pathologie und Hygiene. February, 1900. Jahrgang II, Heft 1, pp. 21-30.]

[Footnote 26: See Scripture: Scientific Child Study. Transactions of the Illinois Society for Child Study, May, 1895, vol. 1, No. 2, pp. 32-37.]

[Footnote 27: Experimentelle Untersuchungen über die Gedächtnissentwickelung bei Schulkindern. Zeits. f. Psychologie, u. Physiologie der Sinnes-organe, November, 1900. Bd. 24. Heft 5, pp. 321-351.]

[Footnote 28: See Note 4, p. 270.]

[Footnote 29: Memory: An Inductive Study. By F.W. Colegrove. Henry Holt and Co., New York, 1900, p. 229. See also Individual Memories. American Journal of Psychology, January, 1899, vol. 10, pp 228-255.]

* * * * *

CHAPTER XI - THE EDUCATION OF GIRLS

Equal opportunities of higher education now open—Brings new dangers to women—Ineradicable sex differences begin at puberty, when the sexes should and do diverge—Different interests—Sex tension—Girls more mature than boys at the same age—Radical psychic and physiological differences between the sexes—The bachelor women—Needed reconstruction—Food—Sleep—Regimen—Manners—Religion—Regularity—The topics for a girls' curriculum—The eternal womanly.

The long battle of woman and her friends for equal educational and other opportunities is essentially won all along the line. Her academic achievements have forced conservative minds to admit that her intellect is not inferior to that of man. The old cloistral seclusion and exclusion is forever gone and new ideals are arising. It has been a noble movement and is a necessary first stage of woman's emancipation. The caricatured maidens "as beautiful as an angel but as silly as a goose" who come from the kitchen to the husband's study to ask how much is two times two, and are told it is four for a man and three for a woman, and go back with a happy "Thank you, my dear"; those who love to be called baby, and appeal to instincts half parental in their lovers and husbands; those who find all the sphere they desire in a doll's house, like Nora's, and are content to be men's pets; whose ideal is the clinging vine, and who take no interest in the field where their husbands struggle, will perhaps soon survive only as a diminishing remainder. Marriages do still occur where woman's ignorance and helplessness seem to be the chief charm to men, and may be happy, but such cases are no farther from the present ideal and tendency on the one hand than on the other are those which consist in intellectual partnerships, in which there is no segregation of interests but which are devoted throughout to joint work or enjoyment.

A typical contemporary writer[1] thinks the question whether a girl shall receive a college education is very like the same question for boys. Even if the four K's, *Kirche, Kinder, Kuchen,* and *Kleider* (which may be translated by the four C's, *Church, Children, Cooking,* and *Clothes*), are her vocation, college may help her. The best training for a young woman is not the old college course that has proven unfit for young men. Most college men look forward to a professional training as few women do. The latter have often greater sympathy, readiness of memory, patience with technic, skill in literature and language, but lack originality, are not attracted by unsolved problems, are less motor-minded; but their training is just as serious and important as that of men. The best results are where the sexes are brought closer together, because their separation generally emphasizes for girls the technical training for the profession of womanhood. With girls, literature and language take precedence over science; expression stands higher than action; the scholarship may be superior, but is not effective; the educated woman "is likely to master technic rather than art; method, rather than substance. She may know a good deal, but she can do nothing." In most separate colleges for women, old traditions are more prevalent than in colleges for men. In the annex system, she does not get the best of the institution. By the coeducation method, "young men are more earnest, better in manners and morals, and in all ways more civilized than under monastic conditions. The women do more work in a more natural way, with better perspective and with saner incentives than when isolated from the influence of the society of men. There is less silliness and folly where a man is not a novelty. In coeducational institutions of high standards, frivolous conduct or scandals of any form are rarely known. The responsibility for decorum is thrown from the school to the woman, and the woman rises to the responsibility." The character of college work has not been lowered but raised by coeducation, despite the fact that most of the new, small, weak colleges are coeducational. Social strain, Jordan thinks, is easily regulated, and the dormitory system is on the whole best, because the college atmosphere is highly prized. The reasons for the present reaction against coeducation are ascribed partly to the dislike of the idle boy to have girls excel him and see his failures, or because rowdyish tendencies are checked by the presence of women. Some think that girls do not help athletics; that men count for most because they are more apt to be heard from later; but the most serious new argument is the fear that woman's standards and amateurishness will take the place of specialization. Women take up higher education because they like it; men because their careers depend upon it. Hence their studies are more objective and face the world as it is. In college the women do as well as men, but not in the university. The half-educated woman as a social factor has produced many soft lecture courses and cheap books. This is an argument for the higher education of the sex. Finally, Jordan insists that coeducation leads to marriage, and he believes that its best basis is common interest and intellectual friendship.

From the available data it seems, however, that the more scholastic the education of women, the fewer children and the harder, more dangerous, and more dreaded is parturition, and the less the ability to nurse children. Not intelligence, but education by present man-made ways, is inversely as fecundity. The sooner and the more clearly this is recognized as a universal rule, not, of course, without many notable and much vaunted exceptions, the better for our civilization. For one, I plead with no whit less earnestness and conviction than any of the feminists, and indeed with more fervor because on nearly all their grounds and also on others, for the higher education of women, and would welcome them to every opportunity available to men if they can not do better; but I would open to their election another education, which every competent judge would pronounce more favorable to motherhood, under the influence of female principals who do not publicly say that it is "not desirable" that women students should study motherhood, because they do not know whether they will marry; who encourage them to elect "no special subjects because they are women," and who think infant psychology "foolish."

Various interesting experiments in coeducation are now being made in England.[2] Some are whole-hearted and encourage the girls to do almost everything that the boys do in both study and play. There are girl prefects; cricket teams are formed sometimes of both sexes, but often the sexes matched against each other; one play-yard, a dual staff of teachers, and friendships between the boys and girls are not tabooed, etc. In other schools the sexes meet perhaps in recitation only, have separate rooms for study, entrances, play-grounds, and their relations are otherwise restricted. The opinion of English writers generally favors coeducation up to about the beginning of the teens, and from there on views are more divided. It is admitted that, if there is a very great preponderance of either sex over the other, the latter is likely to lose its characteristic qualities, and something of this occurs where the average age of one sex is distinctly greater than that of the other. On the other hand, several urge that, where age and numbers are equal, each sex is more inclined to develop the best qualities peculiar to itself in the presence of the other.

Some girls are no doubt far fitter for boys' studies and men's careers than others. Coeducation, too, generally means far more assimilation of girls' to boys' ways and work than conversely. Many people believe that girls either gain or are more affected by coeducation, especially in the upper grades, than boys. It is interesting, however, to observe the differences that still persist. Certain games, like football and boxing, girls can not play; they do not fight; they are not flogged or caned as English boys are when their bad marks foot up beyond a certain aggregate; girls are more prone to cliques; their punishments must be in appeals to school sentiment, to which they are exceedingly sensitive; it is hard for them to bear defeat in games with the same dignity and unruffled temper as boys; it is harder for them to accept the school standards of honor that condemn the tell-tale as a sneak, although they soon learn this. They may be a little in danger of being roughened by boyish ways and especially by the crude and unique language, almost a dialect in itself, prevalent among schoolboys. Girls are far more prone to overdo; boys are persistingly lazy and idle. Girls are content to sit and have the subject-matter pumped into them by recitations, etc., and to merely accept, while boys are more inspired by being told to do things and make tests and experiments. In this, girls are often quite at sea. One writer speaks of a certain feminine obliquity, but hastens to say that girls in these schools soon accept its code of honor. It is urged, too, that singing classes the voices of each sex are better in quality for the presence of the other. In many topics of all kinds boys and girls are interested in different aspects of the same theme, and therefore the work is broadened. In manual training, girls excel in all artistic work; boys, in carpentry. Girls can be made not only less noxiously sentimental and impulsive, but their conduct tends to become more thoughtful; they can be made to feel responsibility for bestowing their praise aright and thus influencing the tone of the school. Calamitous as it world be for the education of boys beyond a certain age to be entrusted entirely or chiefly to women, it would be less so for that of girls to be given entirely to men. Perhaps the great women teachers, whose life and work have made them a power with girls comparable to that of Arnold and Thring with boys, are dying out. Very likely economic motives are too dominant for this problem to be settled on its merits only. Finally, several writers mention the increased healthfulness of moral tone. The vices that infest boys' schools, which Arnold thought a quantity constantly changing with every class, are diminished. Healthful thoughts of sex, less subterranean and base imaginings on the one hand, and less gushy sentimentality on the other, are favored. For either sex to be a copy of the other is to be weakened, and each comes normally to respect more and to prefer its own sex.

Not to pursue this subject further here, it is probable that many of the causes for the facts set forth are very different and some of them almost diametrically opposite in the two sexes. Hard as it is *per se*, it is after all a comparatively easy matter to educate boys. They are less peculiarly responsive in mental tone to the physical and psychic environment, tend more strongly and early to special interests, and react more vigorously against the obnoxious elements of their surroundings. This is truest of the higher education, and more so in proportion as the tendencies of the age are toward special and vocational training. Woman, as we saw, in every fiber of her soul and body is a more generic creature than man, nearer to the race, and demands more and more with advancing age an education that is essentially liberal and humanistic. This is progressively hard when the sexes differentiate in the higher grades. Moreover, nature decrees that with advancing civilization the sexes shall not approximate, but differentiate, and we shall probably be obliged to carry sex distinctions, at least of method, into many if not most of the topics of the higher education. Now that woman has by general consent attained the right to the best that man has, she must seek a training that fits her own nature as well or better. So long as she strives to be manlike she will be inferior and a pinchbeck imitation, but she must develop a new sphere that shall be like the rich field of the cloth of gold for the best instincts of her nature.

Divergence is most marked and sudden in the pubescent period—in the early teens. At this age, by almost world-wide consent, boys and girls separate for a time, and lead their lives during this most critical period more or less apart, at least for a few years, until the ferment of mind and body which results in maturity of functions then born and culminating in nubility, has done its work. The family and the home abundantly recognize this tendency. At twelve or fourteen, brothers and sisters develop a life more independent of each other than before. Their home occupations differ as do their plays, games, tastes. History, anthropology, and sociology, a well as home life, abundantly illustrate this. This is normal and biological. What our schools and other institutions should do, is not to obliterate these differences but to make boys more manly and girls more womanly. We should respect the law of sexual differences, and not forget that motherhood is a very different thing from fatherhood. Neither sex should copy nor set patterns to the other, but all parts should be played harmoniously and clearly in the great sex symphony.

I have here less to say against coeducation in college, still less in university grades after the maturity which comes at eighteen or twenty has been achieved; but it is high time to ask ourselves whether the theory and practise of identical coeducation, especially in the high school, which has lately been carried to a greater extreme in this country than the rest of the world recognizes, has not brought certain grave dangers, and whether it does not interfere with the natural differentiations seen everywhere else. I recognize, of course, the great argument of economy. Indeed, we should save money and effort could we unite churches of not too diverse creeds. We could thus give better preaching, music, improve the edifice, etc. I am by no means ready to advocate the radical abolition of coeducation, but we can already sum up in a rough, brief way our account of profit and loss with it. On the one hand, no doubt each sex develops some of its own best qualities best in the presence of the other, but the question still remains, how much, when, and in what way, identical coeducation secures this end?

As has been said, girls and boys are often interested in different aspects of the same topic, and this may have a tendency to broaden the view-point of both and bring it into sympathy with that of the other, but the question still remains whether one be not too much attracted to the sphere of the other, especially girls to that of boys. No doubt some girls become a little less gushy, their conduct more thoughtful, and their sense of responsibility greater; for one of woman's great functions, which is that of bestowing praise aright, is increased. There is also much evidence that certain boys' vices are mitigated; they are made more urbane and their thoughts of sex made more healthful. In some respects boys are stimulated to good scholarship by girls, who in many schools and topics excel them. We should ask, however, What is nature's way at this stage of life? Whether boys, in order to be well virified later, ought not to be so boisterous and even rough as to be at times unfit companions for girls; or whether, on the other hand, girls to be best matured ought not to have their sentimental periods of instability, especially when we venture to raise the question, whether for a girl in the early teens, when her health for her whole life depends upon normalizing the lunar month, there is not something unhygienic, unnatural, not to say a little monstrous, in school associations with boys when she must suppress and conceal her feelings and instinctive promptings at those times which suggest withdrawing, to let nature do its beautiful work of inflorescence. It is a sacred time of reverent exemption from the hard struggle of existence in the world and from mental effort in the school. Medical specialists, many of the best of whom now insist that through this period she should be, as it were, "turned out to grass," or should lie fallow, so far as intellectual efforts go, one-fourth the time, no doubt often go too far, but their unanimous voice should not entirely be disregarded.

It is not this, however, that I have chiefly in mind here, but the effects of too familiar relations and, especially, of the identical work, treatment, and environment of the modern school.

We have now at least eight good and independent statistical studies which show that the ideals of boys from ten years on are almost always those of their own sex, while girls' ideals are increasingly of the opposite sex, or those of men. That the ideals of pubescent girls are not found in the great and noble women of the world or in their literature, but more and more in men, suggests a divorce between the ideals adopted and the line of life best suited to the interests of the race. We are not furnished in our public schools with adequate womanly ideals in history or literature. The new love of freedom which women have lately felt inclines girls to abandon the home for the office. "It surely can hardly be called an ideal education for women that permits eighteen out of one hundred college girls to state boldly that they would rather be men than women." More than one-half of the schoolgirls in these censuses choose male ideals, as if those of femininity are disintegrating. A recent writer,[3] in view of this fact, states that "unless there is a change of trend, we shall soon have a female sex without a female character." In the progressive numerical feminization of our schools most teachers, perhaps naturally and necessarily, have more or less masculine ideals, and this does not encourage the development of those that constitute the glory of womanhood. "At every age from eight to sixteen, girls named from three to twenty more ideals than boys." "These facts indicate a condition of diffused interests and lack of clear-cut purposes and a need of integration."

When we turn to boys the case is different. In most public high schools girls preponderate, especially in the upper classes, and in many of them the boys that remain are practically in a girls' school, sometimes taught chiefly, if not solely, by women teachers at an age when strong men should be in control more than at any other period of life. Boys need a different discipline and moral regimen and atmosphere. They also need a different method of work. Girls excel them in learning and memorization, accepting studies upon suggestion or authority, but are often quite at sea when set to make tests and experiments that give individuality and a chance for self-expression, which is one of the best things in boyhood. Girls preponderate in our overgrown high school Latin and algebra, because custom and tradition and, perhaps, advice incline them to it. They preponderate in English and history classes more often, let us hope, from inner inclination. The boy sooner grows restless in a curriculum where form takes precedence over content. He revolts at much method with meager matter. He craves utility, and when all these instincts are denied, without knowing what is the matter, he drops out of school, when with robust tone and with a truly boy life, such as prevails at Harrow, Eton, and Rugby, he would have fought it through and have done well. This feminization of the school spirit, discipline, and personnel is bad for boys. Of course, on the whole, perhaps, they are made more gentlemanly, more at ease, their manners improved, and all this to a woman teacher seems excellent, but something is the matter with the boy in early teens who can be truly called "a perfect gentleman." That should come later, when the brute and animal element have had opportunity to work themselves off in a healthful normal way. They still have football to themselves, and are the majority perhaps in chemistry, and sometimes in physics, but there is danger of a settled eviration. The segregation, which even some of our schools are now attempting, is always in some degree necessary for full and complete development. Just as the boys' language is apt to creep into that of the girl, so girls' interests, ways, standards and tastes, which are crude at this age, sometimes attract boys out of their orbit. While some differences are emphasized by contact, others are compromised. Boys tend to grow content with mechanical, memorized work and, excelling on the lines of girls' qualities, fail to develop those of their own. There is a little charm and bloom rubbed off the ideal of girlhood by close contact, and boyhood seems less ideal to girls at close range. In place of the mystic attraction of the other sex that has inspired so much that is best in the world, familiar comradeship brings a little disenchantment. The impulse to be at one's best in the presence of the other sex prows lax and sex tension remits, and each comes to feel itself seen through, so that there is less motive to indulge in the ideal conduct which such motives inspire, because the call for it is incessant. This disillusioning weakens the motivation to marriage sometimes on both sides, when girls grow careless in their dress and too negligent in their manners, one of the best schools of woman's morals; and when boys lose all restraints which the presence of girls usually enforces, there is a subtle deterioration. Thus, I believe, although of course it is impossible to prove, that this is one of the factors of a decreasing percentage of marriage among educated young men and women.

At eighteen or twenty the girl normally reaches a stage of first maturity when her ideas of life are amazingly keen and true; when, if her body is developed, she can endure a great deal; when she is nearest, perhaps, the ideal of feminine beauty and perfection. Of this we saw illustrations in Chapter VIII. In our environment, however, there is a little danger that this age once well past there will slowly arise a slight sense of aimlessness or lassitude, unrest, uneasiness, as if one were almost unconsciously feeling along the wall for a door to which the key was not at hand. Thus some lose their bloom and, yielding to the great danger of young womanhood, slowly lapse to a anxious state of expectancy, or desire something not within their reach, and so the diathesis of restlessness slowly supervenes. The best thing about college life for girls is, perhaps, that it postpones this incipient disappointment; but it is a little pathetic to me to read, as I have lately done, the class letters of hundreds of girl graduates, out of college one, two, or three years, turning a little to art, music, travel, teaching, charity work, one after the other, or trying to find something to which they can devote themselves, some cause, movement, occupation, where their capacity for altruism and self-sacrifice can find a field. The tension is almost imperceptible, perhaps quite unconscious. It is everywhere overborne by a keen interest in life, by a desire to know the world at first hand, while susceptibilities are at their height. The apple of intelligence has been plucked at perhaps a little too great cost of health. The purely mental has not been quite sufficiently kept back. The girl wishes to know a good deal more of the world and perfect her own personality, and would not marry, although every cell of her body and every unconscious impulse points to just that end. Soon, it may be in five or ten years or more, the complexion of ill health is in these notes, or else life has been adjusted to independence and self-support. Many of these bachelor women are magnificent in mind and body, but they lack wifehood and yet more — motherhood.

In fine, we should use these facts as a stimulus to ask more searchingly the question whether the present system of higher education for both sexes is not lacking in some very essential elements, and if so what these are. Indeed, considering the facts that in our social system man makes the advances and that woman is by nature more prone than man to domesticity and parenthood, it is not impossible that men's colleges do more to unfit for these than do those for women. One cause may be moral. Ethics used to be taught as a practical power for life and reënforced by religious motives. Now it is theoretical and speculative and too often led captive by metaphysical and epistemological speculations. Sometimes girls work or worry more over studies and ideals than is good for their constitution, and boys grow idle and indifferent, and this proverbially tends to bad habits. Perhaps fitting for college has been too hard at the critical age of about eighteen, and requirements of honest, persevering work during college years too little enforced, or grown irksome by physiological reaction of lassitude from the strain of fitting and entering. Again, girls mature earlier than boys; and the latter who have been educated with them tend to certain elements of maturity and completeness too early in life, and their growth period is shortened or its momentum lessened by an atmosphere of femininity. Something is clearly wrong, and more so here than we have at present any reason to think is the case among the academic male or female youth of other lands. To see and admit that there is an evil very real, deep, exceedingly difficult and complex in its causes, but grave and demanding a careful reconsideration of current educational ideas and practises, is the first step; and this every thoughtful and well-informed mind, I believe, must now take.

It is utterly impossible without injury to hold girls to the same standards of conduct, regularity, severe moral accountability, and strenuous mental work that boys need. The privileges and immunities of her sex are inveterate, and with these the American girl in the middle teens fairly tingles with a new-born consciousness. Already she occasionally asserts herself in the public high school against a male teacher or principal who seeks to enforce discipline by methods boys respect, in a way that suggests that the time is at hand when popularity with her sex will be as necessary in a successful teacher as it is in the pulpit. In these interesting oases where girl sentiment has made itself felt in school it has generally carried parents, committeemen, the press, and public sentiment before it, and has already made a precious little list of martyrs whom, were I an educational pope, I would promptly canonize. The progressive feminization of secondary education works its subtle demoralization on the male teachers who remain. Public sentiment would sustain them in many parental exactions with boys which it disallows in mixed classes. It is hard, too, for male principals of schools with only female teachers not to suffer some deterioration in the moral tone of their virility and to lose in the power to cope successfully with men. Not only is this often confessed and deplored, but the incessant compromises the best male teachers of mixed classes must make with their pedagogic convictions in both teaching and discipline make the profession less attractive to manly men of large caliber and of sound fiber. Again, the recent rapid increase of girls, the percentage of which to population in high schools has in many communities doubled in but little more than a decade, almost necessarily involves a decline in the average quality of girls, perhaps as much greater for them as compared with boys as their increase has been greater. When but few were found in these institutions they were usually picked girls with superior tastes and ability, but now the average girl of the rank and file is, despite advanced standard, of admission, of an order natively lower. From this deterioration both boys and teachers suffer, even though the greatest good for the greatest number may be enhanced. Once more, it is generally admitted that girls in good boarding-schools, where evenings, food, and regimen are controlled, are in better health than day pupils with social, church, and domestic duties and perhaps worries to which boys are less subject. This is the nascent stage of periodicity to the slow normalization of which, during these few critical years, everything that interferes should yield. Some kind of tacit recognition of this is indispensable, but in mixed classes every form of such concession is baffling and demoralizing to boys.

The women who really achieve the higher culture should make it their "cause" or "mission" to work out the new humanistic or liberal education which the old college claimed to stand for and which now needs radical reconstruction to meet the demands of modern life. In science they should aim to restore the humanistic elements of its history, biography, its popular features at their best, and its applications in all the more non-technical fields, as described in Chapter XII, and feel responsibility not to let the moral, religious, and poetic aspects of nature be lost in utilities. Woman should be true to her generic nature and take her stand against all premature specialization, and when the *Zeitgeist* [Spirit of the Times] insists on specialized training for occupative pursuits without waiting for broad foundations to be laid, she should resist all these influences that make for psychological precocity. *Das Ewig-Weibliche* [The eternal womanly] is no iridescent fiction but a very definable reality, and means perennial youth. It means that woman at her best never outgrows adolescence as man does, but lingers in, magnifies and glorifies this culminating stage of life with its all-sided interests, its convertibility of emotions, its enthusiasm, and zest for all that is good, beautiful, true, and heroic. This constitutes her freshness and charm, even in age, and makes her by nature more humanistic than man, more sympathetic and appreciative. It is not chiefly the 70,000 superfluous Massachusetts women of the last census, but representatives of every class and age in the 4,000 women's clubs of this country that now find some leisure for general culture in all fields, and in which most of them no doubt surpass their husbands. Those who still say that men do not like women to be their mental superiors and that no man was ever won by the attraction of intellect, on the one hand, and those who urge that women really want husbands to be their intellectual superiors, both misapprehend. The male in all the orders of life is the agent of variation and tends by nature to expertness and specialisation, without which his individuality is incomplete. In his chosen line he would lead and be authoritative, and he rarely seeks partnership in it in marriage. This is no subjection, but woman instinctively respects and even reveres, and perhaps educated woman coming to demand, it in the man of her whole-hearted choice. This granted, man was never more plastic to woman's great work of creating in him all the wide range of secondary sex qualities which constitute his essential manhood. In all this, the pedagogic fathers we teach in the history of education are most of them about as luminous and obsolete as is patristics for the religious teacher, or as methods of other countries are coming to be in solving our own peculiar pedagogic problems. The relation of the academically trained sexes is faintly typified by that of the ideal college to the ideal university, professional or technical school. This is the harmony of counterparts and constitutes the best basis of psychic amphimixis. For the reinstallation of the humanistic college, the time has come when cultivated woman ought to come forward and render vital aid. If she does so and helps to evolve a high school and an A.B. course that is truly liberal, it will not only fit her nature and needs far better than anything now existing, but young men at the humanistic stage of their own education will seek to profit by it, and she will thus repay her debt to man in the past by aiding him to de-universitize the college and to rescue secondary education from its gravest dangers.

But even should all this be done, coeducation would by means be thus justified. If adolescent boys normally pass through a generalized or even feminized stage of psychic development in which they are peculiarly plastic to the guidance of older women who have such rare insight into their nature, such infinite sympathy and patience with all the symptoms of their storm and stress metamorphosis, when they seek everything by turns and nothing long, and if young men will forever afterward understand woman's nature better for living out more fully this stage of their lives and will fail to do so if it is abridged or dwarfed, it by no means follows that intimate daily and class-room association with girls of their own age is necessary or best. The danger of this is that the boy's instinct to assert his own manhood will thus be made premature and excessive, that he will react against general culture, in the capacity for which girls, who are older than boys at the same age, naturally excel them. Companionship and comparisons incline him to take premature refuge in some one talent that emphasizes his psycho-sexual difference too soon. Again, he is farther from nubile maturity than the girl classmate of his own age, and coeducation and marriage between them are prone to violate the important physiological law of disparity that requires the husband to be some years the wife's senior, both in their own interests, as maturity begins to decline to age, and in those of their offspring. Thus the young man with his years of restraint and probation ahead, and his inflammable desires, is best removed from the half-conscious cerebrations about wedlock, inevitably more insistent with constant girl companionship. If he resists this during all the years of his apprenticeship, he grows more immune and inhibitive of it when its proper hour arrives, and perhaps becomes in soul a bachelor before his time. In this side of his nature he is forever incommensurate with and unintelligible to woman, be she even teacher, sister, or mother. Better some risk of gross thoughts and even acts, to which phylogeny and recapitulation so strongly incline him, than this subtle eviration. But if the boy is unduly repelled from the sphere of girls' interests, the girl is in some danger of being unduly drawn to his, and, as we saw above, of forgetting some of the ideals of her own sex. Riper in mind and body than her male classmate, and often excelling him in the capacity of acquisition, nearer the age of her full maturity than he to his, he seems a little too crude and callow to fulfil the ideals of manhood normal to her age which point to older and riper men. In all that makes sexual attraction best, a classmate of her own age is too undeveloped, and so she often suffers mute disenchantment, and even if engagement be dreamed of, it would be, on her part, with unconscious reservations if not with some conscious renunciation of ideals. Thus the boy is correct in feeling himself understood and seen through by his girl classmates to a degree that is sometimes quite distasteful to him, while the girl finds herself misunderstood by and disappointed in men. Boys arrive at the humanistic stage of culture later than girls and pass it sooner; and to find them already there and with their greater aptitude excelling him, is not an inviting situation, and so he is tempted to abridge or cut it out and to hasten on and be mature and professional before his time, for thus he gravitates toward his normal relation to her sex of expert mastership on some bread- or fame-winning line. Of course, these influences are not patent, demonstrable by experiment, or measurable by statistics; but I have come to believe that, like many other facts and laws, they have a reality and a dominance that is all-pervasive and inescapable, and that they will ultimately prevail over economic motives and traditions.

To be a true woman means to be yet more mother than wife. The madonna conception expresses man's highest comprehension of woman's real nature. Sexual relations are brief, but love and care of offspring are long. The elimination of maternity is one of the great calamities, if not diseases, of our age. Marholm[4] points out at length how art again to-day gives woman a waspish waist with no abdomen, as if to carefully score away every trace of her mission; usually with no child in her arms or even in sight; a mere figurine, calculated perhaps to entice, but not to bear; incidentally degrading the artist who depicts her to a fashion-plate painter, perhaps with suggestions of the arts of toilet, cosmetics, and coquetry, as if to promote decadent reaction to decadent stimuli. As in the Munchausen tale, the wolf slowly ate the running nag from behind until he found himself in the harness, so in the disoriented woman the mistress, virtuous and otherwise, is slowly supplanting the mother. Please she must, even though she can not admire, and can so easily despise men who can not lead her, although she become thereby lax and vapid.

The more exhausted men become, whether by overwork, unnatural city life, alcohol, recrudescent polygamic inclinations, exclusive devotion to greed and pelf; whether they become weak, stooping, blear-eyed, bald-headed, bow-legged, thin-shanked, or gross, coarse, barbaric, and bestial, the more they lose the power to lead woman or to arouse her nature, which is essentially passive. Thus her perversions are his fault. Man, before he lost the soil and piety, was not only her protector and provider, but her priest. He not only supported and defended, but inspired the souls of women, so admirably calculated to receive and elaborate suggestions, but not to originate them. In their inmost souls even young girls often experience disenchantment, find men little and no heroes, and so cease to revere and begin to think stupidly of them as they think coarsely of her. Sometimes the girlish conceptions of men are too romantic and exalted; often the intimacy of school and college wear off a charm, while man must not forget that today he too often fails to realize the just and legitimate expectations and ideals of women. If women confide themselves, body and soul, less to him than he desires, it is not she, but he, who is often chiefly to blame. Indeed, in some psychic respects, it seems as if in human society the processes of subordinating the male to the female, carried so far in some of the animal species, had already begun. If he is not worshiped as formerly, it is because he is less worshipful or more effeminate, less vigorous and less able to excite and retain the great love of true, not to say great, women. Where marriage and maternity are of less supreme interest to an increasing number of women, there are various results, the chief of which are as follows:

1. Women grow dollish; sink more or less consciously to man's level; gratify his desires and even his selfish caprices, but exact in return luxury and display, growing vain as he grows sordid; thus, while submitting, conquering, and tyrannizing over him, content with present worldly pleasure, unmindful of the past, the future, or the above. This may react to intersexual antagonism until man comes to hate woman as a witch, or, as in the days of celibacy, consider sex a wile of the devil. Along these lines even the stage is beginning to represent the tragedies of life.

2. The disappointed woman in whom something is dying comes to assert her own ego and more or less consciously to make it an end, aiming to possess and realize herself fully rather than to transmit. Despairing of herself as a woman, she asserts her lower rights in the place of her one great right to be loved. The desire for love may be transmuted into the desire for knowledge, or outward achievement become a substitute for inner content. Failing to respect herself as a productive organism, she gives vent to personal solutions; seeks independence; comes to know very plainly what she wants; perhaps becomes intellectually emancipated, and substitutes science for religion, or the doctor for the priest, with the all-sided impressionability characteristic of her sex which, when cultivated, is so like an awakened

child. She perhaps even affects mannish ways, unconsciously copying from those not most manly, or comes to feel that she has been robbed of something; competes with men, but sometimes where they are most sordid, brutish, and strongest; always expecting, but never finding, she turns successively to art, science, literature, and reforms; craves especially work that she can not do; and seeks stimuli for feelings which have never found their legitimate expression.

3. Another type, truer to woman's nature, subordinates self; goes beyond personal happiness; adopts the motto of self-immolation; enters a life of service, denial, and perhaps mortification, like the Countess Schimmelmann; and perhaps becomes a devotee, a saint, and, if need be, a martyr, but all with modesty, humility, and with a shrinking from publicity.

In our civilization, I believe that bright girls of good environment of eighteen or nineteen, or even seventeen, have already reached the above-mentioned peculiar stage of first maturity, when they see the world at first hand, when the senses are at their very best, their susceptibilities and their insights the keenest, tension at its highest, plasticity and all-sided interests most developed, and their whole psychic soil richest and rankest and sprouting everywhere with the tender shoots of everything both good and bad. Some such—Stella Klive, Mary MacLane, Hilma Strandberg, Marie Bashkirtseff—have been veritable epics upon woman's nature; have revealed the characterlessness normal to the prenubile period in which everything is kept tentative and plastic, and where life seems to have least unity, aim, or purpose. By and by perhaps they will see in all their scrappy past, if not order and coherence, a justification, and then alone will they realize that life is governed by motives deeper than those which are conscious or even personal. This is the age when, if ever, no girl should be compelled. It is the experiences of this age, never entirely obliterated in women, that enable them to take adolescent boys seriously, as men can rarely do, in whom these experiences are more limited in range though no less intense. It is this stage in woman which is most unintelligible to man and even unrealized to herself. It is the echoes from it that make vast numbers of mothers pursue the various branches of culture, often half secretly, to maintain their position with their college sons and daughters, with their husbands, or with society.

But in a very few years, I believe even in the early twenties with American girls, along with rapidly in creasing development of capacity there is also observable the beginnings of loss and deterioration. Unless marriage comes there is lassitude, subtle symptoms of invalidism, the germs of a rather aimless dissatisfaction with life, a little less interest, curiosity, and courage, certain forms of self-pampering, the resolution to be happy, though at too great cost; and thus the clear air of morning begins to haze over and unconsciously she begins to grope. By thirty, she is perhaps goaded into more or less sourness; has developed more petty self-indulgences; has come to feel a right to happiness almost as passionately as the men of the French Revolution and as the women in their late movement for enfranchisement felt for liberty. Very likely she has turned to other women and entered into innocent Platonic pairing-off relations with some one. There is a little more affectation, playing a rôle, and interest in dress and appearance is either less or more specialized and definite. Perhaps she has already begun to be a seeker who will perhaps find, lose, and seek again. Her temper is modified; there is a slight stagnation of soul; a craving for work or travel; a love of children with flitting thoughts of adopting one, or else aversion to them; an analysis of psychic processes until they are weakened and insight becomes too clear; sense of responsibility without an object; a slight general *malaise* and a sense that society is a false "margarine" affair; revolt against those that insist that in her child the real value of a woman is revealed. There are alternations between excessive self-respect which demands something almost like adoration of the other sex and self-distrust, with, it may be, many dreameries about forbidden subjects and about the relations of the sexes generally.

A new danger, the greatest in the history of her sex, now impends, viz., arrest, complacency, and a sense of finality in the most perilous first stage of higher education for girls, when, after all, little has actually yet been won save only the right and opportunity to begin reconstructions, so that now, for the first time in history, methods and matter could be radically transformed to fit the nature and needs of girls. Now most female faculties, trustees, and students are content to ape the newest departures in some one or more male institutions as far as their means or obvious limitations make possible with a servility which is often abject and with rarely ever a thought of any adjustment, save the most superficial, to sex. It is the easiest, and therefore the most common, view typically expressed by the female head of a very successful institution,[5] who was "early convinced in my teaching experience that the methods for mental development for boys and girls applied equally without regard to sex, and I have carried the same thought when I began to develop the physical, and filled my gymnasium with the ordinary appliances used in men's gymnasia." There is no sex in mind or in science, it is said, but it might as well be urged that there is no age, and hence that all methods adapted to teaching at different stages of development may be ignored. That woman can do many things as well as man does not prove that she ought to do the same things, or that man-made ways are the best for her. Mrs. Alice Freeman Palmer[6] was right in saying that woman's education has all the perplexities of that of man, and many more, still more difficult and intricate, of its own.

Hence, we must conclude that, while women's colleges have to a great extent solved the problem of special technical training, they have done as yet very little to solve the larger one of the proper education of woman. To assume that the latter question is settled, as is so often done, is disastrous. I have forced myself to go through many elaborate reports of meetings where female education was discussed by those supposed to be competent; but as a rule, not without rare, striking exceptions, these proceedings are smitten with the same sterile and complacent artificiality that was so long the curse of woman's life. I deem it almost reprehensible that, save a few general statistics, the women's colleges have not only made no study themselves of the larger problems that impend, but have often maintained a repellent attitude toward others who wished to do so. No one that I know of connected with any of these institutions, where the richest material is going to waste, is making any serious and competent research on lines calculated to bring out the psycho-physiological differences between the sexes and those in authority are either conservative by constitution or else intimidated because public opinion is still liable to panics if discussion here becomes scientific and fundamental, and so tend to keep prudery and the old habit of ignoring everything that pertains to sex in countenance.

Again, while I sympathize profoundly with the claim of woman for every opportunity which she can fill, and yield to none in appreciation of her ability, I insist that the cardinal defect in the woman's college is that it is based upon the assumption, implied and often expressed, if not almost universally acknowledged, that girls should primarily be trained to independence and self-support, and that matrimony and motherhood, if it come, will take care of itself, or, as some even urge, is thus best provided for. If these colleges are, as the above statistics indicate, chiefly devoted to the training of those who do not marry, or if they are to educate for celibacy, this is right. These institutions may perhaps come to be training stations of a new-old type, the agamic or even agenic woman, be she nut, maid—old or young—nun, school-teacher, or bachelor woman. I recognize the very great debt the world owes to members of this very diverse class in the past. Some of them have illustrated the very highest ideals of self-sacrifice, service, and devotion in giving to mankind what was meant for husband and children.

Some of them belong to the class of superfluous women, and others illustrate the noblest type of altruism and have impoverished the heredity of the world to its loss, as did the monks, who Leslie Stephens thinks contributed to bring about the Dark Ages, because they were the best and most highly selected men of their age and, by withdrawing from the function of heredity and leaving no posterity, caused Europe to degenerate. Modern ideas and training are now doing this, whether for racial weal or woe, can not yet be determined, for many whom nature designed for model mothers.

The bachelor woman is an interesting illustration of Spencer's law of the inverse relation of individuation and genesis. The completely developed individual is always a terminal representative in her line of descent. She has taken up and utilized in her own life all that was meant for her descendants, and has so overdrawn her account with heredity that, like every perfectly and completely developed individual, she is also completely sterile. This is the very apotheosis of selfishness from the standpoint of every biological ethics. While the complete man can do and sometimes does this, woman has a far greater and very peculiar power of overdrawing her reserves. First she loses mammary functions, so that should she undertake maternity its functions are incompletely performed because she can not nurse, and this implies defective motherhood and leaves love of the child itself defective and maimed, for the mother who has never nursed can not love or be loved aright by her child. It crops out again in the abnormal or especially incomplete development of her offspring, in the critical years of adolescence, although they may have been healthful before, and a less degree of it perhaps is seen in the diminishing families of cultivated mothers in the one-child system. These women are the intellectual equals and often the superiors of the men they meet; they are very attractive as companions, like Miss Mehr, the university student, in Hauptmann's "Lonely Lives," who alienated the young husband from his noble wife; they enjoy all the keen pleasures of intellectual activity; their very look, step, and bearing is free; their mentality makes them good fellows and companionable in all the broad intellectual spheres; to converse with them is as charming and attractive for the best men as was Socrates's discourse with the accomplished hetaerae; they are at home with the racquet and on the golf links; they are splendid friends; their minds, in all their widening areas of contact, are as attractive as their bodies; and the world owes much and is likely to owe far more to high Platonic friendships of this kind. These women are often in every way magnificent, only they are not mothers, and sometimes have very little wifehood in them, and to attempt to marry them to develop these functions is one of the unique and too frequent tragedies of modern life and literature. Some, though by no means all, of them are functionally castrated; some actively deplore the necessity of child-bearing, and perhaps are parturition phobiacs, and abhor the limitations of married life; they are incensed whenever attention is called to the functions peculiar to their sex, and the careful consideration of problems of the monthly rest are thought "not fit for cultivated women."

The slow evolution of this type is probably inevitable as civilization advances, and their training is a noble function. Already it has produced minds of the greatest acumen who have made very valuable contributions to science, and far more is to be expected of them in the future. Indeed, it may be their noble function to lead their sex out into the higher, larger life, and the deeper sense of its true position and function, for which I plead. Hitherto woman has not been able to solve her own problems. While she has been more religious than man, there have been few great women preachers; while she has excelled in teaching young children, there have been few Pestalozzis, or even Froebels; while her invalidism is a complex problem, she has turned to man in her diseases. This is due to the very intuitiveness and naïveté of her nature. But now that her world is so rapidly widening, she is in danger of losing her cue. She must be studied objectively and laboriously as we study children, and partly by men, because their sex must of necessity always remain objective and incommensurate with regard to woman, and therefore more or less theoretical. Again, in these days of intense new interest in feelings, emotions, and sentiments, when many a psychologist now envies and, like Schleiermacher, devoutly wishes he could become a woman, he can never really understand *das Ewig-Weibliche*, [The eternal womanly] one of the two supreme oracles of guidance in life, because he is a man; and here the cultivated woman must explore the nature of her sex as man can not, and become its mouthpiece. In many of the new fields opening in biology since Darwin, in embryology, botany, the study of children, animals, savages (witness Miss Fletcher), sociological investigation, to say nothing of all the vast body of work that requires painstaking detail, perseverance, and conscience, woman has superior ability, or her very sex gives her peculiar advantages where she is to lead and achieve great things in enlarging the kingdom of man. Perhaps, too, the present training of women may in the end develop those who shall one day attain a true self-knowledge and lead n the next step of devising a scheme that shall fit woman's nature and needs.

For the slow evolution of such a scheme, we must first of all distinctly and ostensively invert the present maxim, and educate primarily and chiefly for motherhood, assuming that, if that does not come, single life can best take care of itself, because it is less intricate and lower and its needs far more easily met. While girls may be trained with boys, coeducation should cease at the dawn of adolescence, at least for a season. Great daily intimacy between the sexes in high school, if not in college, tends to rub of the bloom and delicacy which can develop in each, and girls suffer in this respect, let us repeat, far more than boys. The familiar comradeship that ignores sex should be left to the agenic class. To the care of their institutions, we leave with pious and reverent hands the ideals inspired by characters like Hypatia, Madame de Staël, the Misses Cobb, Martineau, Fuller, Bronté, by George Eliot, George Sand, and Mrs. Browning; and while accepting and profiting by what they have done, and acknowledging every claim for their abilities and achievements, prospective mothers must not be allowed to forget a still larger class of ideal women, both in history and literature, from the Holy Mother to Beatrice Clotilda de Vaux, and all those who have inspired men to great deeds, and the choice and far richer anthology of noble mothers.

We must premise, too, that she must not be petted or pampered with regimen or diet unsuited to her needs; left to find out as best she can, from surreptitious or worthy sources, what she most of all needs to know; must recognize that our present civilization is hard on woman and that she is not yet adjusted to her social environment; that as she was of old accused of having given man the apple of knowledge of good and evil, so he now is liable to a perhaps no less serious indictment of having given her the apple of intellectualism and encouraged her to assume his standards at the expense of health. We must recognize that riches are probably harder on her, on the whole, than poverty, and that poor parents should not labor too hard to exempt her from its wholesome discipline. The expectancy of change so stamped upon her sex by heredity as she advances into maturity must not be perverted into uneasiness or her soul sown with the tares of ambition or fired by intersexual competition and driven on, to quote Dr. R.T. Edes, "by a tireless sort of energy which is a compound of conscience, ambition, and desire to please, plus a peculiar female obstinacy." If she is bright, she must not be overworked in the school factory, studying in a way which parodies Hood's "Song of the Shirt"; and if dull or feeble, she should not be worried by preceptresses like a eminent lady principal,[7] who thought girls' weakness is usually imaginary or laziness, and that doctors are to blame for suggesting illness and for intimating that men will have to choose between a healthy animal and an educated invalid for a wife.

Without specifying here details or curricula, the ideals that should be striven toward in the intermediate and collegiate education of adolescent girls with the proper presupposition of motherhood, and which are already just as practicable as Abbotsholme[8] or *L'Ecole des Roches*,[9] may be rudely indicated somewhat as follows.

First, the ideal institution for the training of girls from twelve or thirteen on into the twenties, when the period most favorable to motherhood begins, should be in the country in the midst of hills, the climbing of which is the best stimulus for heart and lungs, and tends to mental elevation and breadth of view. There should be water for boating, bathing, and skating, aquaria and aquatic life; gardens both for kitchen vegetables and horticulture; forests for their seclusion and religious awe; good roads, walks, and paths that tempt to walking and wheeling: playgrounds and space for golf and tennis, with large covered but unheated space favorable for recreations in weather really too bad for out-of-door life and for those indisposed; and plenty of nooks that permit each to be alone with nature, for this develops inwardness, poise, and character, yet not too great remoteness from the city for a wise utilization of its advantages at intervals. All that can be called environment is even more important for girls than boys, significant as it is for the latter.

The first aim, which should dominate every item, pedagogic method and matter, should be health—a momentous word that looms up beside holiness, to which it is etymologically akin. The new hygiene of the last few years should be supreme and make these academic areas soared to the cult of the goddess Hygeia. Only those who realize what advances have been made in health culture and know something of its vast new literature can realize all that this means. The health of woman is, as we have seen, if possible even more important for the welfare of the race than that of man; and the influence of her body upon her mind is, in a sense, greater, so that its needs should be supreme and primary. Foods should favor the completest digestion, so that metabolism be on the highest plane. The dietary should be abundant, plain, and varied, and cooked with all the refinements possible in the modern cooking-school, which should be one of its departments, with limited use of rich foods or desserts and stimulating drinks, but with wholesome proximity to dairy and farm. Nutrition is the first law of health and happiness, the prime condition and creator of euphoria; and the appetite should be, as it always is if unperverted, like a kind of somatic conscience steadfastly pointing toward the true pole of needs.

Sleep should be regular, with a fixed retiring hour and curfew, on plain beds in rooms of scrupulous neatness reserved chiefly for it with every precaution for quiet, and, if possible, with windows more or less open the year round, and, like other rooms, never overheated. Bathing in moderation, and especially dress and toilet should be almost raised to fine arts and objects of constant suggestion. Each student should have three rooms, for bath, sleep, and study, respectively, and be responsible for their care, with every encouragement for expressing individual tastes; but will, an all-dominant idea of simplicity, convenience, refinement, and elegance, without luxury. Girls need to go away from home a good part of every year to escape the indiscretion and often the coddling of parents and to learn self-reliance; and a family dormitory system, with but few, twelve to twenty, in each building, to escape nervous wear and distraction, to secure intimacy and acquaintance with one or more matrons or teachers and to ensure the most pedagogic dietetics, is suggested.

Exercise comes after regimen, of which it is a special reform. Swedish gymnastics should be abandoned or reduced to a minimum of best points, because it is too severe and, in forbidding music, lays too little stress upon the rhythm element. Out-of-door walks and games should have precedence over all else. The principle sometimes advocated, that methods of physical training should apply to both boys and girls without regard to sex, and with all the ordinary appliances found in the men's gymnasia introduced, should be reversed and every possible adjustment made to sex. Free plays and games should always have precedence over indoor or uniform *commando* exercises. Boating and basket-ball should be allowed, but with the competition element sedulously reduced, and with dancing of many kinds and forms the most prominent of indoor exercises. The dance cadences the soul; the stately minuet gives poise; the figure dances train the mind; and pantomime and dramatic features should be introduced and even specialties, if there are strong individual predispositions. The history of the dance, which has often been a mode of worship, a school of morals, and which is the root of the best that is in the drama, the best of all exercises and that could be again the heart of our whole educational system, should be exploited, and the dancing school and class rescued from its present degradation. No girl is educated who can not dance, although she need not know the ballroom in its modern form.[10]

Manners, a word too often relegated to the past as savoring of the primness of the ancient dame school or female seminary, are really minor or sometimes major morals. They can express everything in the whole range of the impulsive or emotional life. Now that we understand the primacy of movement over feeling, we can appreciate what a school of bearing and repose in daily converse with others means. I would revive some of the ancient casuistry of details, but less the rules of the drawing-room, call and party, although these should not be neglected, than the deeper expressions of true ladyhood seen in an exquisite, tender and unselfish regard for the feelings of others. Women's ideal of compelling every one whom they meet to like them is a noble one, and the control of every automatism is not only a part of good breeding, but nervous health.

Regularity should be another all-pervading norm. In the main, even though he may have "played his sex symphony too harshly," E.H. Clark was right. Periodicity, perhaps the deepest law of the cosmos, celebrates its highest triumphs in woman's life. For years everything must give way to its thorough and settled establishment. In the monthly Sabbaths of rest, the ideal school should revert to the meaning of the word leisure. The paradise of stated rest should be revisited, idleness be actively cultivated; reverie, in which the soul, which needs these seasons of withdrawal for its own development, expatiates over the whole life of the race, should be provided for and encouraged in every legitimate way, for, in rest, the whole momentum of heredity is felt in ways most favorable to full and complete development. Then woman should realize that *to be* is greater than *to do*; should step reverently aside from her daily routine and let Lord Nature work. In this time of sensitiveness and perturbation, when anemia and chlorosis are so peculiarly immanent to her sex, remission of toil should not only be permitted, but required; and yet the greatest individual liberty should be allowed to adjust itself to the vast diversities of individual constitutional needs. (See Chapter VII on this point.) The cottage home, which should take the place of the dormitory, should always have special interest and attractions for these seasons.

There should always be some personal instruction at these seasons during earlier adolescent years. I have glanced over nearly a score of books and pamphlets that are especially written for girls; while all are well meant and far better than the ordinary modes by which girls acquire knowledge of their own nature if left to themselves, they are, like books for boys, far too prolix, and most are too scientific and plain and direct. Moreover, no two girls need just the same instruction, and to leave it to reading is too indirect and causes the mind to dwell on it for too long periods. Best of all is individual instruction at the time, concise, practical, and never, especially in the early years, without a certain mystic and religious tone which should pervade all and make everything sacred. This should not be given by male physicians—and indeed most female doctors would make it too professional, and the maiden teacher must forever lack reverence for it — but it should come from one whose soul and body are full of wifehood and motherhood and who is old enough to know and is not without the necessary technical knowledge.

Another principle should be to broaden by retarding; to keep the purely mental back and by every method to bring the intuitions to the front; appeals to tact and taste should be incessant; a purely intellectual man is no doubt biologically a deformity, but a purely intellectual woman is far more so. Bookishness is probably a bad sign in a girl; it suggests artificiality, pedantry, the lugging of dead knowledge. Mere learning is not the ideal, and prodigies of scholarship are always morbid. The rule should be to keep nothing that is not to become practical; to open no brain tracts which are not to be highways for the daily traffic of thought and conduct; not to overburden the soul with the impedimenta of libraries and records of what is afar off in time or zest, and always to follow truly the guidance of normal and spontaneous interests wisely interpreted.

Religion will always bold as prominent a place in woman's life as politics does in man's, and adolescence is still more its seedtime with girls than with boys. Its roots are the sentiment of awe and reverence, and it is the great agent in the world for transforming life from its earlier selfish to its only really mature form of altruism. The tales of the heroes of virtue, duty, devotion, and self-sacrifice from the Old Testament come naturally first; then perhaps the prophets paraphrased as in the pedagogic triumph of Kent and Saunders's little series; and when adolescence is at its height then the chief stress of religious instruction should be laid upon Jesus's life and work. He should be taught first humanly, and only later when the limitations of manhood seem exhausted should His Deity be adduced as welcome surplusage. The supernatural is a reflex of the heart; each sustains and neither can exist without the other. If the transcendent and supernal had no objective existence, we should have to invent and teach it or dwarf the life of feeling and sentiment. Whatever else religion is, therefore, it is the supremest poetry of the soul, reflecting like nothing else all that is deepest, most generic and racial in it. Theology should be reduced to a minimum, but nothing denied where wanted. Paul and his works and ways should be for the most part deferred until after eighteen. The juvenile well as the cyclone revivalist should be very carefully excluded; and yet in every springtime, when nature is recreated, service and teaching should gently encourage the revival and even the regeneration of all the religious instincts. The mission recruiter should be allowed to do his work outside these halls, and everything in the way of infection and all that brings religion into conflict with good taste and good sense should be excluded, while esthetics should supplement, reënforce, and go hand in hand with piety. Religion is in its infancy; and woman, who has sustained it in the past, must be the chief agent in its further and higher development. Orthodoxies and all narrowness should forever give place to cordial hospitality toward every serious view, which should be met by the method of greater sympathy rather than by that of criticism.

Nature in her many phases should, of course, make up a large part of the entire curriculum, but here again the methods of the sexes should differ somewhat after puberty. The poetic and mythic factors and some glimpses of the history of science should be given more prominence; the field naturalist rather than the laboratory man of technic should be the ideal especially at first; nature should be taught as God's first revelation, as an Old Testament related to the Bible as a primordial dispensation to a later and clearer and more special one. Reverence and love should be the motive powers, and no aspect should be studied without beginning and culminating in interests akin to devotion. Mathematics should be taught only in its rudiments, and those with special talents or tastes for it should go to agamic schools. Chemistry, too, although not excluded, should have a subordinate place. The average girl has little love of sozzling and mussing with the elements, and cooking involves problems in organic chemistry too complex to be understood very profoundly, but the rudiments of household chemistry should be taught. Physics, too, should be kept to elementary stages. Meteorology should have a larger, and geology and astronomy increasingly larger places, and are especially valuable because, and largely in proportion as, they are taught out of doors, but the general principles and the untechnical and practical aspects should be kept in the foreground. With botany more serious work should be done. Plant-lore and the poetic aspect, as in astronomy, should have attention throughout, while Latin nomenclature and microscopic technic should come late if at all, and vulgar names should have precedence over Latin terminology. Flowers, gardening, and excursions should never be wanting. Economic and even medical aspects should appear, and prominent and early should come the whole matter of self cross-fertilization and that by insects. The moral value of this subject will never be fully understood till we have what might almost be called a woman's botany, constructed on lines different from any of the text-books I have glanced at. Here much knowledge interesting in itself can be early taught, which will spring up into a world of serviceable insights as adolescence develops and the great law of sex unfolds.

Zoology should always be taught with plenty of pets, menagerie resources, and with aquaria, aviaries, apiaries, formicaries, etc., as adjuncts.

It should start in the environment like everything else. Bird and animal lore, books, and pictures should abound in the early stages, and the very prolific chapter of instincts should have ample illustration, while the morphological nomenclature and details of structure should be less essential. Woman has domesticated nearly all the animals, and is so superior to man in insight into their modes of life and psychoses that many of them are almost exemplifications of moral qualities to her even more than to man. The peacock is an embodied expression of pride; the pig, of filth; the fox, of cunning; the serpent, of subtle danger; the eagle, of sublimity; the goose, of stupidity; and so on through all the range of human qualities, as we have seen. At bottom, however, the study of animal life is coming to be more and more a problem of heredity, and its problems should have dominant position and to them the other matter should grade up.

This shades over into and prepares for the study of the primitive man and child so closely related to each other. The myth, custom, belief, domestic practises of savages, vegetative and animal traits in infancy and childhood, the development of which is a priceless boon for the higher education of women, open of themselves a great field of human interest where she needs to know the great results, the striking details, the salient illustrations, the basal principles rather than to be entangled in the details of anthropometry, craniometry, philology, etc.

All this lays the basis for a larger study of modern man—history, with the biographical element very prominent throughout, with plenty of stories of heroes of virtue, acts of valor, tales of saintly lives and the personal element more prominent, and specialization in the study of dynasties, wars, authorities, and controversies relegated to a very subordinate place. Sociology, undeveloped, rudimentary, and in some places suspected as it is, should have in the curriculum of her higher education a place above political economy. The stories of the great reforms, and accounts of the constitution of society, of the home, church, state, and school, and philanthropies and ideals, should to the fore.

Art in all its forms should be opened at least in a propædeutic way and individual tastes amply and judiciously fed, but there should be no special training in music without some taste and gift, and the aim should be to develop critical and discriminative appreciation and the good taste that sees the vast superiority of all that is good and classic over what is cheap and fustian.

In literature, myth, poetry, and drama should perhaps lead, and the knowledge of the great authors in the vernacular be fostered. Greek, Hebrew, and perhaps Latin languages should be entirely excluded, not but that they are of great value and have their place, but because a smattering knowledge is bought at too high a price of ignorance of more valuable things. German, French, and Italian should be allowed and provided for by native teachers and by conversational methods if desired, and in their proper season.

In the studies of the soul of man, generally called the philosophic branches, metaphysics and epistemology should have the smallest, and logic the next least place. Psychology should be taught on the genetic basis of animals and children, and one of its tap-roots should be developed from the love of infancy and youth, than which nothing in all the world is more worthy. If a woman Descartes ever arises, she will put life before theory, and her watchword will be not *cogito, ergo sum*, [I think, therefore I am] but *sum, ergo cogito* [I am, therefore I think]. The psychology of sentiments and feelings and intuitions will take precedence of that of pure intellect; ethics will be taught on the basis of the whole series of practical duties and problems, and the theories of the ultimate nature of right or the constitution of conscience will have small place.

Domesticity will be taught by example in some ideal home building by a kind of laboratory method. A nursery with all carefully selected appliances and adjuncts, a dining-room, a kitchen, bedroom, closets, cellars, outhouses, building, its material, the grounds, lawn, shrubbery, hothouse, library, and all the other adjuncts of the hearth will be both exemplified and taught. A general course in pedagogy, especially its history and ideals, another in child study, and finally a course in maternity the last year taught broadly, and not without practical details of nursing, should be comprehensive and culminating. In its largest sense maternity might be the heart of all the higher training of young women.

Applied knowledge will thus be brought to a focus in a department of teaching as one of the specialties of motherhood and not as a vocation apart. The training should aim to develop power of maternity in soul as well as in body, so that home influence may extend on and up through the plastic years of pubescence, and future generations shall not rebel against these influences until they have wrought their perfect work.

The methods throughout should be objective, with copious illustrations by way of object-lessons, apparatus, charts, pictures, diagrams, and lectures, far less book work and recitation, only a limited amount of room study, the function of examination reduced to a minimum, and everything as suggestive and germinal as possible. Hints that are not followed up; information not elaborated into a thin pedagogic sillabub or froth; seed that is sown on the waters with no thought of reaping; faith in a God who does not pay at the end of each week, month, or year, but who always pays abundantly some time; training which does not develop hypertrophied memory-pouches that carry, or creative powers that discover and produce—these are lines on which such an institution should develop. Specialization has its place, but it always hurts a woman's soul more than a man's, should always come later, and if there is special capacity it should be trained elsewhere. Unconscious education is a power of which we have yet to learn the full ranges.

In most groups in this series of ideal departments there should be at least one healthful, wise, large-souled, honorable, married and attractive man, and, if possible, several of them. His very presence in an institution for young women gives poise, polarizes the soul, and gives wholesome but long-circuited tension at root no doubt sexual, but all unconsciously so. This mentor should not be more father than brother, though he should combine the best of each, but should add another element. He need not be a doctor, a clergyman, or even a great scholar, but should be accessible for confidential conferences even though intimate. He should know the soul of the adolescent girl and how to prescribe; he should be wise and fruitful in advice, but especially should be to all a source of contagion and inspiration for poise and courage even though religious or medical problems be involved. But even if he lack all these latter qualities, though he so poised that impulsive girls can turn their hearts inside out in his presence and perhaps even weep on his shoulder, the presence of such a being, though a complete realization of this ideal could be only remotely approximated, would be the center of an atmosphere most wholesomely tonic.

In these all too meager outlines I have sketched a humanistic and liberal education and have refrained from all details and special curriculization. Many of the above features I believe would be as helpful for boys as for girls, but woman has here an opportunity to resume her exalted and supreme position, to be the first in this higher field, to lead man and pay her debt to his educational institutions, by resuming her crown. The ideal institutions, however, for the two will always be radically and probably always increasingly divergent.

As a psychologist, penetrated with the growing sense of the predominance of the heart over the mere intellect, I believe myself not alone in desiring to make a tender declaration of being more and more passionately in love with woman as I conceive she came from the hand of God. I keenly envy my Catholic friends their Maryolatry. Who ever asked if the Holy Mother, whom the wise men adored, knew the astronomy of the Chaldees or had studied Egyptian or Babylonian, or even whether she knew how to read or write her own tongue, and who has ever thought of caring? We can not conceive that she bemoaned any limitations of her sex, but she has been an object of adoration all these centuries because she glorified womanhood by being more generic, nearer the race, and richer in love, pity, unselfish devotion and intuition than man. The glorified madonna ideal shows us how much more whole and holy it is to be a woman than to be artist, orator, professor, or expert, and suggests to our own sex that to be a man is larger than to be gentleman, philosopher, general, president, or millionaire.

But with all this love and hunger in my heart, I can not help sharing in the growing fear that modern woman, at least in more ways and places than one, is in danger of declining from her orbit; that she is coming to lack just confidence and pride in her sex as such, and is just now in danger of lapsing to mannish ways, methods, and ideals, until her original divinity may become obscured. But, if our worship at her shrine is with a love and adoration a little qualified and unsteady, we have a fixed and abiding faith without which we should have no resource against pessimism for the future of our race, that she will ere long evolve a sphere of life and even education which fits her needs as well as, if not better than those of man fit his.

Meanwhile, if the eternally womanly seems somewhat less divine, we can turn with unabated faith to the eternally childish, the best of which in each are so closely related. The oracles of infancy and childhood will never fail. Distracted as we are in the maze of new sciences, skills, ideals, knowledges that we can not fully coördinate by our logic or curriculize by our pedagogy; confused between the claims of old and new methods; needing desperately, for survival as a nation and a race, some clue to thrid the mazes of the manifold modern cultures, we have now at least one source to which we can turn—we have found the only magnet in all the universe that points steadfastly to the undiscovered pole of human destiny. We know what can and will ultimately coördinate in the generic, which is larger than the logical order, all that is worth knowing, teaching, or doing by the best methods, that will save us from misfits and the waste ineffable of premature and belated knowledge, and that is in the interests and line of normal development in the child in our midst that must henceforth ever lead us which epitomizes in its development all the stages, human and prehuman; that is the proper object of all that strange new love of everything that is naive, spontaneous, and unsophisticated in human nature. The heart and soul of growing childhood is the criterion by which we judge the larger heart and soul of mature womanhood; and these are ultimately the only guide into the heart of the new education which is to be, when the school becomes what Melanchthon said it must be—a true workshop of the Holy Ghost—and what the new psychology, when it rises to the heights of prophecy, foresees as the true paradise of restored intuitive human nature.

[Footnote 1: David Starr Jordan: The Higher Education of Women. Popular Science Monthly, December, 1902, vol. 62, pp. 97-107. See also my article on this subject in Munsey's Magazine, February, 1906, and President Jordan's reply in the March number, 1906.]

[Footnote 2: Coeducation. A series of essays by various authors, edited by Alice Woods, with an introduction by M.E. Sadler. Longmans, Green and Co., London 1903, p. 148 *et seq.*]

[Footnote 3: The Evolution of Ideals. W.G. Chambers, Pedagogical Seminary, March, 1903, vol. 10, pp. 101-143. Also, B.E. Warner: The Young Woman in Modern Life. Dodd, Mead & Co., New York, 1903, p. 218.]

[Footnote 4: The Psychology of Woman. Translated by G.A. Etchison. Richards, London, 1899.]

[Footnote 5: Physical Development of Women and Children. By Miss M.E. Allen. American Association for Physical Education., April, 1890.]

[Footnote 6: A Review of the Higher Education of Women. Forum, September, 1891, vol. 12, pp 25-40. See also G. von Bunge: Die zunehmende Unfähigkeit der Frauen ihre Kinder zu stillen. München Reinhardt, 1903, 3d ed. Also President Harper's Decennial Report, pp. xciv-cxi.]

[Footnote 7: Physical Hindrances to Teaching Girls, by Charlotte W. Porter. Forum, September, 1891, vol. 12, pp. 41-49.]

[Footnote 8: Abbotsholme, 1889-1899: or Ten Years' Work in an Educational Laboratory, by Cecil Reddie, G. Allen London, 1900.]

[Footnote 9: See L'Ecole des Roches, a school of the Twentieth Century, by T.R. Croswell. Pedagogical Seminary, December, 1900, vol. 7, pp. 479-491.]

[Footnote 10: See Chapter VI.]

* * * * *

CHAPTER XII - MORAL AND RELIGIOUS TRAINING

Dangers of muscular degeneration and overstimulus of brain—Difficulties in teaching morals—Methods in Europe—Obedience to commands—Good habits should be mechanized—Value of scolding—How to flog aright—Its dangers—Moral precepts and proverbs—Habituation—Training will through intellect—Examinations—Concentration—Originality—Froebel and the naive—First ideas of God—Conscience—Importance of Old and New Testaments—Sex dangers—Love and religion—Conversion.

From its nature as well as from its central importance it might be easily shown that the will is no less dependent on the culture it receives than is the mind. It is fast becoming as absurd to suppose that men can survive in the great practical strain to which American life subjects all who would succeed, if the will is left to take its doubtful chances of training and discipline, as to suppose that the mind develops in neglect. Our changed conditions make this chance of will-culture more doubtful than formerly. A generation or two ago[1] most school-boys had either farm work, chores, errands, jobs self-imposed, or required by less tender parents; they *made* things, either toys or tools, out of school. Most school-girls did house-work, more or less of which is, like farm-work, perhaps the most varied and most salutary as well as most venerable of all schools for the youthful body and mind. They undertook extensive works of embroidery, bed-quilting, knitting, sewing, mending, if not cleaning, and even spinning and weaving their own or others' clothing, and cared for the younger children. The wealthier devised or imposed tasks for will-culture, as the German Kaiser has his children taught a trade as part of their education. Ten days at the hoe-handle, axe, or pitchfork, said an eminent educator lately in substance, with no new impression from without, and one constant and only duty, is a schooling in perseverance and sustained effort such as few boys now get in any shape; while city instead of country life brings so many new, heterogeneous and distracting impressions of motion rather than rest, and so many privileges with so few corresponding duties, that with artificial life and bad air the will is weakened, and eupeptic minds and stomachs, on which its vigor so depends, are rare. Machines supersede muscles, and perhaps our athleticism gives skill too great preponderance over strength, or favors intense rather than constant, long-sustained, unintermittent energy. Perhaps too many of our courses of study are better fitted to turn out many-sided but superficial paragraphists, than men who can lay deep plans, and subordinate many complex means to one remote end. Meanwhile, if there is any one thing of which our industries and practical arts are in more crying need than another, it is the old-fashioned virtue of thoroughness, of a kind and degree which does not address merely the eye, is not limited by the letter of a contract, but which has some regard for its products for their own sake, and some sense for the future. Whether in science, philosophy, morals, or business, the fields for long-ranged cumulative efforts are wider, more numerous, and far more needy than in the days when it was the fashion for men contentedly to concentrate themselves to one vocation, life-work, or mission, or when cathedrals or other yet vaster public works were transmitted, unfinished but ever advancing, from one generation of men to another.

It is because the brain is developed, while the muscles are allowed to grow flabby and atrophied, that the deplored chasm between knowing and doing is so often fatal to the practical effectiveness of mental and moral culture. The great increase of city and sedentary life has been far too sudden for the human body—which was developed by hunting, war, agriculture, and manifold industries now given over to steam and machinery—to adapt itself healthfully or naturally to its new environment. Let any of us take down an anatomical chart of the human muscles, and reflect what movements we habitually make each day, and realize how disproportionately our activities are distributed compared with the size or importance of the muscles, and how greatly modern specialization of work has deformed our bodies. The muscles that move the scribbling pen are insignificant fraction of those in the whole body, and those that wag the tongue and adjust the larynx are also comparatively few and small. Their importance is, of course, not underrated, but it is disastrous to concentrate education upon them too exclusively or too early in life. The trouble is that few realize what physical vigor is in man or woman, or how dangerously near weakness often is to wickedness, how impossible healthful energy of will is without strong muscles which are its organ, or how endurance and self-control, no less than great achievement, depend on muscle-habits. Both in Germany and Greece, a golden age of letters was preceded, by about a generation, by a golden age of national gymnastic enthusiasm which constitutes, especially in the former country, one of the most unique and suggestive chapters in the history of pedagogy. Symmetry and grace, hardihood and courage, the power to do everything that the human body can do with and without all conceivable apparatus, instruments, and even tools, are culture ideals that in Greece, Rome, and Germany respectively have influenced, as they might again influence, young men, as intellectual ideals never can do save in a select few. We do not want "will-virtuosos," who perform feats hard to learn, but then easy to do and good for show; nor spurtiness of any sort which develops an erethic habit of work, temper, and circulation, and is favored by some of our popular sports but too soon reacts into fatigue. Even will-training does not reach its end till it leads the young up to taking a intelligent, serious and life-long interest in their own physical culture and development. This is higher than interest in success in school or college sport; and, though naturally later than these, is one of the earliest forms of will-culture in which it is safe and wise to attempt to interest the young for its own sake alone. In our exciting life and trying climate, in which the experiment of civilization has never been tried before, these thoughts are merely exercises.

But this is, of course, preliminary. Great as is the need, the practical difficulties in the way are very great. First, there are not only no good text-books in ethics, but no good manual to guide teachers. Some give so many virtues or good habits to be taught per term, ignoring the unity of virtue as well as the order in which the child's capacities for real virtue unfold. Advanced text-books discuss the grounds of obligation, the nature of choice or freedom, or the hedonistic calculus, as if pleasures and pains could be balanced as measurable quantities, etc., so that philosophic morality is clearly not for children or teachers. Secondly, evolution encourages too often the doubt whether virtue can be taught, when it should have the opposite effect. Perversity and viciousness of will are too often treated as constitutional disease; and insubordination or obstinacy, especially in school, are secretly admired as strength, instead of being vigorously treated as crampy disorders of will, and the child is coddled into flaccidity. Becomes the lowest develops first, there is danger that it will interfere with the development of the higher, and thus, if left to his own, the child may come to have no will. The third and greatest difficulty is, that with the best effort to do so, so few teachers can separate morality from religious creed. So vital is the religions sentiment here that it is hard to divorce the end of education from the end of life, proximate from ultimate grounds of obligation, or finite from infinite duties. Those whose training has been more religious than ethical can hardly teach morality *per se* satisfactorily to the *noli me tangere* [Touch me not] spirit of denominational freedom so wisely jealous of conflicting standards and sanctions for the young.

How then can we ever hope to secure proper training for the will?

More than a generation ago Germany developed the following method: Children of Lutheran, Catholic and Jewish parentage, which include most

German children, were allowed one afternoon a week for several years, and two afternoons a week for a few months preceding confirmation, to spend half of a school day with instructors of these respective professions, who were nominated by the church, but examined by the state as to their competence. These teachers are as professional, therefore, as those in the regular class work. Each religion is allowed to determine its own course of religious instruction, subject only to the approval of the cultus minister or the local authorities. In this way a rupture between the religious sentiments and teaching of successive generations is avoided and it is sought to bring religious training to bear upon morals. These classes learn Scripture, hymns, church service, — the Catholics in Latin and the Jewish in Hebrew, — the history of their church and people, and sometimes a little systematic theology. In some of these schools, there are prizes and diplomas, and the spirit of competition is appealed to. A criticism sometimes made against them, especially against the Lutheran religious pedagogy, is that it is too intellectual. It is, of course, far more systematic and effective from this point of view than the American Sunday School, so that whatever may be said of its edifying effects, the German child knows these topics far better than the American. This system, with modifications, has been adopted in some places in France, England and in America, more often in private than in public schools, however.

The other system originated in France some years after the Franco-Prussian War when the clerical influence in French education gave way to the lay and secular spirit. In these classes, for which also stated times are set apart and which are continued through all the required grades under the name of moral and civic instruction, the religious element is entirely absent, except that there are a few hymns, Bible passages and stories which all agree upon as valuable. Most of the course is made up of carefully selected maxims and especially stories of virtue, records of heroic achievements in French history and even in literature and the drama. Everything, however, has a distinct moral lesson, although that lesson is not made offensively prominent. We have here nearly a score of these textbooks, large and small. It would seen as though the resources of the French records and literature had been ransacked, and indeed many deeds of heroism are culled from the daily press. The matter is often arranged under headings such as cleanliness, acts of kindness, courage, truthfulness versus lying, respect for age, good manners, etc. Each virtue is thus taught in a way appropriate to each stage of childhood, and quite often bands of mercy, rescue leagues and other societies are the outgrowth of this instruction. It is, of course, exposed to much criticism from the clergy on the cogent ground that morality needs the support of religion, at the very least, in childhood. This system has had much influence in England where several similar courses have been evolved, and in this country we have at least one very praiseworthy effort in this direction, addressed mainly, however, to older children.

Besides this, two ways suggest themselves. First, we may try to assume, or tediously enucleate a consensus of religious truth as a basis of will training, e.g., God and immortality, and, ignoring the minority who doubt these, vote them into the public school. Pedagogy need have nothing whatever to say respecting the absolute truth or falsity of these ideas, but there is little doubt that they have an influence on the will, at a certain stage of average development, greater and more essential than any other; so great that even were their vitality to decay like the faith in the Greek or German mythology, we should still have to teach God and a future life as the most imperative of all hypotheses in a field where, as in morals, nothing is so practical as a good theory; and we should have to fall to teaching the Bible as a moral classic, and cultivate a critical sympathy for its view of life. But this way ignores revelation and supernatural claims, while some have other objections to emancipating or "rescuing" the Bible from theology just yet. Indeed, the problem how to teach anything that the mind could not have found out for itself, but that had to be revealed, has not been solved by modern pedagogy, which, since Pestalozzi, has been more and more devoted to natural and developing methods. The latter teaches that there must not be too much seed sown, too much or too high precept, or too much iteration, and that, in Jean Paul's phrase, the hammer must not rest on bell, but only tap and rebound, to bring out a clear tone. Again, a consensus of this content would either have to be carefully defined and would be too generic and abstract for school uses, or else differences of interpretation, which so pervade and are modified by character, culture, temperament, and feeling, would make the consensus itself nugatory. Religious training must be specific at first, and, omitting qualifications, the more explicit the denominational faith the earlier may religious motives affect the will.

This is the way of our hopes, to the closer consideration of which we intend to return in the future, though it must be expected that the happiest consensus will be long quarantined from most schools. Meanwhile a second way, however unpromising, is still open. Noble types of character may rest on only the native instincts of the soul or even on broadly interpreted utilitarian considerations. But if morality without religion were only a bloodless corpse or a plank in a shipwreck, there is now need enough for teachers to study its form, drift, and uses by itself alone. This, at least, is our purpose in considering the will, and this only.

The will, purpose, and even mood of small children when alone, are fickle, fluctuating, contradictory. Our very presence imposes one general law on them, viz., that of keeping our good will and avoiding our displeasure. As the plant grows towards the light, so they unfold in the direction of our wishes, felt as by divination. They respect all you smile at, even buffoonery; look up in their play to call your notice, to study the lines of your sympathy, as if their chief vocation was to learn your desires. Their early lies are often saying what they think will please us, knowing no higher touchstones of truth. If we are careful to be wisely and without excess happy and affectionate when they are good, and saddened and slightly cooled in manifestations of love if they do wrong, the power of association in the normal, eupeptic child will early choose right as surely as pleasure increases vitality. If our love is deep, obedience is an instinct if not a religion. The child learns that while it can not excite our fear, resentment or admiration, etc., it can act on our love, and this should be the first sense of its own efficiency. Thus, too, it first learns that the way of passion and impulse is not the only rule of life, and that something is gained by resisting them. It imitates our acts long before it can understand our words. As if it felt its insignificance, and dreaded to be arrested in some lower phase of its development, its instinct for obedience becomes almost a passion. As the vine must twine or grovel, so the child comes unconsciously to worship idols, and imitates bad patterns and examples in the absence of worthy ones. He obeys as with a deep sense of being our chattel, and, at bottom, admires those who coerce him, if the means be wisely chosen. The authority must, of course, be ascendancy over heart and mind. The more absolute such authority the more the will is saved from caprice and feels the power of steadiness. Such authority excites the unique, unfathomable sense of reverence, which measures the capacity for will-culture, and is the strongest and soundest of all moral motives. It is also the most comprehensive, for it is first felt only towards persons, and personality is a bond, enabling any number of complex elements to act or be treated as whole, as everything does and is in the child's soul, instead of in isolation and detail. In the feeling of respect culminating in worship almost all educational motives are involved, but especially those which alone can bring the will to maturity; and happy the child who is bound by the mysterious and constraining sympathy of dependence, by which, if unblighted by cynicism, a worthy mentor directs and lifts the will. This unconscious reflection of our character and wishes is the diviner side of childhood, by which it is quick and responsive to everything in its moral environment. The child may not be able to tell whether its teacher often smiles, dresses in this way or that, speaks loud or low, has many rules or not, though every element of her personality affects him profoundly. His acts of will have not been *choices*, but a mass of psychic causes far greater than consciousness can estimate have laid a basis of character, than which heredity alone is deeper, before the child knows he has a will. These influences are not transient but life-long, for if the conscious and intentional may anywhere be said to be only a superficial wave over the depths of the unconscious, it is in the sphere of will-culture.

But command and obedience must also be specific to supplant nature. Here begins the difficulty. A young child can know no general commands. "Sit in your chair," means sit a moment, a sort of trick, with no prohibition to stand the next instant. Any just-forbidden act may be done in the next room. All is here and now, and patient reiteration, till habit is formed, and no havoc-making rules which it cannot understand or remember, is our cue. Obedience can, however, be instinct even here, and is its chief virtue, and there is no more fear of weakening the will by it than in the case of soldiers. As the child grows older, however, and as the acts commanded are repugnant, or unusual, there should be increasing care, lest authority be compromised, sympathy ruptured, or lest mutual timidity and indecision, if not mutual insincerity and dissimulation, as well as parodied disobedience, etc., to test us, result. We should, of course, watch for favorable moods, assume no unwonted or preternatural dignity or owlish air of wisdom, and command in a low voice which does not too rudely break in upon the child's train of impressions. The acts we command or forbid should be very few at first, but inexorable. We should be careful not to forbid where we cannot follow a untrusty child, or what we can not prevent. Our own will should be a rock and not a wave. Our requirements should be uniform, with no whim, mood, or periodicity of any sort about them. If we alternate from caresses to severity, are fields and capricious instead of commanding by a fixed and settled plan, if we only now and then take the child in hand, so he does not know precisely what to expect, we really require the child to change its nature with every change in us, and well for the child who can defy such a changeable authority, which not only unsettles but breaks up character anew when it is just at the beginning of the formative period. Neglect is better than this, and fear of inconsistency of authority makes the best parents often jealous of arbitrariness in teachers. Only thus can we develop general habits of will and bring the child to know general maxims of conduct inductively, and only thus by judicious boldness and hardihood in command can we bring the child to feel the conscious strength that comes only from doing unpleasant things. Even if instant obedience be only external at first, it will work inward, for moods are controlled by work, and it is only will which enlarges the bounds of personality.

Yet we must not forget that even morality is relative, and is one thing for adults and often quite another for children. The child knows nothing of absolute truth, justice, or virtues. The various stimuli of discipline are to enforce the higher though weaker insights which the child has already unfolded, rather than to engraft entirely unintuited good. The command must find some ally, feeble though it be, in the child's own soul. We should strive to fill each moment with as little sacrifice or subordination, as mere means or conditions to the future, as possible, for fear of affectation and insincerity. But yet the hardier and sounder the nature, the more we may address training to barely nascent intuitions, with a less ingredient of immediate satisfaction, and the deeper the higher element Of interest will be grounded in the end. The child must find as he advances towards maturity, that every new insight, or realization of his own reveals the fact that you have been there before with commands, cultivating sentiments and habits, and not that he was led to mistake your convenience or hobby for duty, or failed to temper the will by temporizing with it. The young are apt to be most sincere at an age when they are also most mistaken, but if sincerity be kept at its deepest and best, will be least harmful and easiest overcome. If authority supplement rather than supersede good motives, the child will so love authority as to overcome your reluctance to apply it directly, and as a final result will choose the state and act you have pre-formed in its slowly-widening margin of freedom, and will be all the less liable to undue subservience to priest or boss, or fashion or tradition later, as obedience gives place to normal, manly independence.

In these and many other ways everything in conduct should be mechanized as early and completely as possible. The child's notion of what is right is what is habitual, and the simple, to which all else is reduced in thought, is identified with the familiar. It is this primitive stratum of habits which principally determines our deepest belief which all must have over and above knowledge — to which men revert in mature years from youthful vagaries. If good acts are a diet and not a medicine, are repeated over and over again, as every new beat of the loom pounds in one new thread, and sense of justice and right is wrought into the very nerve-cells and fibers; if this ground texture of the soul, this "memory and habit-plexus," this sphere of thoughts we oftenest think and acts we oftenest do, is early, rightly and indiscerptibly wrought, not only does it become a web of destiny for us, so all-determining is it, but we have something perdurable to fall back on if moral shock or crisis or change or calamity shall have rudely broken up the whole structure of later associations. Not only the more we mechanize thus, the more force of soul is freed for higher work, but we are insured against emergencies in which the choice and deed is likely to follow the nearest motive, or that which acts quickest, rather than to pause and be influenced by higher and perhaps intrinsically stronger motives. Reflection always brings in a new set of later-acquired motives and considerations, and if these are better than habit-mechanism, then pause is good; if not, he who deliberates is lost. Our purposive volitions are very few compared with the long series of desires, acts and reactions, often contradictory, many of which were never conscious, and many once willed but now lapsed to reflexes, the traces of which crowding the unknown margins of the soul, constitute the organ of the conscious will.

It is only so far as this primitive will is wrong by nature or training, that drastic reconstructions of any sort are needed. Only those who mistake weakness for innocence, or simplicity for candor, or forget that childish faults are no less serious because universal, deny the, at least, occasional depravity of all children, or fail to see that fear and pain are among the indispensables of education, while a parent, teacher, or even a God, *all* love, weakens and relaxes the will. Children do not cry for the alphabet; the multiplication table is more like medicine than confectionery, and it is only affected thoroughness that omits all that is hard. "The fruits of learning may be sweet, but its roots are always bitter," and it is this alone that makes it possible to strengthen the will while instructing the mind. The well-schooled will comes, like Herder, to scorn the luxury of knowing without the labor of learning. We must anticipate the future penalties of sloth as well as of badness. The will especially is a trust we are to administer for the child, not as he may now wish, but as he will wish when more mature. We must now compel what he will later wish to compel himself to do. To find his habits already formed to the same law that his mature will and the world later enjoin, cements the strongest of all bonds between mentor and child. Nothing, however, must be so individual as punishment. For some, a threat at rare intervals is enough; while for others, however ominous threats may be, they become at once "like scarecrows, on which the foulest birds soonest learn to perch." To scold well and wisely is an art by itself. For some children, pardon is the worst punishment; for others, ignoring or neglect; for others, isolation from friends, suspension from duties; for others, seclusion—which last, however, is for certain ages beset with extreme danger—and for still others, shame from being made conspicuous. Mr. Spencer's "natural penalties" can be applied to but few kinds of wrong, and those not the worst. Basedow tied boys who fell into temptation to a strong pillar to brace them up; if stupid and careless, put on a fool's cap and bells; if they were proud, they were suspended near the ceiling in a basket, as Aristophanes represented Socrates. Two boys who quarreled, were made to look into each other's eyes before the whole school till their angry expressions gave way before the general sense of the ridiculous. This is more ingenious than wise. The object of discipline is to avoid punishment, but even flogging should never be forbidden. It maybe reserved, like a sword in its scabbard, but should not get so rusted in that it can not be drawn on occasion. The law might even limit the size and length of the rod, and place of application, as in Germany, but it should be of no less liberal dimensions here than there. punishment should, of course, be minatory and reformatory, and not vindictive, and we should not forget that certainty is more effective than severity, nor that it is apt to make motives sensuous, and delay the psychic restraint which should early preponderate over the physical. But will-culture for boys is rarely as thorough as it should be without more or less flogging. I would not, of course, urge the extremes of the past. The Spartan beating as a gymnastic drill to toughen, the severity which prevailed in Germany for a long time after its Thirty Years' Wars,[2] the former fashion in many English schools of walking up not infrequently to take a flogging as a plucky thing to do, and with no notion of disgrace attaching to it, shows at least an admirable strength of will. Severe constraint gives poise, inwardness, self-control, inhibition, and not-willingness, if not willingness, while the now too common habit of coquetting for the child's favor, and tickling its ego with praises and prizes, and pedagogic pettifogging for its good-will, and sentimental fear of a judicious slap to rouse a spoiled child with no will to break, to make it keep step with the rest in conduct, instead of delaying a whole school-room to apply a subtle psychology of motives on it, is bad. This reminds one of the Jain who sweeps the ground before him lest he unconsciously tread on a worm. Possibly it may be well, as Schleiermacher suggests, not to repress some one nascent bad act in some natures, but let it and the punishment ensue for the sake of Dr. Spankster's tonic. Dermal pain is not the worst thing in the world, and by a judicious knowledge of how it feels at both ends of the rod, by flogging and being flogged, far deeper pains may be forefended. Insulting defiance, deliberative disobedience, ostentatious carelessness and bravado, are diseases of the will, and, in very rare cases of Promethean obstinacy, the severe process of breaking the will is needful, just as in surgery it is occasionally needful to rebreak a limb wrongly set, or deformed, to set it over better. It is a cruel process, but a crampy will in childhood means moral traumatism of some sort in the adult. Few parents have the nerve to do this, or the insight to see just when it is needed. It is, as some one has said, like knocking a man down to save him from stepping off a precipice. Even the worst punishments are but very faint types of what nature has in store in later life for some forms of perversity of will, and are better than sarcasm, ridicule, or tasks, as penalties. The strength of obstinacy is admirable, and every one ought to have his own will; but a false direction, though almost always the result of faulty previous training when the soul more fluid and mobile, is all the more fatal. While so few intelligent parents are able to refrain from the self-indulgence of too much rewarding or giving, even though it injures the child, it is perhaps too much to expect the hardihood which can be justly cold to the caresses of a child who seeks, by displaying all its stock of goodness and arts of endearment, to buy back good-will after punishment has been deserved. If we wait too long, and punish in cold blood, a young child may hate us; while, if we punish on the instant, and with passion, a little of which is always salutary, on the principle, *ohne Affekt kein Effekt*, [Without passion, no effect] an older child may fail of the natural reactions of conscience, which should always be secured. The maxim, *summum jus summa injuria*, [The rigor of the law may be the greatest wrong] we are often told, is peculiarly true in school, and so it is; but to forego all punishment is no less injustice to the average child, for it is to abandon one of the most effective means of will-culture. We never punish but a part, as it were, of the child's nature; he has lied, but is not therefore a liar, and we deal only with the specific act, and must love all the rest of him.

And yet, after all, indiscriminate flogging is so bad, and the average teacher is so inadequate to that hardest and most tactful of all his varied duties, viz., selecting the right outcrop of the right fault of the right child at the right time and place, mood, etc., for best effect, that the bold statement of such principles as above is perhaps not entirely without practical danger, especially in two cases which Madame Necker and Sigismund have pointed out, and in several cases of which the present writer has notes. First, an habitually good child sometimes has a saturnalia of defiance and disobedience; a series of insubordinate acts are suddenly committed which really mark the first sudden epochful and belated birth of the instinct of independence and self-regulation, on which his future manliness will depend. He is quite irresponsible, the acts are never repeated, and very lenient treatment causes him, after the conflict of tumultuous feelings has expanded his soul, to react healthfully into habitual docility again, if some small field for independent action be at once opened him. The other case is that of *ennui*, of which children suffer such nameless qualms. When I should open half a dozen books, start for a walk, and then turn back, wander about in mind or body, seeking but not finding content in anything, a child in my mood will wish for a toy, an amusement, food, a rare indulgence, only to neglect or even reject it petulantly when granted. These flitting "will-spectres" are physical, are a mild form of the many fatal dangers of fatigue; and punishment is the worst of treatment. Rest or diversion is the only cure, and the teacher's mind must be fruitful of purposes to that end. Perhaps a third case for palliative treatment is, those lies which attend the first sense of badness. The desire to conceal it occasionally accompanies the nascent effort to reform and make the lie true. These cases are probably rare, while the temptation to lie is far greater for one who does ill than for one who does well, for fear is the chief motive, and a successful lie which concealed would weaken the desire to cure a fault.

We have thus far spoken of obedience, and come now to the later necessity of self-guidance, which, if obedience has wrought its perfect work, will be natural and inevitable. It is very hard to combine reason and coercion, yet it is needful that children think themselves free long before we cease to determine them. As we slowly cease to prescribe and begin to inspire, a very few well-chosen mottoes, proverbs, maxims, should be taught very simply, so that they will sink deep. Education has been defined as working against the chance influences of life, and it is certain that without some precepts and rules the will will not exert itself. If reasons are given, and energy is much absorbed in understanding, the child will assent but will not do. If the mind is not strong, many wide ideas are very dangerous. Strong wills are not fond of arguments, and if a young person falls to talking or thinking beyond his experience, subjective or objective, both conduct and thought are soon confused by chaotic and incongruous opinions and beliefs; and false expectations, which are the very seducers of the will, arise. There can be little will-training by words, and the understanding can not realize the ideals of the will. All great things are dangerous, as Plato said, and the truth itself is not only false but actually immoral to unexpanded minds. Will-culture is intensive, not extensive, and the writer knows a case in which even a vacation ramble with a moralizing fabulist has undermined the work of years. Our precepts must be made very familiar, copiously illustrated, well wrought together by habit and attentive thought, and above all clear cut, that the pain of violating them may be sharp and poignant. Vague and too general precepts beyond the horizon of the child's real experience do not haunt him if they are outraged. Now the child must obey these, and will, if he has learned to obey well the command of others.

One of the best sureties that he will do so is muscle-culture, for if the latter are weaker than the nerves and brain, the gap between knowing and doing appears and the will stagnates. Gutsmuths, the father of gymnastics in Germany before Jahn, used to warn men not to fancy that the few tiny muscles that moved the pen or tongue had power to elevate men. They might titillate the soul with words and ideas; but rigorous, symmetrical muscle-culture alone, he and his Turner societies believed, could regenerate the Fatherland, for it was one thing to paint the conflict of life, and quite another to bear arms in it. They said, "The weaker the body the more it commands; the stronger it is the more it obeys."

In this way we shall have a strong, well-knit soul-texture, made up of volitions and ideas like warp and woof. Mind and will will be so compactly organized that all their forces can be brought to a single point. Each concept or purpose will call up those related to it, and once strongly set toward its object, the soul will find itself borne along by unexpected forces. This power of totalizing, rather than any transcendent relation of elements, constitutes at least the practical unity of the soul, and this unimpeded association of its elements is true or inner freedom of will. Nothing is wanting or lost when the powers of the soul are mobilized for a great task, and its substance is impervious to passion. With this organization, men of really little power accomplish wonders. Without it great minds are confused and lost. They have only velleity or caprice. The will makes a series of vigorous, perhaps almost convulsive, but short, inconsistent efforts. As Jean Paul says, there is sulphur, charcoal, and saltpetre in the soul, but powder is not made, for they never find each other. To understand this will-plexus is preeminent among the new demands now laid on educators.

But, although this focalizing power of acting with the whole rather than with a part of the soul, gives independence of many external, conventional, proximate standards of conduct, deepening our interests in life, and securing us against disappointment by defining our expectations, while such a sound and simple will-philosophy is proof against considerable shock and has firmness of texture enough to bear much responsibility, there is, of course, something deeper, without which all our good conduct is more or less hollow. This is that better purity established by mothers in the plastic heart, before the superfoetation of precept is possible, or even before the "soul takes flight in language"; it is perhaps pre-natal or hereditary. Much every way depends on how aboriginal our goodness is, whether the will acts with effort, as we solve an intricate problem, in solitude, or as we say the multiplication table, which only much distraction can confuse, or as we repeat the alphabet, which the din of battle could not hinder. Later and earlier training should harmonize with each other and with nature. Thrice happy he who is so wisely trained that he comes to believe he believes what his soul deeply does believe, to say what he feels and feel what he really does feel, and chiefly whose express volitions square with the profounder drift of his will as the resultant of all he has desired or wished, expected, attended to, or striven for. When such an one comes to his moral majority by standing for the first time upon his own careful conviction, against the popular cry, or against his own material interests or predaceous passions, and feels the constraint and joy of pure obligation which comes up from this deep source, a new, original force is brought into the world of wills. Call it inspiration, or Kant's transcendental impulse above and outside of experience, or Spencer's deep reverberations from a vast and mysterious past of compacted ancestral experiences, the most concentrated, distilled and instinctive of all psychic products, and as old as Mr. Tyndall's "fiery cloud" — the name or even source is little. We would call it the purest, freest, most prevailing, because most inward, will or conscience.

This free, habitual guidance by the highest and best, by conviction with no sense of compulsion or obligation, impractical if not dangerous ideal, for it can be actually realized only by the rarest moral genius. For most of us, the best education is that which makes us the best and most obedient servants. This is the way of peace and the way of nature, for even if we seriously try to keep up a private conscience at all, apart from feeling, faction, party or class spirit, or even habit, which are our habitual guides, the difficulties are so great that most hasten, more or less consciously and voluntarily, to put themselves under authority again, serving only the smallest margin of independence in material interests, choice of masters, etc, and yielding to the pleasing and easy illusion that inflates the minimum to seem the maximum of freedom, and uses the noblest ideal of history, viz., that of pure autonomous oughtness, as a pedestal for idols of selfishness, caprice and conceit. The trouble is in interpreting these moral instincts, for even the authorities lack the requisite self-knowledge in which all wisdom culminates. The moral interregnum which the *Aufklärung* [Enlightenment] has brought will not end till these instincts are rightly interpreted by in intelligence. The richest streams of thought must flow about them, the best methods must peep and pry till their secrets are found and put into the idea-pictures in which most men think.

This brings us, finally, to the highest and also immediately practical method of moral education, viz., training the will by and for intellectual work. Youth and childhood must not be subordinated as means to maturity. Learning is more useful than knowing. It is the way and not the goal, the work and not the product, the acquiring and not the acquisition, that educates will and character. To teach only results, which are so simple, without methods by which they were obtained, which are so complex and hard, to develop the sense of possession without the strain of activity, to teach great matters too easily or even as play, always to wind along the lines of least resistance into the child's mind, is imply to add another and most enervating luxury to child-life. Only the sense and power of effort, which made Lessing prefer the search to the possession of truth, which trains the will in the intellectual field, which is becoming more and more the field of its activity, counts for character and makes instruction really educating. This makes mental work a series of acts, or living thoughts, and not merely words. Real education, that we can really teach, and that which is really most examinable, is what we do, while those who acquire without effort may be extremely instructed without being truly educated.

It is those who have been trained to put forth mental power that come to the front later, while it is only those whose acquisitions are not transpeciated into power who are in danger of early collapse.

It is because of this imperfect appropriation through lack of volitional reaction that mental training is so often dangerous, especially in its higher grades. Especially wherever good precepts are allowed to rest peacefully beside undiscarded bad habits, moral weakness is directly cultivated. Volitional recollection, or forcing the mind to reproduce a train of impressions, strengthens what we may call the mental will; while if multifarious impressions which excite at the time are left to take their chances, at best, fragmentary reproduction, incipient amnesia, the prelude of mental decay, may be soon detected. Few can endure the long working over of ideas, especially if at all fundamental, which is needful to full maturity of mind, without grave moral danger. New standpoints and ideas require new combinations of the mental elements, with constant risk that during the process, what was already secured will fall back into its lower components. Even oar immigrants suffer morally from the change of manners and customs and ideas, and yet education menus change; the more training the more change, as a rule, and the more danger during the critical transition period while we oscillate between control by old habits, or association within the old circle of thought, and by the new insights, as a medical student often suffers from trying to bring the regulation of his physical functions under new and imperfect hygienic insights. Thus most especially if old questions, concerning which we have long since ceased to trust ourselves to give reasons, need to be reopened, there is especial danger that the new equilibrium about which the dynamic is to be re-resolved into static power will be established, if at all, with loss instead of with gain. Indeed, it is a question not of schools but of civilization, whether mental training, from the three R's to science and philosophy, shall really make men better, as the theory of popular education assumes, and whether the genius and talent of the few who can receive and bear it can be brought to the full maturity of a knowledge fully facultized—a question paramount, even in a republic, to the general education of the many.

The illusion is that beginnings are hard. They are easy. Almost any mind can advance a little way into almost any subject. The feeblest youth can push on briskly in the beginning of a new subject, but he forgets, and so does the examiner who marks him, that difficulties increase not in arithmetical but in almost geometrical ratio as he advances. The fact, too, that all topics are taught by all teachers and that we have no specialized teaching in elementary branches, and that examinations are placed in the most debilitating part of our peculiarly debilitating spring, these help us to solve the problem which China has solved so well, viz., how to instruct and not to educate. A pass mark, say of fifty, should be given not for mastery of the first half of the book, or for knowledge of half the matter in it, but for that of three-fourths or more. Suppose one choose the easier method of tattooing his mind by attaining the easy early stages of proficiency in many subjects, as is possible and even encouraged in too many of our school and college curricula, he weakens the will-quality of his mind. Smattering is dissipation of energy. Only great, concentrated and prolonged efforts in one direction really train the mind, because only *they* train the will beneath it. Many little, heterogeneous efforts of different sorts leave the mind in a muddle of heterogeneous impressions, and the will like a rubber band is stretched to flaccidity around one after another bundle of objects too large for it to clasp into unity. Here again, *in der Beschränkung zeigt sich der Meister* [The master shows himself in self-limitation]; all-sidedness through one-sidedness; by stalking the horse or cow out in the spring time, till he gnaws his small allotted circle of grass to the ground, and not by roving and cropping at will, can he be taught that the sweetest joint is nearest the root, are convenient symbols of will-culture in the intellectual field. Even a long cram, if only on one subject, which brings out the relations of the parts, or a "one-study college," as is already devised in the West, or the combination of several subjects even in primary school grades into a "concentration series," as devised by Ziller and Rein, the university purpose as defined by Ziller of so combining studies that each shall stand in the course next to that with which it is inherently closest connected by matter and method, or the requirements of one central and two collateral branches for the doctorate examination—all these devices no doubt tend to give a sense of efficiency, which is one of the deepest and proudest joys of life, in the place of a sense of possession so often attended by the exquisite misery of conscious weakness. The unity of almost any even ideal purpose is better than none, if it tend to check the superficial one of learning to repeat again or of boxing the whole compass of sciences and liberal arts, as so many of our high schools or colleges attempt.

Finally, in the sphere of mental productivity and originality, a just preponderance of the will-element makes men distrust new insights, quick methods, and short cuts, and trust chiefly to the genius of honest and sustained work, in power of which perhaps lies the greatest intellectual difference between men. When ideas are ripe for promulgation they have been condensed and concentrated, thought traverses them quickly and easily—in a word, they have become practical, and the will that waits over a new idea patiently and silently, without anxiety, even though with a deepening sense of responsibility, till all sides have been seen, all authorities consulted, all its latent mental reserves heard from, is the man who "talks with the rifle and not with the water-hose," or, in a rough farmer's phrase, "boils his words till he can give his hearers sugar and not sap." Several of the more important discoveries of the present generation, which cost many weary months of toil, have been enumerated in a score or two of lines, so that every experimenter could set up his apparatus and get the results in a few minutes. Let us not forget that, in most departments of mental work, the more we revise and reconstruct our thought, the longer we inhibit its final expression, while the oftener we return to it refreshed from other interests, the clearer and more permeable for other minds it becomes, because the more it tends to express itself in terms of willed action, which is "the language of complete men."

So closely bound together are moral and religious training that a discussion of one without the other would be incomplete. In a word, religion is the most generic kind of culture as opposed to all systems or departments which are one sided. All education culminates in it because it is chief among human interests, and because it gives inner unity to the mind, heart, and will. How now should this common element of union be taught?

To be really effective and lasting, moral and religious training must begin in the cradle. It was a profound remark of Froebel that *the unconsciousness of a child is rest in God*. This need not be understood in guy pantheistic sense. From this rest in God the childish soul should not be abruptly or prematurely aroused. Even the primeval stages of psychic growth are rarely so all-sided, so purely unsolicited, spontaneous, and unprecocious, as not to be in a sense a fall from Froebel's unconsciousness or rest in God. The sense of touch, the mother of all the other senses, is the only one which the child brings into the world already experienced; but by the pats, caresses, hugs, etc., so instinctive with young mothers, varied feelings and sentiments are communicated to the child long before it recognizes its own body as distinct from things about it. The mother's face and voice are the first conscious objects as the infant soul unfolds, and she soon comes to stand in the very place of God to her child. All the religion of which the child is capable during this by no means brief stage of its development consists of those sentiments—gratitude, trust, dependence, love, etc., now felt only for her—which are later directed toward God. The less these are now cultivated toward the mother, who is now their only fitting if not their only possible object, the more feebly they will later be felt toward God. This, too, adds greatly to the sacredness and the responsibilities of motherhood. Froebel perhaps is right that thus fundamental religious sentiments can be cultivated in the earliest months of infancy. It is of course impossible not to seem, perhaps even not to be, sentimental upon this theme, for the infant soul has no other content than sentiments, and because upon these rests the whole superstructure of religion in child or adult. The mother's emotions, and physical and mental states, indeed, imparted and reproduced in the infant so immediately, unconsciously, and through so many avenues, that it is no wonder that these relations see mystic. Whether the mother is habitually under the influence of calm and tranquil emotions, or her temper is fluctuating or violent, or her movements are habitually energetic or soft and caressing, or she be regular or irregular in her ministrations to the infant in her arms, all these characteristics and habits are registered in the primeval language of touch upon the nervous system of the child. From this point of view, poise and calmness, the absence of all intense annuli and of sensations or transitions which are abrupt or sudden, and an atmosphere of quieting influences, like everything which retards by broadening, is in the general line of religious culture. The soul of an infant is well compared to a seed planted in a garden. It is not pressed or moved by the breezes which rustle the leaves overhead. The sunlight does not fall upon it, and even dew and evening coolness scarcely reach it; but yet there is not a breath of air or a ray of sunshine, nor a drop of moisture to which it is responsive, and which does not stir all its germinant forces. The child is a plant, must live out of doors in proper season, and there must be no forcing. Religion, then, at this important stage, at least, is naturalism pure and simple, and religious training is the supreme art of standing out of nature's way. So implicit is the unity of soul and body at this formative age that care of the body is the most effective ethico-religious culture.

Next to be considered are the sentiments which unfold under the influence of that fresh and naive curiosity which attends the first impressions of natural objects from which both religion and science spring as from one common root. The awe and sublimity of a thunderstorm, the sights and sounds of a spring morning, objects which lead the child's thoughts to what is remote in time and space, old trees, ruins, the rocks, and, above all, the heavenly bodies—the utilization of these lessons is the most important task of the religious teacher during the *kindergarten* stage of childhood. Still more than the undevout astronomer, the undevout child under such influences is abnormal. In these directions the mind of the child is as open and plastic as that of the ancient prophet to the promptings of the inspiring Spirit. The child can recognize no essential difference between nature and the supernatural, and the products of mythopoeic fancy which have been spun about natural objects, and which have lain so long and so warm about the hearts of generations and races of men, are now the best of all nutriments for the soul. To teach scientific rudiments only about nature, on the shallow principle that nothing should be taught which must be unlearned, or to encourage the child to assume the critical attitude of mind, is dwarfing the heart and prematurely forcing the head. It has been said that country life is religion for children at this stage. However this may be, it is clear that natural religion is rooted in such experiences, and precedes revealed religion in the order of growth and education, whatever its logical order in systems of thought may be. A little later, habits of truthfulness[3] are best cultivated by the use of the senses in exact observation. To see a simple phenomenon in nature and report it fully and correctly is no easy matter, but the habit of trying to do so teaches what truthfulness is and leaves the impress of truth upon the whole life and character. I do not hesitate to say, therefore, that elements of science should be taught to children for the moral effects of its influences. At the same time all truth is not sensuous, and this training alone at this age tends to make the mind pragmatic, dry, and insensitive or unresponsive to that other kind of truth the value of which is not measured by its certainty so much as by its effect upon us. We must learn to interpret the heart and our native instincts as truthfully as we do external nature, for our happiness in life depends quite as largely upon bringing our beliefs into harmony with the deeper feelings of our nature as it does upon the ability to adapt ourselves to our physical environment. Thus not only all religious beliefs and moral acts will strengthen if they truly express the character instead of cultivating affectation and insincerity in opinion, word, and deed, as with mistaken pedagogic methods they may do. This latter can be avoided only by leaving all to naturalism and spontaneity at first, and feeding the soul only according to its appetites and stage of growth. No religious truth must be taught as fundamental—especially as fundamental to morality—which can be seriously doubted or even misunderstood. Yet it must be expected that convictions will be transformed and worked over and over again, and only late, if at all, will an equilibrium between the heart and the truth it clings to as finally satisfying be attained. Hence most positive religious instruction, or public piety, if taught at all, should be taught briefly as most serious but too high for the child yet, or as rewards to stimulate curiosity for them later, but sacred things should not become too familiar or be conventionalized before they can be felt or understood.

The child's conception of God should not be personal or too familiar *at first*, but He should appear distant and vague, inspiring awe and reverence far more than love; in a word, as the God of nature rather than as devoted to serviceable ministrations to the child's individual wants. The latter should be taught to be a faithful servant rather than a favorite of God. The inestimable pedagogic value of the God-idea consists in that it widens the child's glimpse of the whole, and gives the first presentment of the universality of laws, such as are observed in its experiences and that of others, so that all things seem comprehended under one stable system or government. The slow realization that God's laws are not like those of parents and teachers, evadible, suspensible, but changeless, and their penalties sure as the laws of nature, is most important factor of moral training. First the law, the schoolmaster, then the Gospel; first nature, then grace, is the order of growth.

The pains or pleasures which follow many acts are immediate, while the results that follow others are so remote or so serious that the child must utilize the experience of others. Artificial rewards and punishments must be cunningly devised so as to simulate and typify as closely as possible the real natural penalty, and they must be administered uniformly and impartially like laws of nature. As commands are just, and as they are gradually perceived to spring from superior wisdom, respect arises, which Kant called the bottom motive of duty, and defined as the immediate determination of the will by law, thwarting self-love. Here the child reverences what is not understood as authority, and to the childish "Why?" which always implies imperfect respect for the authority, however displeasing its behest, the teacher or parent should always reply, "You cannot understand why yet," unless quite sure that a convincing and controlling insight can be given, such as shall make all future exercise of outward authority in this particular unnecessary. From this standpoint the great importance of the character and native dignity of the teacher is best seen. Daily contact with some teachers is itself all-sided ethical education for the child without a spoken precept. Here, too, the real advantage of male over female teachers, especially for boys, is seen in their superior physical strength, which often, if highly estimated, gives real dignity and commands real respect, and especially in the unquestionably greater uniformity of their moods and their discipline.

During the first years of school life, a point of prime importance in ethico-religious training is the education of conscience. This latter is the most complex and perhaps the most educable of all our so-called "faculties." A system of carefully arranged talks, with copious illustrations from history and literature, about such topics as fair play, slang, cronies, dress, teasing, getting mad, prompting in class, white lies, affectation, cleanliness, order, honor, taste, self-respect, treatment of animals, reading, vacation pursuits, etc., can be brought quite within the range of boy-and-girl interests by a sympathetic and tactful teacher, and be made immediately and obviously practical. All this is nothing more or less than conscience-building. The old superstition that children have innate faculties of such a finished sort that they flash up and grasp the principle of things by a rapid sort of first "intellection," an error that made all departments of education so trivial, assumptive and dogmatic for centuries before Comenius, Basedow and Pestalozzi, has been banished everywhere save from moral and religious training, where it still persists in full force. The senses develop first, and all the higher intuitions called by the collective name of conscience gradually and later in life. They first take the form of sentiments without much insight, and are hence liable to be unconscious affectation, and are caught insensibly from the environment with the aid of inherited predisposition, and only made more definite by such talks as the above. But parents are prone to forget that healthful and correct sentiments concerning matters of conduct are, at first, very feeble, and that the sense of obligation needs the long and careful guardianship of external authority. Just as a young medical student with a rudimentary notion of physiology and hygiene is sometimes disposed to undertake a more or less complete reform of his diet, regimen, etc., to make it "scientific" in a way that an older and a more learned physician would shrink from, so the half-insights of boys into matters of moral regimen are far too apt, in the American temperament, to expend, in precocious emancipation and crude attempts at practical realization, the force which is needed to bring their insights to maturity. Authority should be relaxed gradually, explicitly, and provisionally over one definite department of conduct at a time. To distinguish right and wrong in their own nature is the highest and most complex of intellectual processes. Most men and all children are guided only by associations of greater or less subtlety. Perhaps the whole round of human duties might be best taught by gathering illustrations of selfishness and tracing it in its countless disguises and ramifications through every stage of life. Selfishness is opposed to a sense of the infinite and is inversely as real religion, and the study of it is not, like systematic ethics, apt to be confused and made unpractical by conflicting theories.

The Bible, the great instrument in the education of conscience, is far less juvenile than it is now the fashion to suppose. At the very least, it expresses the result of the ripest human experience, the noblest traditions of humanity. Old Testament history, even more than most very ancient history, is distilled to an almost purely ethical content. For centuries Scripture was withheld from the masses for the same reason that Plato refused at first to put his thoughts into writing, because it would be sure to be misunderstood by very many and lead to that worst of errors and fanaticism caused by half-truths. Children should not approach it too lightly.

The Old Testament, perhaps before or more than the New, is the Bible for childhood. A good, protracted course of the law pedagogically prepares the way for the apprehension of the Gospel. Then the study of the Old Testament should begin with selected tales, told, as in the German schools, impressively, in the teacher's language, but objectively, and without exegetical or hortatory comment. The appeal is directly to the understanding only at first, but the moral lesson is brought clearly and surely within the child's reach, but not personally applied after the manner common with us.

Probably the most important changes for the educator to study are those which begin between the ages of twelve and sixteen and are completed only some years later, when the young adolescent receives from nature a new capital of energy and altruistic feeling. It is physiological second birth, and success in life depends upon the care and wisdom with which this new and final invoice of energy is husbanded. These changes constitute a natural predisposition to a change of heart, and may perhaps be called, in Kantian phrase, its *schema*. Even from the psychophysic standpoint it is a correct instinct which has slowly led churches to center so much of their cultus upon regeneration. In this I, of course, only assert here the neurophysical side, which is everywhere present, even if everywhere subordinate to the spiritual side. As everywhere, so here, too, the physical may be called in a sense regulative rather than constitutive. It is therefore not surprising that statistics show that far more conversions, proportionately, take place during the adolescent period, which does not normally end before the age of twenty-four or five, than during any other period of equal length. At this age most churches confirm.

Before this age the child lives in the present, is normally selfish, deficient in sympathy, but frank and confidential, obedient to authority, and without affectation save the supreme affectation of childhood, viz., assuming the words, manners, habits, etc., of those older than itself. But now stature suddenly increases, and the power of physical and mental endurance and effort diminishes for a time; larynx, nose, chin change, and normal and morbid ancestral traits and features appear. Far greater and more protracted, though unseen, are the changes which take place in the nervous system, both in the development of the cortex and expansion of the convolutions and the growth of association-fibers by which the elements shoot together and relation of things are seen, which hitherto seemed independent, to which it seems as if for a few years the energies of growth were chiefly directed. Hence this period is so critical and changes in character are so rapid. No matter how confidential the relations with the parent may have been, an important domain of the soul now declares its independence. Confidences are shared with those of equal age and withheld from parents, especially by boys, to an extent probably little suspected by most parents. Education must be addressed to freedom, which recognizes only self-made law, and spontaneity of opinion and conduct is manifested, often in extravagant and grotesque forms. There is now a longing for that kind of close sympathy and friendship which makes cronies and intimates; there is a craving for strong emotions which gives pleasure in exaggerations; and there are nameless longings for what is far, remote, strange, which emphasizes the self-estrangement which Hegel so well describes, and which marks the normal rise of the presentiment of something higher than self. Instincts of rivalry and competition now grow strong in boys, and girls grow more conscientious and inward, and begin to feel their music, reading, religion, painting, etc., and to realize the bearing of these upon their future adult life. There is often a strong instinct of devotion and self-sacrifice toward some, perhaps almost any, object, or in almost any cause which circumstances may present. Moodiness and perhaps a love of solitude are developed. "Growing fits" make hard and severe labor of body and mind impossible without dwarfing or arresting the development, by robbing of its nutrition some part of the organism—stomach, lungs, chest, heart, back, brain, etc.—which is peculiarly liable to disease later. It is never so hard to tell the truth plainly and objectively and without any subjective twist. The life of the mere individual ceases and that of person, or better, of the race, begins. It is a period of realization, and hence often of introspection. In healthy natures it is the golden age of life, in which enthusiasm, sympathy, generosity, and curiosity are at their strongest and best, and when growth is so rapid that, e.g., each college class is conscious of a vast interval of development which separates it from the class below; but it is also a period subject to Wertherian crises, such as Hume, Richter, J.S. Mill, and others passed through, and all depends on the direction given to these new forces.

The dangers of this period are great and manifest. The chief of these, far greater even than the dangers of intemperance, is that the sexual elements of soul and body will be developed prematurely and disproportionately. Indeed, early maturity in this respect is itself bad. If it occurs before other compensating and controlling powers are unfolded, this element is hypertrophied and absorbs and dwarfs their energy and it is then more likely to be uninstructed and to suck up all that is vile in the environment. Far more than we realize, the thoughts and feelings of youth center about this factor of his nature. Quite apart, therefore, from its intrinsic value, education should serve the purpose of preoccupation, and should divert attention from an element of our nature the premature or excessive development of which dwarfs every part of soul and body. Intellectual interests, athleticism, social and esthetic tastes, should be cultivated. There should be some change in external life. Previous routine and drill-work must be broken through and new occupations resorted to, that the mind may not be left idle while the hands are mechanically employed. Attractive home-life, friendships well chosen and on a high plane, and regular habits, should of course be cultivated. Now, too, though the intellect is not frequently judged insane, so that pubescent insanity is comparatively rare, the feelings, which are yet more fundamental to mental sanity, are most often perverted, and lack of emotional steadiness, violent and dangerous impulses, unreasonable conduct, lack of enthusiasm and sympathy, are very commonly caused by abnormalities here. Neurotic disturbances, such as hysteria, chorea, and, in the opinion of some physicians, sick-headache and early dementia are peculiarly liable to appear and become seated during this period. In short, the previous selfhood is broken up like the regulation copy handwriting of early school years, and a new individual is in process of crystallization. All is solvent, plastic, peculiarly susceptible to external influences.

Between love and religion, God and nature have wrought a strong and indissoluble bond. Flagellations, fasts, exposure, excessive penances of many kinds, the Hindoo cultus of quietude, and mental absorption in vacuity and even one pedagogic motive of a cultus of the spiritual and supernatural, e. g. in the symposium of Plato, are all designed as palliatives and alteratives of degraded love. Change of heart before pubescent years, there are several scientific reasons for thinking means precocity and forcing. The age signalized by the ancient Greeks as that at which the study of what was comprehensively called music should begin, the age at which Roman guardianship ended, as explained by Sir Henry Maine, at which boys are confirmed in the modern Greek, Catholic, Lutheran and Episcopal churches, and at which the child Jesus entered the temple, is as early as any child ought consciously to go about his heavenly Father's business. If children are instructed in the language of these sentiments too early, the all-sided deepening and broadening of soul and of conscience which should come with adolescent years will be incomplete. Revival sermon which the writer has heard preached to very young children are analogous to exhorting them to imagine themselves married people and inculcating the duties of that relation. It is because this precept is violated in the intemperate haste for immediate results that we may so often hear childish sentiments and puerile expressions so strangely mingled in the religious experience of otherwise apparently mature adults, which remind one of a male voice constantly modulating from manly tones into boyish falsetto. Some one has said of very early risers that they were apt to be conceited all the forenoon, and stupid and uninteresting all the afternoon and evening. So, too, precocious infant Christians are apt to be conceited and full of pious affectations all the forenoon of life, and thereafter commonplace enough in their religious life. One is reminded of Aristotle's theory of Catharsis, according to which the soul was purged of strong or bad passions by listening to vivid representations of them on the stage. So, by the forcing method we deprecate, the soul is given just enough religious stimulus to act as an inoculation against deeper and more serious interest later. At this age the prescription of a series of strong feelings is very apt to cause attention to concentrate on physical states in a way which may culminate in the increased activity of the passional nature, or may induce that sort of self-flirtation which is expressed in morbid love of autobiographic confessional outpourings, or may issue in the supreme selfishness of incipient and often unsuspected hysteria. Those who are led to Christ normally by obeying conscience are not apt to endanger the foundation of their moral character if they should later chance to doubt the doctrine of verbal inspiration or some of the miracles, or even get confused about the Trinity, because their religious nature is not built on the sand. The art of leading young men through college without ennobling or enlarging any of the religious notions of childhood is anti-pedagogic and unworthy philosophy, and is to leave men puerile in the highest department of their nature.

At the age we have indicated, when the young man instinctively takes the control of himself into his own hands, previous ethico-religious training should be brought to a focus and given a personal application, which, to be most effective, should probably, in most cases, be according to the creed of the parent. It is a serious and solemn epoch, and ought to be fittingly signalised. Morality now needs religion, which cannot have affected life much before. Now duties should be recognised as divine commands, for the strongest motives, natural and supernatural, are needed for the regulation of the new impulses, passions, desires, half insights, ambitions, etc., which come to the American temperament so suddenly before the methods of self-regulation can become established and operative. Now a deep personal sense of purity and impurity are first possible, and indeed inevitable, and this natural moral tension is a great opportunity to the religious teacher. A serious sense of God within, and of responsibilities which transcend this life as they do the adolescent's power of comprehension; a feeling for duties deepened by a realization and experience of their conflict such as some have thought to be the origin of religion itself in the soul—these, too, are elements of the "theology of the heart" revealed at this age to every serious youth, but to the judicious emphasis and utilization of which, the teacher should lend his consummate skill. While special lines of interest leading to a career must be now well grounded, there must also be a culture of the ideal and an absorption in general views and remote and universal ends. If all that is pure and disciplining in what is transcendent, whether to the Christian believers, the poet or the philosopher, had even been devised only for the better regulation of human energies set free at this age, but not yet fully defined or realized, they would still have a most potent justification on this ground alone. At any rate, what is often wasted in excess here, if husbanded, ripens into philosophy, the larger love to the world, the true and the good, in a sense not unlike that in the symposium of Plato.

Finally, there is danger lest this change, as prescribed and formulated by the church, be too sudden and violent, and the capital of moral force which should last a lifetime be consumed in a brief, convulsive effort, like the sudden running down of a watch if its spring be broken. Piety is naturally the slowest because the most comprehensive kind of growth. Quetelet says that the measure of the state of civilization in a nation is the way in which it achieves its revolutions. As it becomes truly civilized, revolutions cease to be sudden and violent, and become gradually transitory and without abrupt change. The same is true of that individual crisis which psychophysiology describes as adolescence, and of which theology formulates a higher spiritual potency as conversion. The adolescent period lasts ten years or more, during all of which development of every sort is very rapid and constant, and it is, as already remarked, intemperate haste for immediate results, of reaping without sowing, which has made so many regard change of heart as an instantaneous conquest rather than as a growth, and persistently to forget that there is something of importance before and after it in healthful religious experience.

[Footnote 1: See author's Boy Life, in Massachusetts Country Town Forty Years Ago. Pedagogical Seminary, June, 1906, vol. 13, pp. 192-207.]

[Footnote 2: Those interested in school statistics may value the record kept by a Swabian schoolmaster named Hauberle, extending over fifty-one years and seven months' experience as a teacher, as follows: 911,527 blows with a cane; 124,010 with a rod; 20,939 with a ruler; 136,715 with the hand; 19,295 over the mouth; 7,905 boxes on the ear; 1,115,800 snaps on the head; 22,763 nota benes with Bible, catechism, hymnbook and grammar; 777 times boys had to kneel on peas; 613 times on triangular blocks of wand; 5,001 had to carry a timber mare; and, 7,701 hold the rod high; the last two being punishments of his own invention. Of the blows with the cane 800,000 were for Latin vowels, and 76,000 of those with the rod for Bible verses and hymns. He used a scolding vocabulary of over 3,000 terms, of which one-third were of his own invention.]

[Footnote 3: For most recent and elaborate study of children's lies see Zeitschrift für pädagogische Psychologie, Pathologie und Hygiene, Juli, 1905. Jahrgang 7, Heft 3, pp. 177-205.]

* * * * *

INDEX

* * * * *

Abstract words, need of Accessory and fundamental movement Accuracy of memory overdone Activity of children, motor Adolescence biography and literature of characterized Agriculture Alternations of physical and psychic states Altruism of country children of woman, cutlet for Amphimixis, psychic, basis of Anger Anthropometry and ideal of gymnastics Arboreal life and the hand Art study Arts and crafts movement Associations devised or guided by adults Astronomy Athletic festivals in Greece Athletics as a conversation topic dangers and defects of records in Attention fostered by *commando* exercises rhythm in spontaneous Authority and adolescence Autobiographies of boyhood Automatisms motor, causes and kinds of control and serialization of danger of premature control of desirable

Bachelor women Basal muscles, development of Basal powers, development of Bathing Beauty, age of feminine Belief, habit and muscle determining Bible, the influence of, in adolescence methods of teaching study of, for girls study of, in German method of will training study of, order in study of, postponed study of, preparation for Biography and adolescence Blood vessels, expansion at puberty Blushing, characteristic of puberty Body training, Greek Botany Boxing Boys age of little affection in dangers of coeducation for differences between, and girls latitude in conduct and studies of, before puberty puberty in, characteristics of Brain action, unity in Bullying Bushido

Cakewalk Castration, functional in women Catharsis, Aristotle's theory of Character and muscles Children faults and crimes of motor activity of motor defects of selfishness of Chivalry, medieval Chorea Christianity, muscular Chums and cronies Church, feminity in the City children vs. country children Civilized men, savages physically superior to Climbing hill muscles, age for exercise of Coeducation, dangers in College coeducation in English requirements of woman's ideal school and Combat, personal, as exercise *Commando* exercises restricted for girls Concentration Concreteness in modern language study, criticized Conduct mechanized of Italian schoolboys tabulated weather and Confessionalism of young women passional inducement to Conflict, *see* Combat Control nervous, through dancing of anger of brute instincts of children's movements Conversation, athletics in degeneration in, causes of Conversion Coördination loosened at adolescence inherited tendencies of muscular Corporal punishment Country children vs. city children Crime, juvenile causes of education and reading and Cruelty, a juvenile fault Culture heroes

    Dancing
Deadly sins, the seven, vs. modern juvenile faults
Debate and will-training
Doll curve
Domesticity
Dramatic instinct of puberty
Drawing, curve of stages of
Dueling

    Education
  art in
  crime and
  industrial
  intellectual
  manual
  moral and religious
  of boys
  of girls
  physical
Effort, as a developing force
Emotions
  dancing completest language of the
  religion directed to
Endurance
Energy and laziness
English
  language and literature, pedagogy of
  pedagogic degeneration in, causes of
  requirements of college
  sense language, dangers of
Ennui
Erect position and true life
Ethics, study of, criticized
Ethical judgments of children
Euphoria and exercise
Evolution, movement as a measure of

Exercise
  health and
  measurements and
  music and
  nascent periods and
  rhythm and
    Farm work Fatigue at puberty chores and not a cause for punishment play and restlessness expressive of result of labor with defective psychic impulsion rhythm of activity and will-culture and Faults of children Favorite sounds and words Fecundity of college women Femininity in the church in the school and college Feminists Fighting Flogging Foreign languages, dangers of France, religious training in Friendships of adolescence Fundamental and accessory Future life, as a school teaching
    Games
  groups
  Panhellenic
Gangs, organized juvenile
Genius, early development of
Germany, will-training in
Girl graduates
  aversion to marriage of
  fecundity of
  sterility of
Girls
  and boys, differences between
  coeducation for, dangers of
  education of
  education of, humanistic
  education of, manners in
  education of, more difficult than of boys
  education of, nature in
  education of, regularity in
  education of, religion in
  ideal school and curriculum for
  overdrawing their energy
Grammar, place of
Greece, athletic festivals in
Greek body training
Group games
Growth
  at puberty

gymnastics and its effect on
of muscle structure and function, measure of
periods
rhythmic
Gymnastics
  effect on growth, its
  ideal of, and anthropometry
  ideals, its four unharmonized, and
  military ideals and
  nascent periods and
  patriotism and
  proportion and measurement for, criticized
  Swedish

Habits and muscle
Hand and arboreal life
Health, exercise and
  of girls
Heredity, a factor in development
High School, the coeducation in
  language study and
Hill-climbing
Historic interest, growth of
Home, restraint of, detrimental
Honor, among hoodlums
  in sports
Hoodlums
Hysteria

Imagination, at puberty
  of children
  play and
Individuality, growth of, at puberty
Industrial education
Industry and movement
Inhibition
Intellect, adolescence in
Intemperance

Knightly ideas of youth
Knowing and doing

Language, concreteness in, degeneration through dangers of, through eye and hand precision curve of *vs.* literature Latin, danger of Laughter

Laziness and energy Lies Literary men, youth of women, youth of Literature and adolescence language *vs.*

Machinery and movement Mammae, loss of function of Manners in girls' education Manual training defects and criticisms of difficulties of Marriage, dangers in delay of influenced by coeducation influenced by college training Mastery in art-craft, equipment for Maternity, dangers of deferred Measurements and exercise Memory, accuracy, age, and kinds of sex curve of types of Military drill ideals and gymnastics Mind and motility Money sense Monthly period and Sabbath Motherhood, training for Motor, activity, primitive automatisms defects of children defects, general economies powers, general growth of precocity psychoses, muscles and recaptulation regularity Movement and industry Movements, passive precocity of Muscle tension and thought Muscles, per cent by weight of body character and motor psychoses and small, and thought will and Muscular Christianity Music and exercise Myths, study of

Nascent periods and exercises
Nature in girls' education

Obedience

Panhellenic games Passive movements Patriotism and gymnastics Peace, man's normal state Periodicity in growth in women Philology, dangers of Plasticity of growth at puberty Play course of study imagination and prehistoric activity and problem sex and stages and ages of work and Plays and games, codification of Precocity, motor in the motor sphere Predatory organizations Primitive motor activity Punishments in school, causes of

Reading age crime and curve Reason, development of Recapitulation and motor heredity Records in athletics Regularity in education of girls Religious training, age for for girls in Europe premature two methods of Retardation as a means of broadening Revivalists Rhythm, exercise and in primitive activities of work and rest

Savages physically superior to civilized men School, language study in need of enthusiasm in punishments in, causes of reading in Scientific men, youth of Sedentary life Selfishness of children Sex, play and sports and Slang curve value of Sleep, in education of girls Sloyd, origin, aims, criticism of Social activities organizations of youth Solitude Sounds, favorite, and words Sports, values of different codification of sexual influence in team work in Spurtiness Sterility of girl graduates Story-telling, interest in Struggle-for-lifeurs Students' associations Stuttering and stammering Swedish gymnastics Swimming

Talent, early development of
Teachers, aversions to
Team spirit
Technical courses, need of
Telegraphic skill
Temibility
Theft, juvenile
Thought and muscle tension
Transitory nature of youthful experiences
Tree life and erect posture
Truancy
Truth-telling
Turner movement

    Unmarried women, dangers to

    Vagabondage

Vagrancy
Virility in the Church

    Weather and conduct

Will, muscles and
 training
Womanly, the eternal
Women, bachelors
 dangers to, in not marrying
 education of, ideal
 young, confessionalism of
Work at its best, play
 play and
 rest and, rhythm of
Wrestling

    Young Men's Christian Association
    * * * * *